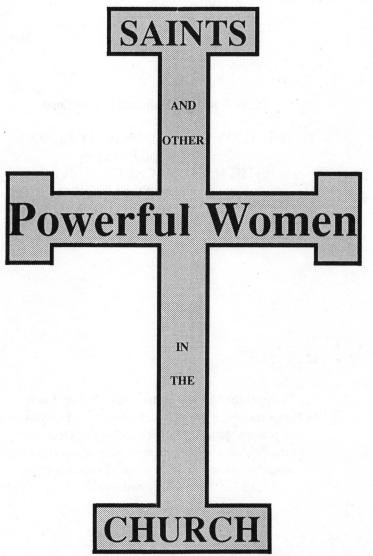

SAINTS

AND

OTHER

Powerful Women

IN

THE

CHURCH

Bob and Penny Lord

Journeys of Faith
31220 La Baya Drive #110 - Westlake Village, CA 91362

Other Books by Bob and Penny Lord

THIS IS MY BODY, THIS IS MY BLOOD
Miracles of the Eucharist
THE MANY FACES OF MARY
a Love Story
WE CAME BACK TO JESUS

ISBN 0-926143-08-5

Dedication

First and foremost, we want to dedicate this book to the greatest woman in history, the *Role Model* by which all others are measured, and that is our best friend, **Mary, the Mother of God.** Without her inspiration and help on a *daily basis*, none of these women would have had the impact they had on the Church. We say that Mary is *touchable*, but we really don't know just how available and helpful she is. In all her Apparitions, Mary reaches out to us, to help us. She becomes vulnerable; she allows herself to be touched. Battle lines are drawn. Attacks from the *fallen* angels are a guarantee. They hate her more than any human being the Lord has put on this earth. Good people are made to do bad things. Unbridled anger, pure hatred spews out of their mouths in denunciation of her. But then good things happen. *"In the end, my Immaculate Heart will triumph."* Mass conversions come about. There are healings of body and soul, reconciliation, return to her Son Jesus in the Eucharist. All of this happens because she is willing to be *Touchable!* And so it is with her *daughters* the Women we've written about in this book. They experienced the same joys and sorrows as Mary. But because she stepped out in faith before them, giving them strength by her *example* of unconditional love for Jesus, they were able to endure, and triumph. We thank you Mary, for your eternal *"Yes"*.

Our Dedications have become books in themselves. But in an instance such as this, there are so many people we must thank, both for their prayers, and their input. The research was extensive. In addition to the need to be as accurate as possible regarding facts on the lives of these powerful women, we reached out to their Communities to discover the *real* Saint, as passed on by their traditions. Also, when writing about women such as Mother Angelica, Sister Briege McKenna, who are alive and very active today, and Mother Thecla Merlo, who died in 1964, we enlisted the aid of people who have known and loved these women.

We want to thank everybody who helped us on this book, but in particular, those who worked so hard with us in getting it right.

And so we give thanks....

To *Luz Elena Sandoval* and *Brother Joseph* for their tireless work on this book. They began by researching the many women we have written about. In addition, they read and reread the manuscripts so many times, looking for errors, typos and insights we may have missed, they can probably recite the book by heart. Their handiwork has its stamp on the cover art, as well as much of the photographic placement throughout the book. Theirs has been a truly *selfless role!*

To the *Carmelite Sisters in Little Rock, Arkansas*, for their prayers that the Holy Spirit inspire us with the entire book, but in particular, that the two T's, Teresa of Avila, and Thérèse of Lisieux, were correct.

To *Fr. George Kennedy, OCD,* and *Yvonne Liddicoat* for their assistance with the chapters on the two T's.

To *Fray Hernandez, OCD*, of Alba de Tormes, for the simple way he expressed his overwhelming love for Teresa of Avila, which gave us the courage to write about her.

To our daughter, *Sister Clare Lord TOSF*, who took her religious name from St. Clare of Assisi, for all the pilgrimages and *l'avventura* we shared and for the strong part she played in our getting to know and love St. Clare; *to Jeanette Humes TOSF*, for her aid with St. Clare, as well.

To *Sister Raphael, Sister Grace Marie* and *Sister Antoinette* in particular, but to all the Sisters of Our Lady of the Angels Monastery, *Mother Mary Gabriel* and the Sister Servants of the Eternal Word, and *Fr. Michael McDonagh* of the Order of the Eternal Word, for their ongoing prayers which sustain us and for their invaluable help with the chapter on Mother Angelica.

To *Jackie Grchan*, Sister Briege's secretary, for all her work and patience, especially in coordinating the photographs and manuscript. Thanks to *Fr. Kevin Scallon* for reading the manuscript on Sister Briege.

To *Fr. Harold Cohen* of New Orleans, for his insights on Sister Briege and for always representing the Priesthood and the Church for us.

To the loyal followers of Mother Thecla Merlo, the Daughters of St. Paul, we say thank you, not only for allowing us to write about this dynamic woman, but for the loving, ongoing support you have given our book Ministry. Particular thanks to *Sister Mary Mark* and *Sister Annette* in Boston, and our special angel, *Sister Joanne* in Metairie.

To the *Augustinian community of Sisters of St. Clare of Montefalco,* for faithfully living a life so rich in the teachings of their Saint, that we found ourselves drawn back time and time again to Montefalco and to our Saint.

To *Fr. Giustino,* of the Augustinian Monastery of St. Rita in Cascia, Italy, for his *living* witness of obedience and faithfulness to his vocation, in the tradition of St. Rita.

To our grandson *Robert Ziminsky* who the Lord put in our ministry at a time when we needed his help on the Saints we have written about in this book. He traveled with us on most of our research pilgrimages, and has been an invaluable source of information in areas we may otherwise have forgotten. Thank you Jesus, for making it possible for us to have Rob with us for this time, for this most important book. And thank you, Rob, for saying "Yes".

†

The above thanks were to people who helped make *this book* possible. There are those we must thank, without whom our *Ministry* would not be possible.

To *Luz Elena Sandoval* and *Brother Joseph*, our family in Christ, whose ongoing, unconditional "yes" make it possible for all the other work to get done so we can concentrate on our books. Together, these two oversee our entire operation, including pilgrimages, books and television ministry, and lecture series. They block us from the outside world, so we can work on our writing. They travel around the country with us when we give talks, taking care of all the details. They put together our *Good Newsletter*, in addition to writing articles for it. They are responsible for distributing the *Good Newsletter* to over 30,000 people four times a year. They are truly *servants of Jesus,* and we thank them, and our Lord Jesus for sending them to us.

To *John and Annabel Joyce* who have been a continuous source of support and strength for us. We thank Our Lord Jesus for their selfless help and *example* over the years.

To *Dr. Jeffrey Mirus* of Trinity Communications in Manassas, Virginia, who's never been too busy to help with a problem, no matter how big or small. The Lord had Dr. Mirus put us into the publishing business, so we guess he's stuck with us. Thank you, Dr. Mirus, for not giving up on us.

There are brothers and sisters here at home, but also in various parts of the country, who open their doors to us, help us with our lecture schedule, bring us from place to place, and are willing to do just about anything to aid us in spreading the Good News. Thank you, *Joe and Nina Amoroso, Bev and Ted Miller, Lynn and Marguerite Waguespack, Fred and Alverta Hasling, Jim and Patti Cunningham, Fannie Ruiz, Mary Bologna, Al and Mary Geiling, and Tom and Lonnie Daggett.*

There are just too many people who are always there to help us. We could not possibly list all of you. But you are dear to us. You are always in our prayers. We thank you, as we thank Our dear Lord Jesus for you. We dedicate this book to you.

Table of Contents

Table of Contents

Introduction

Women of our Church, we salute you! We stand in the light of your strength and accomplishments, your will power and determination to stand up against unbelievable odds to do God's work, to take giant strides towards the salvation of our Church and our world.

Woman has always played a *major* part in God's plan. When God made woman of man's rib, He formed *unity.* *"That is why a man leaves his father and mother and is united with his wife, and they become one."* (Gen 2:24-25)

It is interesting to note that Adam, from whom Eve was taken, was placed by God into a deep sleep. Was it that Eve was to be brought forth by God Himself, *of* man but not *by* man? Could it be that God did not want Eve to be a cause of *pain* for Adam but a loving partner and companion?

When Eve disobeyed God's mandate not to eat the forbidden fruit, her action was to cause a reaction that not only would affect her happiness and life but that of her Adam and all generations to come. It reverberated down through the centuries, not to be overturned until, thousands of years later, *another woman,* a second Eve, was to make her Fiat with the words *"I am the handmaiden of the Lord. Let it be done unto me according to your will."* (Luke 1:38)

Eve's act of disobedience was to give birth to other acts against our loving God by the family of man that would follow. But God is a God of mercy, love and forgiveness, a *forever* God of Faithfulness to a very often unfaithful people. When I think of how lovingly God fashioned Adam and Eve, the joy He felt as He looked about at the life they would have, I cannot help grieve with Him as He, the Loving

Parent saw them throw it all away. But our Compassionate God could not close the door on His Children.

To know of God's Love for *woman* down through the centuries, one only has to begin with the women of the Old Testament. If we listen to God's Word carefully, we see Mother Mary, the New Eve in God's promise to the serpent, of the woman whose *"offspring will crush your head."* (Gen 3:15) As one woman's *"yes"* was to lead to betrayal, God accepted another woman's *"yes"* to redeem that betrayal.

The echoes of the women before us resound even to the most sacred times in our lives. During the Holy Sacrament of Matrimony, one reading recalls Ruth's faithful response to her mother-in-law Naomi's plea for Ruth to leave her, *"Wherever you go, I will go; wherever you live, I will live. Your people will be my people, and your God will be my God."* (Ruth 1:16)

Under pain of death, mid-wives disobeyed Pharaoh's order to kill all male children born to Israelite women. Because of one *woman's* courage, his mother, Moses was born and sent down the river in a basket. Another *woman*, Pharaoh's daughter, showed her *strength* by taking the *Jewish* baby Moses into her home and raising him. Because of their yes'es, the Jews were freed from the clutches of Pharaoh, and brought to the Promised Land. (Exodus 2:1-10)

In the tradition of our Jewish ancestors, for centuries *women* have begun the Sabbath on Friday night with the lighting of candles and recitation of prayers. The Faith of the Jews is passed on by the *woman*; for the children to be Jewish, the *mother*, not the father, must be Jewish.

Children have been taught by the mother from time immemorial. In our own modern society, the tradition is carried on. We gave a talk to a group of women in Louisiana. We said to them, "Are you aware that 85% of what is taught in your home to your children *and your husband*, is done by the wife? The bulk of informational material that comes into the house comes from the wife and mother."

We believe it's been part of God's plan from before the creation of man, that woman could bring us to the depths of despair, or to the heights of ecstasy. They have been given this power by God to be instruments of the greatest good, as with Mother Mary or, as in the case of *Eve*, the worst evil.

The focus of this book is on those who have *glorified* God, who have given their sisters *role models* to follow, reason to hold their heads high. These are women who have contributed to a heritage of which we can all be truly proud. When we began researching the lives of *powerful women in the Church,* living and dead, we were hoping to be able to find something in them that could be used to affirm the women of today. We really believe that women have been victims of a plot to separate them from the Church, by destroying their self worth. We were praying that something we would find could be used to lift their spirits, and let them know how important they are to the Church.

What we found was such an abundance of contributions, such a bastion of *strength*, such love, such example, not only in those who have lived and died, but in those who are still among us. They have all fought against the same defeatist elements, those that would destroy not only women, but the Church itself, only to rise up victoriously against the enemy, and to shine brightly in the heavens. We thought at the beginning that our major problem would be finding *enough* women we could hold up as examples. What we found was that there were and are so *many*, we have to eliminate some or there would be so many pages, and the book would be so heavy, it would be impossible to ever finish it. *But how can you eliminate so many women who have made such an impact on the life of the Church?* You don't. You write a *second* volume. We felt such an urgency to get this book out to you in the shortest possible time, we committed to a Volume II, and a Volume III, if necessary. Whatever it takes to let women know what a heritage they have in their sisters of yesterday and today, we'll undertake it.

The Lord has given us a message through this book, which we gladly pass on to you. *Have faith!* Go before the Blessed Sacrament and lay your problems out before the Lord. These are simple teachings that we learned in Grade School, but have either forgotten, or given up on. When the latest theories in Science or Psychology come along, we throw away the power the Lord has given us in simple things, like having faith, and appealing to Jesus in His Blessed Sacrament. *But they work!* They always have. They worked for Mother Thecla, St. Bernadette, Teresa of Avila, Thérèse of Lisieux; they work today for Mother Angelica, for Sister Briege, and for all the women we're writing about in this book. Why would you think they wouldn't work for you? We hear excuses like *"They (the saints) aren't relevant today!"* or *"It's different now!"*, or *"Our problems are unique to our time"*. Think again! Read the struggles of the women in this book. Don't buy into the lie.

We have to share a little problem we have had in writing this book. It's easy to write about the virtues, the holiness and spirituality of *canonized* Saints like the Saints we've chosen for this first volume. It's all after the fact. The Church has already proclaimed them Saints.

We have never written about *living* Saints before. We talk of them often, because we truly believe that these special people are doing God's work on earth. There are times when speaking about people like Mother Angelica, Sister Briege or Mother Thecla, that we can't help putting them in the same category as the brothers and sisters before us who have been proclaimed members of the Communion of Saints.

We don't believe for a minute that Sainthood is a hit-and-miss proposition. We're all called to be Saints. It's a decision *we* make. Little Thérèse of Lisieux knew for a *fact* that she would be a Saint, and you know the power Our Lord Jesus has given her. Penny and I maintain that we will be in the Kingdom. We probably will *never* be canonized, and we most likely will take a little side trip to *Purgatory*, but we're on our way there. We believe the Lord has called Mother Angelica, Mother Thecla Merlo, Sister Briege, and many more of the women of this world who are making a mark in the fiber of our Church, to be with Him in the Kingdom, to be Saints.

We don't mean that we're anticipating, or trying to dictate what decisions the official Church will or should make regarding the sanctity of any of us. Canonization is a gift from God given for a specific reason, which we're not required to understand. But there are Saints all around us. We have seen Sainthood in action, and met Saints in our lives. We believe the people we're writing about are some of those Saints. So bear with us when we speak of what we term "*Living Saints*" with a little awe. We've studied these women. We know them. They've earned the love and respect of the mystical body of Christ.

A gift the Lord has given us in researching and writing the biographies of these powerful women in the Church, is the *effect* they have had on the generations *to come*. It's nice to be able to read about attributes that the people of God, our relatives the Saints, have had in their lifetimes. We get warm and fuzzy, and a little proud of our Church when we read these stories. *But warm and fuzzy do not necessarily mean power.* The ladies the Lord has chosen for this first volume of *Saints and other Powerful Women in the Church*, have been women who have left their mark not only on the Church of their day, but on the *women* to follow them.

There is a cross-section of personalities of the women in this book. There is something in each of the accounts that will touch a woman of *today*. But in addition, we believe there is a special *sister* waiting for you in these pages whom you can embrace wholeheartedly, because there is so much in her that you can relate to, no matter who you are.

Because of the sensitivity of the subject matter, and the high visibility of the powerful women we have written about in this book, we have taken great care to be as factual as possible. We have enlisted the aid of many researchers more knowledgeable in the lives of these women than we. But there are times when there are blank spaces in the biographies, one-liners that tell such stories, or insights that cry out for us to go down on our knees and beg the inspiration of the Holy Spirit to fill in the gaps. At these few times, we have asked the Lord to guide us in employing the *"What if"* or *"Dare to Dream"* philosophy into our narrative.

While these instances are few and far between, they are used to bridge the gap between what is known, and what *might have been*. We have come to know and love these women so dearly, and have become so much a part of them, we feel justified in these few artistic licenses. We are encouraged in this by the words of author Murray Bodo in his Foreword on the life of St. Clare of Assisi[1]. He states,

> *"The story is not necessarily always factual, but to me it is true. And if you believe, as I do, that the imagination sometimes brings us closer to truth than does fact, then perhaps you can dare to believe that the imagination can also remember something history has failed to record."*

We invite you now, ladies and gentlemen, to let your hearts fill with pride, as you share the joys and sorrows of your sisters, *Saints and Other Powerful Women in the Church*.

---

[1]Clare: a Light in the garden, Murray Bodo, St. Anthony Messenger Press, 1979 - Pg X

St. Clare of Assisi

Sister Moon to Francis' Brother Sun

"Always be lovers of God and your souls and the souls of your Sisters, and always be eager to observe what you have promised to the Lord"

It would be very easy for *anyone*, even someone as well known and loved as our Pope John Paul II to be dwarfed by the aura and the presence of the little *poverello*, St. Francis, to be totally *overshadowed* by the essence of Francis which continues to cover Assisi. Unless, however, that *anyone* happened to be Clare, the fairest in the land, the noble lady who gave her whole life over to Jesus through the inspiration of His little messenger on earth, Francis. As Mother Mary is the moon, reflecting the Light of Jesus, so Clare is sister moon, reflecting the light of Francis.

When a pilgrim approaches the great hill of Assisi from the valley of Santa Maria degli Angeli, he cannot help but notice the two largest, most imposing buildings in Assisi. At one end of town, on the Hill of Hell, later renamed the Hill of Paradise, looms the grand tribute to Francis, the Basilica of St. Francis. On the other end of town, somewhat smaller, so as not to outshine the Seraphic Father, rises the Basilica of St. Clare. It was originally called the Chapel of St. George. After Francis' death, it became his resting place until the grand Basilica was built. Appropriately, it is *now* the resting place of St. Clare. It's almost as if they're looking at each other. As in life, the love of Francis for Clare and Clare for Francis is permanently etched in the skyline of the city, through the buildings dedicated to each of them.

While it's true that most people do not get to meet Clare until they've met and gotten to know Francis, somewhat as if he were introducing you to the most important member of his family, once you have met Clare, you are immediately taken back by *her own unique* power and spirituality.

Her body has never decomposed, after over 700 years. She is the instrument the Lord used to give us a *Miracle of the Eucharist*[1] in Assisi, and is called the patron Saint of television and the airwaves. Clare, do we need you now! The order she co-founded under the tutelage of St. Francis, his second order, the Poor Clares are *powerful movers in the Church.* One Poor Clare we write about in this book, Mother Angelica of EWTN, strengthened and encouraged by the fact that her mother in faith, *St. Clare*, was patroness of the airwaves, spreads the Gospel through *television* around the United States. Sister Briege McKenna of the Congregation of the Sisters of *St. Clare*, uses the airwaves by means of *telephone* to do the Lord's healing work. And so, through her daughters, the spirit of St. Clare continues to live on and touch the Church.

But who is Clare? Is she a female clone of St. Francis, or is she her own woman? Why was she able to attract so many followers during her lifetime, and why has her Community of Sisters become so widespread down through the ages? We don't want to go out of sequence, but later on in the story, we will tell you of an instance where Clare led her ladies on a *hunger strike*, how she singlehandedly dispersed an army of Saracens, how she was also able to write her *own* Rule, against all opposition, and how she got her way with Popes and Cardinals. This is just the tip of the iceberg, but it gives some insight as to who she was.

---

[1]Miracle of the Eucharist of Assisi - described in detail in Bob and Penny Lord's book, *This Is My Body, This Is My Blood, Miracles of the Eucharist.*

Clare, the fairest in the land

Clare was born of the nobility of Assisi in 1193. At that time, Francis was about twelve years old. He had not yet started any trouble in Assisi. There was a great distinction in those days placed on those who were *nobility*, and those who were *rich*. They were not always the same people. Clare's family was noble; Francis' family was rich. The nobility always looked down on the rich as being beneath them, while the rich knew they could very often buy and sell the nobility, but really wanted to be part of the *club*.

Clare had two sisters, Agnes and Beatrice. Her mother was Ortolana, and her father Faverone Offreduccio. There is not too much known about Clare's childhood and teenage years, but we see a similarity between Clare and Francis even as youths. We learn that Clare was a *good and spiritual young girl*, even before she gave her life over to Jesus through Francis. She was obedient to her parents, caring for the poor, loving to others, very unlike many young women of her station. Francis was a *good boy*. But he was a normal young man, involved in the world and its attractions. He loved to party. He learned to play five instruments. He wore the best clothes. He had to have the best suit of armor and horse to go off and fight in the wars. His conversion was not so much from evil to good, but from the treasures of the *world* to the treasures of the Gospel, from materialism to poverty for the love of Jesus. And so it was with Clare.

The first accounts we have of Clare are when she was eighteen years old. Her father had died; her mother was in charge of all the Faverone girls, under the guidance of their uncles, led by Monaldo. At that time, young women carried a high price in the marriage market. Not that they were actually bought and sold, but marriage partners were arranged based on the *attributes* of the girl, and the *wealth* of the boy's family. Very often, marriages were negotiated during the childhood of the bride and groom. This was not the situation, however, in Clare's case. *She* had a mind of her own. She was breathtakingly beautiful. She had long blonde hair, which just added to her value as a highly desirable wife in the *marketplace*. Clare was determined not to marry, though she did not know why. The Lord had touched her heart from childhood. *He* was to be her spouse. But it would take someone she respected to make this known to her. While her mother and uncles tried to interest her in various young men, she kept asking about the di Bernardone boy, Francis, who was thirty by this time.

Clare and Francis

Possibly the only thing the nobility and merchants in Assisi agreed on was the anger that rose up in them when they heard the name of Francis di Bernardone. To their way of thinking, he had disgraced his family, and stolen from his father to give to beggars and lepers. *He must surely be crazy.* To add to their indignation, many of the sons of the nobility of Assisi kept flocking to Francis, joining him in his insanity. They were spellbound by him. They had left their homes, given their possessions away, and donned the heavy, coarse sack cloth tunic that Francis wore. There were families in Assisi who would have liked to wring Francis' neck.

Clare knew the reaction she would get from her relatives every time she mentioned Francis' name, but she couldn't help it. She found him so fascinating! What he had done, and what he was preaching was so contrary to anything she had ever heard before. She had known him over the years. She most likely bumped into him from time to time, lowering her eyes as he passed by. She may have witnessed the public trial Francis' father had subjected him to, when Francis took off all his clothes, gave them to his father, and proclaimed from that time, *God* was his father.

Clare had never spoken to Francis. *She had to meet him!* One day, she chose to go out walking on the very road

she knew he would be taking. They met. Francis had known
of her since she was a child. Hers was one of the few noble
families living in Assisi. Francis could see in Clare that very
special quality that Jesus would use some day. When their
eyes met, the heavens opened up and the Holy Spirit entered
into them. They could not break the fixed look. They gazed
into each other's souls. Finally, Francis spoke to Clare.
"You will have to know how to die."

Clare looked at him questioningly, and perhaps a little
apprehensively. Never taking her eyes off Francis, she
pleaded, *"What do you mean?"*

Francis replied, tenderly, *"On the cross with Christ."*
She still did not understand what he meant, but felt an
unexplainable excitement surge through her. His words
remained with her. She could not get them out of her mind.
She met with him frequently over the next few months,
listening in awe as Francis shared the overpowering love he
had for Jesus and the Gospel life. He impressed on Clare
the dignity and beauty of a girl like her, giving herself over to
Jesus as a spotless virgin, to be His bride. His words were
like arrows of love from the Lord penetrating her heart,
burning her with an insatiable desire for more.

She went to the Church of San Giorgio[1] for a Lenten
service. Francis spoke that evening. She was inspired by his
powerful *witnessing* of the Gospel life; lifted up by the joy he
transmitted in his poverty; and drawn to the *Living* Jesus so
visible through him and his words. There was such a light in
his eyes, a fire in his voice. She went to him after the service.
She knew she, too, was being called to live the life of the

---

[1]Church of San Giorgio - This is the church where Clare's decision to
follow Francis was made. It is also the church where Francis was buried
for two years, and where the incorrupt body of St. Clare is kept today.
The Basilica of St. Clare is built on this spot. The original little church
of Saint George is still there.

Gospel. She asked him to help her achieve that goal. They planned for her to enter the Community on Palm Sunday.

The next Sunday was Palm Sunday. Clare went with all the young ladies of Assisi to the Palm Sunday services at the Cathedral in Assisi. The Bishop conducted the liturgy. As part of the Mass, after the readings and homily, the Bishop blessed and distributed palms to the faithful. The entire congregation filed up to the altar to receive them. The young unmarried girls of Assisi, of which Clare was a part, were to be last in the procession. They rose from their seats, resplendently outfitted in the latest Spring fashions, and glided up to the altar to receive the palms; all, that is, *except Clare*. She remained in her seat with her head down. She wasn't sure what she was doing, or why she was doing it. Her thoughts must have been running amuck; *Was she being holy, or shy?* She honestly did not know. She just knew that was what she was supposed to do. The Bishop noticed her absence at the altar, as did the whole town. After presenting all the young girls with blessed palms, the Bishop rose, and walked over to where Clare was seated. He blessed her and placed a palm in her hands. Then he returned to the altar to continue the Mass. Clare just sat there looking down, her palm branch clutched to her heart. What had happened to her? *She had been touched, and would never be the same.*

That same Palm Sunday evening, Clare left her home for the last time, exiting through the Door of the Dead[1], which signified a complete break with her family. Waiting for her at the door of her house was her faithful friend, Pacifica Guelfuccio. They walked together through the

---

[1]Door of the Dead - A door which was kept closed except when a dead person was taken out of the home. It is somewhat higher off the ground than the entrance door.

woods, to Santa Maria degli Angeli, where the Portiuncola[2] was located. At that time, it was almost a forest, with the Chapel in the middle. Francis had built little huts around the modest little church. Two of the friars were waiting for Clare and Pacifica. They led the girls through the brush, the thorns on the bushes ripping away at their good Palm Sunday clothes. Finally, they arrived at the Portiuncola. Before presenting Clare to Francis, Pacifica removed all Clare's jewelry. She replaced Clare's delicately embroidered Palm Sunday dress with a coarse habit, tied at the waist with a cord. Clare stepped over the gown that had fallen to the ground and out of her shoes, to a new walk and a new life.

Clare was brought before Francis. He was versed in the proper procedure for receiving a woman into a Religious Order. We have to believe the Bishop was aware of what was about to happen because one of the friars, Fr. Sylvester, stood in as his *delegate*. Francis asked Clare, *"What do you want, my daughter?"* She knelt before him while he sheared her magnificent blonde hair from her head.[1] He then placed a coarse piece of woolen cloth over her head. Being very proper, Francis brought her to stay with the Benedictine Sisters of St. Paul in Bastia, until he could set up a convent for her. Meanwhile, Pacifica left and went home. We believe she told the family what had happened to Clare.

Uncle Monaldo to the Rescue

As soon as word got out that Clare had run away to Francis, war broke out. The uncles, who had sworn to protect the daughters of Faverone, gathered as one, with Monaldo in charge, and stormed the Portiuncola. When they found that Clare had been moved to the Benedictine

---

[2]Portiuncola - little portion - a dilapidated chapel owned by the Benedictines, which was given to Francis and his followers for the rental of a bucket of fish per year.

[1]All these items, her dress and blonde hair have been miraculously preserved and can be seen today in the Basilica of St. Clare in Assisi.

convent of St. Paul in Bastia, a short distance from Assisi, they converged on that place. They yelled; they threatened; they cursed; but trying to get into a cloistered convent is like trying to get into the Pope's apartments, almost impossible.

Monaldo saw he was getting nowhere, so he changed his tactic from anger to syrupy sweet. *He only wanted to be sure of his niece's well-being. If he could just speak to her, he and his men would go home.* Clare finally acquiesced, with the provision the church would be the meeting-place. Monaldo and his men left all their weapons outside, before entering the church. They saw Clare, as she stood at the altar, her hand clutching the altar cloth. This was a clear *symbol* that she was under the protection and asylum of the Church. Monaldo was aware of this!

At first, he spoke softly and sweetly to Clare. He tried to hide his displeasure. He had planned a very suitable marriage for Clare, and she was not interested. His focus was to get her out of this place at all costs. When it was obvious his sweet tact was not going to work, he resorted to anger again. He and his men began tugging at Clare. At one point, the cloth was pulled halfway off the altar. But she resisted, and prayed to Jesus, Mary, the Angels and Saints to protect her. It was as if all the legions of Angels were called down from Heaven, with St. Michael in the lead. No matter how hard Monaldo or his men tried, they could not pry Clare loose from the altar. Finally, she removed the woolen cloth from her head. They saw that her hair had been cut off. They were shocked; to them she was dead. She looked at them for a moment, then turned and disappeared inside the cloister. They were never to see her again.

But we have not heard the last of Uncle Monaldo. A few days later, Francis moved Clare from Bastia to the Convent of Sant' Angelo di Panzo, on the hillside of Mount Subasio, right outside Assisi. Each day, her sister Agnes would go to visit Clare there. She was struck by the happiness she saw in Clare. It was as if this were not her sister, but someone else living in Clare's body. Clare shared how all the things they had been taught to hold onto so dearly all their lives, were meaningless. The only thing that meant anything was the love of Jesus. Agnes was so overcome with the change that had taken place in Clare, she decided to stay with her and become a follower. She sent word back to her family that she would not be returning.

Uncle Monaldo went into a rage! This was too much! It was one thing with Clare. *She had been possessed by Francis; but she was eighteen, old enough to go crazy if she chose.* But Agnes was only fifteen years old! She was still under her guardian's supervision. Since the death of Agnes' father Faverone, he, Monaldo, was in charge of her well-being. *He would have none of this!* So he gathered together a little army. How many soldiers would they need to bring back one girl! They went to the Monastery of Sant' Angelo di Panzo. They found Agnes outside, walking around the grounds. They grabbed her and managed to drag her away from the Monastery. Agnes called out to Clare to help her, but Clare appeared oblivious to all that was going on. Agnes could see Clare was in plain view of her abduction, but she was not lifting a finger to help her.

Monaldo's soldiers dragged Agnes through the dense forest; the thickets slashing away at her body, the branches pulling at her blonde hair. Whole strands of hair were ripped out of her head. She actually left a trail of blood and blonde hair all the way down the hill. Finally, out of pain and exhaustion, she collapsed. The uncle, not really caring about the well-being of the girl, but more interested in beating out Clare and especially Francis, shouted out to his men to pick her up. *They would drag her home!* Two soldiers stooped over to pick her up, but she would not budge. It was as if she were weighted down with lead. They tried again, to no avail. Finally, Monaldo, overcome with anger, raised his arm to strike her. It became paralyzed in mid-air; he cried out a blood-curdling scream, so excruciating was his pain. The soldiers scattered, fearing they had gone too far against Our Lord Jesus. Monaldo also ran off, never to return.

Very calmly, Clare followed the trail of blonde hair and blood left by her sister, to the place where she had collapsed. She bent down, and gently picked up her sister. All the cuts and bruises left Agnes. She was completely relaxed, remembering nothing of what had happened. It was as if she had just awakened from a peaceful sleep.

The Convent of San Damiano

Francis moved the ladies again, this time to the grounds of the Church of San Damiano. This was a very special place for him, as it was here the Lord spoke to him from the Cross, telling him to "*go out and repair My Church, which as you can see, is in ruins.*" Clare knew how important this church was to Francis; what a sacrifice it would be for him to give it away to her, because once she and her ladies moved in, Francis would be hesitant about coming back again. It was his own rule. He made a point of keeping a very respectable distance from Clare and her ladies. For her part, Clare stayed at the Convent of San Damiano for the rest of her life.

If there had ever been any doubt as to the sincerity of Clare's vocation, if anyone had thought she did it for the love of Francis, they had but to visit the Poor Ladies, as they were called, in their convent of San Damiano. When we visit there today with pilgrims, it seems charming and romantic, but we wouldn't want to live there. It has been repaired extensively since the time that Clare and her ladies took it as their refuge, and still, you wouldn't want to do more than visit. *Clare was used to the finest.* It's not that she was haughty or spoiled; she just never knew anything other than luxury. Here was the total other end of the spectrum, and she longed for it. While Francis wanted to embrace poverty, Clare *was determined to be poverty*.

Before very long, Clare attracted women from all over Italy, indeed, from all over Europe. Many of them were from well-to-do families. This was the amazing thing about it. The more austere Clare's Rule was, the more she attracted ladies from nobility. The ladies wore no stockings or sandals at any time of the year. They lived in the worst possible conditions at San Damiano. They had no beds. They slept on twigs, with patched hemp for blankets. There were cracks in the ceiling of the upper floor of the convent, which served as sleeping quarters. Wind and rain seeped through the openings. They ate very little, no meat at all. But whatever they did eat was food they *begged* for. Clare made sure that she fasted more than anyone else. If the meager amount of food the extern Sisters[1] brought home was not enough to feed all of them, Clare made sure the other Sisters ate, and she fasted. Once, while Francis was still alive, he and the local bishop had to order Clare to sleep on a mattress, and take at least *some* nourishment every day.

Despite this way of life, or maybe because of it, the followers of Clare were the most beautiful young girls from the best families in Assisi. In the same way that Francis' life had attracted the young men of noble families, Clare's did the same. More and more girls came to San Damiano to visit, never to leave again. Her best friend, Pacifica Guelfuccio, who had gone with her that first Palm Sunday evening to Francis, could not stay away. She had returned home for a time, but found she *had* to be with Clare and Agnes. The better families in Assisi stood guard, in an attempt to keep their daughters from running off in the night, to join Clare and her companions.

---

[1]Extern Sister - A member of a cloistered religious community who was given permission to go outside the cloister to handle matters of the community. In Clare's case, the externs went out and begged for food.

When Clare's family realized that neither she nor Agnes were about to return to their old way of life, their mother Ortolana, gave away all the beautiful things she had collected for her daughters' dowries. She took off her sandals, left their beautiful home near the Church of San Ruffino, and joined her daughters in poverty at the Convent of San Damiano. True to her name, *ortolana* meaning lady gardener, she took care of the gardens at San Damiano.

Clare's influence on young women didn't end in Assisi, either. Young ladies from noble families in Florence, and ultimately, all of Italy came to join her. They began to arrive from *different* parts of Europe. Convents cropped up in France and Germany. Blessed Agnes, the daughter of the King of Bohemia, came to Assisi for a time, to learn under the instruction of Clare. Then she went back to her homeland to begin a Poor Clare convent in that country. She took on the personality of Clare so much that Clare referred to her as "*my half self*".

The way the Lord works is so beautiful! Francis loved Jesus so much he wanted to emulate *Him* in all things. Clare loved Francis and the Jesus she saw in Francis so much, she wanted to be like *him* in all things. Francis did not want her to imitate him, but the Jesus in him. He was afraid Clare might mistake Francis for the Jesus she saw in him. Francis was not Jesus. Clare was not Francis. The Lord used the individual, unique qualities He had given each of these two children before they were born. Therefore the Jesus they projected to the world was completely different, One from the Other. The end result was two distinct role models of Jesus, in the form of Francis and Clare. Francis gathered thousands of followers about him. For her part, Clare embraced and touched thousands of followers that Francis might not have been able to touch. But through the two of them, Jesus was the One who touched His children. Thus when Blessed Agnes was referred to as "my half self" by

Clare, Agnes was reflecting the love of Jesus that projected from Clare. She was a completely different person, who then gathered her own little chickens under her wing. An ardent follower of St. Clare, Mother Angelica of EWTN, once taught her Sisters,

"Show me one Saint who imitated another Saint to become holy. You can't, because you can't be somebody else and be a Saint. You must be yourself imitating Jesus.

"You never read that Jesus remade His apostles. He never sat down and told them, 'Now, Peter, you're impulsive and blustering. You must become someone else.' No, Our Divine Lord used what He found in their individual natures and worked from there - grace building on nature"[1]

Clare was extremely wise for her age. When the Order of Poor Clares was formed, Francis suggested Clare for the Superior. It made sense in that she had been the first member of the Order, and her sister Agnes, the second. Clare refused the position for three years, however, until she reached twenty-one years of age. So we have to remember that this great movement had for its beginnings, a teenage leader. But she had the wisdom and love of a woman of much greater years. A perfect example occurred when her mother entered her Community. Here was a daughter who had to be responsible for the spiritual and physical well-being of her *own* mother. She never lauded it over her mother, however, but treated Ortolana with such tenderness and love, it became an extension and *sign* of the mother she was to all her ladies. She watched over them as they slept at night. She tucked them in when their bedclothes became undone. She washed the feet of the externs when they came in at night from begging for bread and provisions. These

---

[1]My Life with Mother Angelica - Sister M. Raphael, P. 20

women were her priority for the *forty years* she was Superior of the community.   She took to heart the words of Jesus, *"Whoever aspires to be a leader must first serve the others."*

The Woman Clare

Clare was a woman, undeniably a holy woman, and a committed woman, but in the final analysis, *a woman.* Two instances in her life bring that point home very clearly. While it's true that Francis was only the catalyst Jesus used to bring Clare into His bosom, there was that attraction. Both she and Francis knew their relationship would never transcend the spiritual and platonic.   But it seemed that as soon as Clare joined Francis' band of disciples, she was *cut off* from him completely.   Francis' reasoning was sound. He did not want even the slightest hint of scandal to shadow his movement, or that of the Poor Ladies, as Clare's group was called.   That was good, but Clare felt the need for the teachings of Francis for her *own* spiritual nourishment, as well as that of her ladies.

Clare was locked away in her little Convent at San Damiano, while Francis traveled about spreading the Gospel. She understood they were called to different walks, that she was to pray and he was to preach, but she had a problem in that he always stayed away from her and her ladies. This one day in particular, when she heard that he had returned from a trip and was at Santa Maria degli Angeli, she sent word with his friars, asking to share a meal with him. *Francis refused.* Even his followers thought he was being too hard on Clare. They told him,

"Father, it does not seem to us that your way of acting accords very well with charity. Clare has given up all the riches of the world; she is a choice plant in your spiritual garden. Why then do you not wish to make her happy in so little a thing as allowing her to have a meal with you?"

In his heart, Francis knew they were right. He really looked forward to being able to share with Clare. He decided, however, rather than going to San Damiano, he would have Clare come to Santa Maria degli Angeli. He felt it would be good for her to get out. So Clare and one of her ladies went to visit him. First she went into the Portiuncola to pray; then Francis took her on a tour of the little community that had been built there. She had fond memories of that Palm Sunday evening when she first went there to join Francis.

They went into the woods. Francis laid out the meager *bread and water* dinner on a stone. But before eating, they began to pray. They were so filled with the Holy Spirit that the entire area became illuminated. There was so bright a light, it could be seen for miles around. Townspeople thought there was a fire in the woods around Santa Maria degli Angeli and came running with buckets of water to put out the flames. When they arrived, they saw Francis and Clare, with their two companions, deep in prayer, covered by a brilliant aura. After their prayer was over, the light went out and the townspeople dispersed. Clare and Francis stood up, spiritually filled, never having touched one drop of food.

The second instance took place some time later. It was very dramatic, in that Clare got her *Italian* up. Francis went back to his old ways of staying away from the ladies at San Damiano. He would come from time to time, but only to peek in the door. He wanted to be sure they were living up to their vow of poverty, which they were. But he never gave them any spiritual direction, never talked about the Lord, nor shared on the joy of living the Gospel life. Clare felt deeply that she and her ladies needed this. She had never regretted trading the luxuries of her life for the way of the Gospel. If there was not enough bread to eat, she could handle that. If there was no wine, that was better yet. But there was a great need for *spiritual* food. She could not allow her ladies to be deprived of *this*. Francis, on the other hand, felt the need to turn Clare and her ladies completely over to the Lord. To add fuel to the fire, he instructed the brothers who brought provisions to San Damiano, not to speak to the ladies of spiritual matters, only their physical needs. Clare felt it was time for action. She and her ladies went on a hunger strike. They would not accept any more food or oil from Francis. She told her ladies, *"If we are to be deprived of our spiritual nourishment, we will be able to manage also without their material help."*

When word got back to Francis of Clare's decision, he immediately moved into action. He went over to San Damiano to speak to the ladies. They were all excited having their spiritual father there to share with them. Francis was somewhat ill-at-ease. They formed a circle around him. They waited for his words. He meditated for a few moments. Then, filled with the Spirit, he spoke words that touched their hearts. The more inspired he became, the more beautiful the words that flowed from him. Then he went into a deep silence, after which he left them. He had not stayed with them long, but that short period was so powerful, the ladies were in Paradise on earth for days. Clare said a prayer of thanksgiving to Our Lord Jesus for coming through once again, with this most special gift.

Clare gave up all material possessions gladly. But one of the most difficult things for her to give up was her beloved Francis. Because of his lifelong goal of spreading the Gospel and saving souls for Jesus, he abused and mistreated his body, which he called Brother Ass. It took its toll after he had received the Stigmata, the five wounds of Jesus, on Mount Alverna in September of 1224. He lived for two years with this gift from Our Lord, but they were to be the most painful he would ever suffer.

The End of the Beginning

During late Spring of 1225, Francis went to the Convent of San Damiano to be nursed by the Sisters. He thought it would be acceptable, because he was considered a *"Crucified Christ."* He was almost blind. He described the pain in his eyes as *"great splinters of glass scratching against his pupils."* He suffered in his sides, hands and feet from the Wounds of Jesus. His internal organs were disintegrating; his stomach ulcerated from fasting, and his spleen destroyed by fatigue. When he arrived at San Damiano, though it was bright daylight, he groped as if he were walking in the dark of night. Clare met him and gently helped him inside. While he allowed them to minister to him inside the Convent, he would not sleep there. A small hut was set up on a balcony, outside the upper room, which is called today, the balcony of the Canticle of the Creatures.

He never told the ladies how he suffered at night, when all God's creatures, whom he loved so much, bit at his toes, and crawled all over his open sores. But one morning, as Clare went to see how he was feeling, she heard him singing a Canticle to the Creatures.

Most High, Omnipotent, Good Lord.
Thine be the praise, the glory, the honor and benediction.
To Thee alone, Most High, they are due,
And no man is worthy to mention Thee.

Be Thou praised, my Lord, with all Thy creatures, above all Brother Sun,
Who gives the day, and lightens us therewith.
And he is beautiful and radiant with great splendor,
Of Thee, Most High, he bears similitude.

Be Thou praised, my Lord, of Sister Moon and the Stars,
In the heavens Thou has formed them, clear and precious and comely.
Be Thou praised, my Lord, of Brother Wind.

*And of the air and the cloud, and of fair and of all
weather,
By which Thou givest to Thy creatures sustenance.
   Be Thou praised, my Lord, of Sister Water,
Which is much useful and humble, precious and pure.
   Be Thou praised, My Lord, of Brother Fire,
By which Thou has lightened the night,
And he is beautiful and joyful, robust and strong.
   Be Thou praised, my Lord, of our Sister Mother Earth,
Which sustains and hath us in rule,
And produces divers fruits with colored flowers and herbs.*

†

We have to believe that the most difficult period in
Clare's entire life was this year and a half, between the time
Francis visited the convent of San Damiano and that fourth
day in October, 1226, when she lost him completely to God.
The Lord gave the Franciscan Community a special gift in
allowing their father in faith to linger for those last two
years. They were able to brace themselves for the inevitable
time when he would die.

It was a mixed blessing for Clare, also. She knew from
the time he staggered blindly away from San Damiano, that
it was just a matter of time. But no matter how much time
the Lord may have given her to adjust to the fact that he
would die, it was not enough. When Sister Death closed in
on Francis, Clare felt as though her heart were being ripped
out of her body. Her whole world crumbled. She was
inconsolable.

Word came from Santa Maria degli Angeli that Francis
had been brought there from the Bishop's residence in
Assisi. Francis knew he was dying; he wanted to be near the
Portiuncola for the end. Clare *had* to be with him. But
because her own life of fasting and austerity had taken a toll
on her health, she, too, was closer to death than life. It was a
touch-and-go situation for a while, as to who would die first,

Francis or Clare. For that reason, he sent word back with one of the friars that she was not to come to visit him. Instead, he sent a blessing for Clare and her ladies. With it there was a prophecy.

"Let her (Clare) know that before she dies, she and all her Sisters will see me again and receive great consolation from me."

Her Sisters were consoled. Clare was thankful to the Lord for this ray of hope that she would see him again. But seeing him *once more* was not enough! She wanted time with him. She wanted Francis alive! She needed the little poverello who had been her Jesus on earth. The journey to their dream had gone so fast. It couldn't end this way! But it did. She wished she did not have to set an example at this time. She wanted to be a normal woman for just an hour, instead of a Mother figure. She wanted to run out, away from San Damiano, over to Santa Maria degli Angeli. She wanted to cradle Francis in her arms; she wanted to bathe him in her tears; she wanted to take away his sickness; she wanted to make him better. She knew the Angel of Death was coming to take her Francis Home to the Father and she did not want him to go, not yet! She wanted to stop Francis from dying! But she couldn't. The Lord mercifully gave her the gift of illness, which kept her a prisoner of her thatched bed, on the upper level of the Convent of San Damiano. Her Master Jesus saved her from her own desires. He cried with her, by her side, as she unleashed all the sorrow in her heart, crying uncontrollably, without stopping, until she heard the sound of the funeral procession coming to the front of the Church of San Damiano. The body of Francis was brought into the church.

Francis had promised Clare she would see him again. Now he was lying dead on a stretcher. Half the town of Assisi was in attendance. This was not what she wanted. She wanted to be with him; she wanted to talk to him; she

wanted to listen to his voice. But that was not the gift the
Lord gave her. *This* was her gift. She accepted it. She
stopped crying. She opened the Grille. The creaking sound
of metal grinding against metal ripped through the silence of
the church. Everyone focused on the lone figure emerging
from behind the enclosure. She walked over to the
stretcher. Before her was her love, her role model, the
instrument the Lord used to change her life. *He was broken.*
The body was frail, gray, lifeless. A cold chill blew through
the church, richocheting off the walls. Francis' hair was
tossed by the wind, as was his tunic. It was the only
movement on his body. Clare looked at him. For a moment,
she thought he had blinked his eyes, but it was the *wind.*
Then the wind died down, and Francis was still again. She
bent over and kissed his wounded hands, his feet and side.
She painfully rose and took a long last look at him. She tried
to memorize every inch of him. It would have to last her
twenty seven years. She turned and disappeared behind the
iron Grille, among a sea of Sisters, weeping and moaning the
loss of their spiritual father. *Clare never looked back.* Francis
had kept his promise.

   We can't say that Clare stood firm on the Rule of her
Community because of loyalty or *in memory of Francis,* who
was now in Heaven with the Father. She had *always* been
true to her call, maintaining her position, uncompromisingly,
even while he was alive. But we can say she became a
ramrod where the Rule of Poverty was concerned, for the
rest of her life. It's very possible this was to keep alive the
dream of Francis, of which she was an integral part, and
which so many were trying to tear down. Perhaps her
insistence on her Community not owning any property, not
accepting money under any conditions, was her way of telling
the friars "*This was the way Francis wanted it to be.*"

   With Francis physically parted from her, she turned her
focus to the two most important things in her life, *keeping*

alive the dream of Francis through the Rule he had started, and shaping the Second Order of St. Francis into the truest representation of his vision. She was tough, but in an elegant way, so that while she would not bend in her beliefs, Cardinals and Popes believed *she* was doing *them* a favor by *their* giving in to *her* demands. Rules were written for the Poor Ladies. She rejected them. *It was inconceivable that a Community could exist without some form of property*, she was told. *The friars were accepting property!* Clare said no! That was not the Rule Francis wrote, and she would not accept it. Everyone backed down from her, but the final Rule, the one she waited for, fought for, didn't come until two days before she died. She was so determined, she even made the Lord wait to take her to Paradise until she got what she wanted.

Miracle of the Eucharist of Assisi

She was firm in the face of adversity. The famous incident, which we call the *Miracle of the Eucharist of Assisi*, took place at San Damiano in 1241, twelve years before Clare died. The catalyst that the Lord used to bring about this miracle was a German prince, Frederick II of Swabia. There is a tradition that Frederick was born in Assisi at the same time as Francis, and was baptized on the same day in the church of San Ruffino. The Pope had treated this Frederick very well, being sure he was brought up comfortably, affording him every courtesy. The young German repaid his kindness by turning on the Pope and the Church, waging a war against them, and the people of the Umbria. He had visions of an empire that would spread itself from Assisi down to Sicily. To this end, he recruited a band of Saracen (Arab) mercenaries to be his army. Reinforced by his band of merciless cutthroats, Frederick proceeded to march against Assisi.

The convent of San Damiano stood between the troops of Frederick II and the city of Assisi. The fact that there was

Above:
Place where Clare Died

Above:
**Eucharistic Miracle
of Assisi**

Right:
**Convent of
San Damiano**

Left:
**Balcony where
St. Francis Wrote
the Canticle
of Creatures**

a group of virgin nuns in the convent was particularly appealing to the Saracens, who hated Christians, and had a lusty appetite for Caucasian women. They proceeded to attack the Convent. Clare was sick in bed at this time. Her ladies rushed to her, crying, in a state of panic. *What would they do? Could she protect them from the attacking soldiers?* One of the Sisters ran into the room to report that she had seen soldiers in the fields close to the convent. A general state of alarm broke out.

Clare had two Sisters help her up out of bed. She went to their little Chapel, and removed a Monstrance containing the Blessed Sacrament. She held it in her hands, pressed her head against it, and prayed to the Lord. She walked to the large open window facing the courtyard below. She spoke to the Lord, and He answered her. She implored, *"Protect, Lord, these your servants, that I now, by myself, cannot protect."*

A very sweet voice, that of a young child, answered her, *"I will take care of you always."*

Clare added another prayer. *"My Lord, protect also, as it pleases you, this city that by your love supports us."*

The reply she received was, *"It will have to go through suffering, but it will be defended by my protection."*

Strengthened by these words, Clare turned to her Sisters, who were terrified by the prospects of the attack of the feared Saracens. *"I guarantee you, my daughters, that you will not suffer any evil. Only have faith in Christ."* She took the monstrance and held it *high* in the air.

The advancing Saracens froze in their tracks at the courtyard of the Convent. They looked up at Clare, at the Monstrance in her hand. Petrified with fear, as if they could recognize the God Who was there, they turned and ran, fleeing from the convent of San Damiano, leaving Clare and her Sisters in peace. The next day, the people of Assisi were pleased, but astonished that the Saracens had not attacked their city. Survival not conquest, uppermost in their minds, the invaders had left without ever setting foot in the town.

The Hot Cross Buns

Penny has a great devotion to St. Anthony of Padua, another Franciscan, another Doctor of the Church. She becomes downright embarrassed when the only reference people can make to this extremely *Powerful Man in the Church* is as the founder of lost articles. But a friar in Padua once told us that St. Anthony has no problem being called upon to find lost things. *"That's how he hooks you,"* we were told. After he finds something for you once or twice, you have a desire to know more about this Saint. That's when St. Anthony gets his greatest followers, helping them *to find* the Jesus he wanted them to know in the first place.

In light of that, I'm willing to tell the story of St. Clare and the Hot Cross buns. After reading this chapter, no one can accuse me of making *Clare's claim to fame* the fact that she instituted the Hot Cross buns.

Pope Gregory IX came to Assisi for the Canonization of St. Francis. He had stopped at the Convent of San Damiano, but wanted to go back one more time before he left Assisi. So, early one morning, bringing his cortege of Cardinals with him, he made the trip out of Assisi to the humble Convent of the Poor Ladies.

When the Sisters of St. Clare heard that their Pope was coming, they decorated the church and choir stalls with garlands of flowers. Everyone was truly in a festive mood as His Holiness entered the Convent. All the Sisters, including Clare, were in rapt attention, their eyes and ears riveted on the Holy Father, eager to hear what he had to say. But he knew he was in the presence of a Saint; he wanted to hear *her* speak. Clare obediently shared with the Pope and all present, the *glory* of God, and the *virtues* of the new Saint,

Francis. As the Holy Spirit filled them through Clare, they became lost to time, and before they knew it, it was noon.

Clare knew the Pope and his Cardinals could not get back to Assisi in time for lunch, so she invited him to join them in their extremely humble fare of stale bread. We really believe the Pope was honored to be able to live the Gospel life with these selfless ladies, if only for this brief time. He joyfully accepted their hospitality.

The hard pieces of bread were placed on the table. Clare asked the Pope to bless the meal. He asked her to bless it. Out of humility, she said she was a sinner, and could not possibly bless the bread, especially in the presence of Christ's vicar on earth. The Pope had no problem with that. He *ordered* Clare to bless the bread. She closed her eyes, raised her arm, and blessed the bread with such reverence, not a sound could be heard. When she was finished, a gasp of amazement escaped from all present. *A large cross* had formed on each piece of the hardened bread. Although it has not been chronicled anywhere, we have to believe that bread was the most delicious anyone had ever eaten.

St. Clare of the Airwaves

We would like to share one other of Clare's experiences, which is recounted in the *Fioretti*, the Little Flowers of St. Clare. It is the foundation for the title she was given, *Patron Saint of the Airwaves*. It took place on Christmas Eve, 1252, the year before she died.

Clare was too ill to go to Midnight Mass services with her Sisters. She was too feeble to get out of bed. She lay there, her heart breaking as she was to be deprived of our Lord Jesus in the Eucharist on this special night. Her thoughts brought her back to the time in Gubbio, when Francis made the first Nativity Scene, after which all Nativity scenes in the future would be fashioned. Christmas had always been a joyous time for both Clare and Francis. She

"St. Clare
Sister Moon
to
St. Francis'
Brother Sun"

Left:
St. Clare of Assisi

Right:
*Incorrupt Body
of St. Clare*

Left:
Clothing of St. Clare

missed not having him with her on earth, but especially at this, so important a time.

She looked about the bare room that served as the sleeping quarters for the Sisters. Suddenly, there was a great light in the room. She could hear the sounds of Christmas hymns being sung at the great Basilica of St. Francis in Assisi. She felt herself being lifted out of her bed. The cool breeze of the December night brushed across her face; she was transported to the church amidst what sounded to her like the voices of angels. She could smell the sweet fragrance of burning candles, and altar incense. *She was taking part in the Midnight Mass at the Basilica.*

Then she was whisked off to the east, to the Bethlehem of 1200 years before. She was brought down to the cave where the Infant Jesus was born. St. Joseph and Mary were there, in the company of the animals whose cave the Holy Family shared. *Our Lord Jesus came to her as a grown man, and placed the Sacred Host in her mouth.* Then she was transported back to the convent of San Damiano in Assisi. When her daughters in Christ came back upstairs from the Church, their joy was overshadowed by the great sorrow they felt because their Mother had missed the beautiful service. She smiled weakly. Her face was flushed, but not from the illness. She told them of her experience, and how the Lord Himself had given her Communion. They sat by her bed listening and smiling. As they all fell off into a peaceful Christmas slumber, the soft, distant sound of angels singing Gloria in Excelsis Deo could be heard.

Going Home

Clare was tired. She missed Francis. It had been twenty-seven years since she had seen him. She wanted to go Home. But she had her obligation to her Sisters. She could not leave them until the Rule was finally cleared up. Towards the end of 1252, Cardinal Raynaldus, the Protector of the Poor Clares, visited Clare on her sickbed, and gave his *verbal approval* for her Rule. She had been fighting for years, and now, she wanted so desperately for the struggle for her Rule, to be over. But this *verbal approval* from the Cardinal was not good enough. She could not leave her ladies with this. She needed *official* word from the *Pope*, himself. So she held onto life, praying that the Pope's "yes" would come before Sister Death.

Our Lord Jesus knew with whom He was dealing. If He were to call her home without the Rule being accepted, she would only insist that she come back to earth to get the final approval. So He waited for her, while she waited for the Pope. It's been said that those last months were the most *physically* excruciating for Clare, but the most *spiritually* rewarding. Her soul seemed to be ready for the journey Home. Her only concern was not receiving the approval of her Rule before she died. She feared that her ladies would not be strong enough, nor have the influence she had to fight for it. Inevitably, the Lord came to her rescue. Why not?

The Pope, Innocent IV, moved his court from Perugia to Assisi. Possibly a worldly reason for this was because the Upper Church of the Basilica of St. Francis was almost completed, and was ready to be consecrated. That may have been the Pope's reason, but not the Lord's. More likely, He did not want Clare to be pestering Him when she arrived in the Kingdom. So He brought the Pope to Clare. Pope Innocent went to visit this lady whom everyone had already proclaimed a Saint. She asked two favors of him. The first was absolution of all her past sins, which he gladly granted. The second was for her Rule to be approved, *as she had written it.* He gave her that assurance also. But Clare needed it in *writing.* She wanted his *Papal Seal* on it. The Holy Father assured her it would be done. This meeting took place during the first week of August.

Clare held out. It took all she had, and all the ministering of the Holy Angels to keep her on earth much longer. Her Sisters stayed by her side day and night, weeping, because they knew it was just a matter of time before she would leave them. Clare could hardly speak. She prayed with her Sisters, but could barely be heard. On August 9, word got back to the Pope, who was staying at the Basilica of Saint Francis, that Clare would die momentarily. *He had promised her the approval of her Rule before she died!* Hurriedly, he wrote a note on the Rule, bypassing the normal chain of command, and stated the reasons why he was doing it. He gave it his formal approval. It was brought over to Clare on the tenth of August, and she kissed it, praising God for answering her prayer. The next day, August 11, she died.

As tough and hard as Clare was, when it was called for, she was also *that* tender and sensitive. Although she was always firm in following the Rule, which was strict in itself, her reasoning, and pleading with her Sisters to be true to the Rule was always out of love. It's sad that most of what she wrote has not survived her. She put her very soul, and all the love she had for her Community, into everything she wrote. The Rule she wrote, which was finally accepted at the eleventh hour, two days before she died, is a compilation of her life and her values. In it, she reaffirms her staunch loyalty to Francis, and his original Rule. She insists on that loyalty from anyone who would succeed her, *and* anyone who would carry on the Poor Clare tradition anywhere in the world. In addition, she focuses on her Community, and the all-important need to do everything from a *sense of love of God and one another.*

It's very interesting and exciting to read the Rule of St. Clare, in that it is so multi-faceted. Her love for Francis is obvious; no one can deny it. Her obedience to the Monastic tradition of the day is spelled out. And yet, the underlying love of her Sisters smacks of the spirit of the Monastic *reforms* of Vatican II. One might wonder if the authors of this section of Vatican II didn't get some of their wisdom from the Rule of St. Clare, written some 700 years before.

Again we see an example of *Infused Knowledge*, given directly by the Lord. Although Clare was an intelligent woman, she was by no means a theologian. Nor was she trained in the workings of a Community, or how to deal with women. We can't chalk it up to instincts, because there's nothing in Clare's background that would indicate the enormous ability she had to *parent*, even to the extent of parenting her own mother.

As Jesus said to Peter, *"Blest are you, Simon son of Jonah! No mere man has revealed this to you, but my Heavenly Father,"* we say the same of Clare. As in the case of sisters to follow, Catherine of Siena and Teresa of Avila, Clare was taught directly by God. *The knowledge was infused.* She is a personification of the words of Mother Mary in the Magnificat, *"My soul magnifies the Lord, and my spirit rejoices in God my Savior, for He has done great things to me, and holy is His Name."*

Clare is a *role model* for all women in headship, not exclusively of the Church, but *especially* of the Church. She may very well have been placed on this earth to be a prototype for Superiors of Religious Communities, male and female, for centuries to come. Clare could easily be the standard bearer for anyone who would lead a community of people, whether it be a Religious Community, as Superior, or a country, as President, Dictator, or King. And her philosophy was not new, or complicated. It was simple. *"Love one another as I have loved you."*

St. Clare of Montefalco

*"If you seek the Cross of Christ, take my heart;
there you will find the Suffering Lord."*

The above statement was made by St. Clare of
Montefalco, Augustinian Nun, or as she is known in her
native Italy, *Santa Chiara de Montefalco*. They were the
parting words of *a Mother* to her Community of Nuns, and
also a clue from Heaven, which would lead them to
investigate the heart of the Saint after her death.

More importantly, these words were to be *hope in*, and
understanding of, the crosses we are called to carry in our
own lives. Jesus could bear the Cross because He knew and
believed in the Love of the Father and His Promise of the
Ressurection. Clare adored and carried the Cross of Jesus,
confident that she could trust in Him and His Promise to
her. I pray our beloved St. Clare will be for you what she has
been for us, *truth in a world that encourages lies, hope in a
world that promotes hopelessness.*

There is a Saint somewhere for each of us. My mother,
God rest her soul, would always say, *"Every Saint has his or
her own followers."* It's funny how God works. He never
sleeps. We heard about Saints whose bodies never
decomposed.[1] One year, our family decided to trace these

---

[1]never decomposed - Bodies which have not suffered the decay
process which normally occurs after death. With Saints and Blesseds
whose bodies have not decomposed, no preservative chemicals have
been injected into their bodies, no embalming or mummification; nor
have any chemicals been found which the bodies could have produced
naturally to cause this preservation. In these cases, there has been no
medical or scientific reason why the body has not decomposed.

Saints all over Europe. What we discovered was God was using the fact that their bodies were incorrupt as bait to bring us to them. When we arrived at each of the Shrines, we realized the *least* of what was important about each of the Saints was that their bodies had *never* known the ravages of death. We found a family, a Communion of Saints who had a message, a "how to" live your life on *earth* for Christ so you would know Him and live with Him forever in *Paradise.* As Jesus is for all time, His Word true and relevant for yesterday, today and tomorrow, so we discovered it is with those He has chosen to be *powerful* witnesses for us to see and emulate in our own lives. Clare of Montefalco is one of those Saints.

To visit Clare took months of preparation and thousands of dollars spent on learning to read and speak Italian. Her body is in a Monastery in a very small, primitive town, Montefalco, where no one speaks English, which is the case in most small towns in Europe.

Clare is one of the 20,000 proclaimed Saints of the Umbrian Valley of Italy. She stands tall in the company of Saints Francis, Clare and Agnes of Assisi, Saint Rita of Cascia, Saint Benedict of Norcia, Saint Veronica Giuliana of Castello, and Blessed Margaret Castello, just to name a very few. The list goes on and on. We could spend six months in the Umbrian Valley alone, and not visit all the Saints who were born there.

Clare is loved not only by the Nuns who have followed her, but by all the townspeople, as well. Little known outside of the Umbria, she becomes the favorite of pilgrims we bring on our yearly pilgrimages throughout Europe and the Holy Land. What is there about her that makes pilgrims pray to her for her intercession, sometimes over the more famous Saints we visit and venerate?

Montefalco, Town of Peace and Reconciliation

Montefalco or Corccorone, as it was known until 1249, was built originally as a castle by Frederick the Red Beard, better known as Frederick Barbarossa, the invader from Germany. Montefalco is called the "balcony of Umbria." This picturesque village looms 475 meters (1425 feet) above sea level. It is located on a hill, as most towns of medieval times were. This was necessary for the defense of the towns, as they could see invaders approaching and pour boiling hot oil on them as they attempted to climb the walls surrounding the town, that is if they had survived the arrows that had flown from the openings in those same walls.

The town is still enclosed by its ancient walls. There are five gates serving as entrances and exits to and from the city. These ancient gates open onto the most breathtaking countryside, filled with olive trees hundreds of years old, still bearing fruit; vines dripping heavily with grapes; gardens, their rich, black soil yielding fragrant flowers and plentiful vegetables. And if that is not enough, multi-shades of green, paint the lush forests which mysteriously frame and complete the masterpiece before us, *Montefalco*. The sight is so awesome, you just know someone special is here by the Lord's Design.

Clare was born into an Umbrian Society that lived a very simple life. The townspeople were reputed to be quite astute and highly ethical in business. Unlike most of the tiny principalities of Medieval Italy, they did not resort to violence in settling their disputes with their neighbors, but rather brought about reconciliation by coming to mutually acceptable agreements and workable compromises. In addition, they were regarded as truly spiritual and religious in word and deed. Proud of their independence, governing themselves with their own laws, they remained nevertheless obedient to the Holy See, under the supervision of the Rector of the Duchy of Spoleto.

As we entered one of the gates and walked inside, hugging the walls, carefully balancing ourselves on cobble stone roads our shoes were not made to walk on, we passed little shops and even an open flea market. And if we were not careful, we would have passed the Convent, as there are no great signs or impressive facade to reveal any of the awesome power inside. I remember walking our feet off the first time our family went on an *"avventura",* looking for the Church. There are eight Churches in this small town!

Finally, we walked up the steps of the Church, pushed aside a dark curtain inside the open door and caught our breath! The altar was *radiant.* By the way the altar was kept, it was truly a sign of a group of women giving glory to their *Lord Present* among them. Magnificent, baroque gold-leaf carving framed the Crucifix and the Tabernacle. We went up to the altar to pay a visit to our Lord in His Blessed Sacrament and to thank Him for bringing us to the *right church.* As we turned to the right, there was a Shrine to the Saint. In the middle lay the incorrupt body of *Saint Clare* of Montefalco. Were we excited! On either side of the glass sarcophagus containing her *incorrupt body,* there were glass cases, in which were other relics of the Saint.

Not satisfied with what we could see, we looked around for someone to explain what was in those cases. We spotted a Grille with a bell to the left of it. The sign read to sound the bell and a Nun would help you. Well, we did and let me tell you, it was definitely with the help of the Holy Spirit and our knowledge of Italian, that we were able to understand and be understood; the first far more important, as the Nuns speak an Umbrian *dialect,* which at best, is difficult to understand.

A Nun appeared at the Grille, Sister Agnese. She had one of the most radiant smiles we had ever seen, stretching from ear to ear. We asked her to explain the relics on either side of the Saint. She moved to the left of the Grille, and turned on some switches. The doors of the cases opened, and lights went on inside. The case on the right side, she told us, contained the heart of Saint Clare, resting in a bronze bust of her. On the left side was a cross, which contained other relics. In the center of the Cross was the shape of our Crucified Lord, formed out of muscle, found on the inside of the heart of the Saint. Nerve endings formed a Crown of Thorns on His Head. Underneath the shape was a tendon, which looked like the whip of flagellation. On the three corners of the Cross were placed three kidney stones, found in the body of Saint Clare, representing the Trinity. In addition, in the back of the case was a black tunic, which had been worn by the Saint just prior to her death.

This was all wonderful, and very exciting, but we still didn't understand the significance of all this. We looked to Sister Agnese questioningly. Her eyes twinkled as she pointed to the door on the left side of the altar. As we approached, it opened slightly. Sister Agnese had pushed another button. We could hear a bell sounding loudly, announcing we were coming into the *cloister* (we found out later), warning the Nuns to leave the rooms we would be visiting. These Nuns, being cloistered, are not allowed, under ordinary circumstances, to have visitors on this side of the Grille. But more on that later.

We found ourselves in a little Chapel. Sister Agnese told us this was where the miracle happened, and also where St. Clare died. *What miracle?* Our smiling hostess pointed to a fresco on the wall of the Chapel. It pictured Saint Clare kneeling in prayer. Above her was Jesus, with His Cross. He was implanting His Cross into her heart! Underneath the painting, in Italian, we could read the following, *"I have waited so long for someone I could trust with my Cross."* This is the story as told to us by *Suora Agnese.*

The hermitages in this village date back to the 12th century, all owing their beginning to *women*. By the close of the 13th Century, there were *five* Convents of Nuns and two houses of Friars, Franciscans (who were there since 1215), and Augustinians. Till today the two Communities of Contemplatives, the Clares and the Augustinians live the same cloistered life (in the case of the Augustinians 700 years old), a short distance from each other. But this is the story of the Augustinians and their beloved Saint Clare or Mother Clare as they still call her.

A Saint is born to us

Clare was born to Damiano and Iacopa Vengente in the year 1268. She was one of four children. The eldest, her sister Giovanna, established a hermitage in the year 1271. Giovanna was twenty years old when she and her friend Andreola set out to live a life of prayer and sacrifice in the tiny hermitage her father built for them. In 1274, it was granted approval by the ecclesiastical authorities. Giovanna was then allowed to receive candidates.

The first candidate was her sister Clare, all of six years old. Her holy parents had great devotion to our Lord and His Mother. That and the ongoing, *living example* of her sister Giovanna and companion Andreola, whom she visited often at the hermitage, surely contributed greatly to Clare's desire to love and serve the Lord through a life of prayer. She was a very *alive* little girl whom everyone found genuine, perceptive and sensible beyond her years, as well as extremely lovable. From the very beginning, though she was much younger (Giovanna seventeen years her senior), Clare kept up with her two companions, spiritually, prayerfully and penitentially, almost surpassing the mortification practiced by the others. From her earliest childhood years, there had been a burning love inside her for our dear Lord, especially in His Passion. This fire inside her was what gave her the energy and the zeal, her *strength* to live a life that would be demanding for most, but near impossible for a little girl.

Although she was a saintly little girl, she was a little girl with a *very healthy appetite*. She was even known to have to fight her craving for some of her mother's homemade dishes *(Author's note: If any of those dishes are like those the Nuns have made for us, I can understand why)*. Because of this fondness for certain foods, Clare made a point of strictly observing not only an ongoing, but an increasingly more stringent fast and abstinence during Lent than what was observed by the others in the hermitage.

As no Religious Rule had been established in the hermitage, it is all the more remarkable that Clare faithfully practiced *strict* obedience to her sister Giovanna, the leader of the group. Once when she broke the rule of silence prescribed to the Community by Giovanna, Clare imposed on herself a penance of standing in a bucket of ice cold water with her arms outstretched high above her head, praying the Lord's Prayer one hundred times.

In 1278, Clare's friend Marina entered the Convent. She was to be followed shortly after, by others, Tommasa, Paola, Illuminata, and Agnese (like our Sr. Agnese of today). This became a problem. *Oh what we would do for such problems in our Church today!* With more and more girls requesting admittance into their company, it was soon evident they would need a larger hermitage. Giovanna consulted with the members of her Community and other individuals as well, and after prayer and fasting, they decided to move to a hill nearer to the town. Damiano, Giovanna and Clare's father, again set about the building of the new hermitage. He never finished it, however, as the Lord called him *Home*. It is believed he died in 1280 or 1281. Clare was 12 years old.

Brother against brother, sister against sister

I will never understand, with all the work there is to be done to spread the Good News of Christ's Kingdom, why

Christians fight among themselves. Maybe more non-believers would know Christ if more Christians recognized what we do on earth is not for the glory we receive here, but to do Christ's Will as we believe He is calling us. *There has always been so much work to do.* Why are we jealous and envious of one another, trying to destroy our brothers and sisters who are answering the call of the Gospel, as they hear it? Does envy, hate and greed very often dictate our every move, rather than our Love for Jesus?

In addition to some lay people who, for selfish reasons, did not want this little raggedy band of Nuns to come closer into town, there were Franciscans as well. The reason they gave was that the town could not support another Community that subsisted on alms. It would be too much of a drain on the people. Things don't change much. Where is the widow's mite Jesus spoke of? *(Author's note: I came from a very poor parish as a child. In those days, men earned six dollars a week. It was the depression. At the Masses where there were the poor old ladies, mostly widows, the basket was filled with dollar bills. At the twelve o'clock Mass, the one all the wealthy politicians and their wives attended, you could hear the tinkling of coins as they fell into the basket.)*

The Franciscans, arm in arm with the other dissenters, called for a meeting of the Town Council. They demanded that the part of the hermitage that had been constructed be torn down and the land be confiscated. Confident they would be able to persuade the official of the Duchy to decide in their favor, a puffed-up delegation set out to do their *dirty work.* As God is just, so is He powerful. The Duchy voted in favor of the little band of women and the hermitage was saved.

There is an expression that there is no fury like a woman scorned. Well, true or false as that may be, these men, upon being denied the pleasure of destroying the little hermits and taking away their dream, unleashed all their anger and frustration on them. How often we kill, in the name of Christ.

The hostility they leveled at the little Community of women turned into wholesale oppression spawning lies, malicious gossip, and when that failed, acts of violence. All their attempts at terrorizing the young women failed to force them to abandon their dream. After all, wasn't the Lord their General and His Mother their Advocate! Holed up in a house with its roof half-completed, wet, cold and hungry, the little Community was sustained by their faith and calling which was stronger than any persecution the townspeople could impose on them. With hardly a person in the town moved to give them a crust of bread as alms, living on wild herbs and what flour they were able to glean from some edible grains, they discovered Clare had a talent as a cook. She went about making cakes from plants, with so much love and good nature, the Sisters fondly remembered it as a time of joy rather than a time of misery. As Jesus said, "*After the baby is born, the mother soon forgets the labor.*" And so, it was with the little hermits.

Giovanna obtained permission, *finally*, to send some of the sisters begging for alms, as was the customary means of support in all the Monasteries. Clare, although barely fifteen years old, pleaded to be the first one to beg for the necessary alms. Her persistence wore down her sister's objections and Clare was on her way. She set out from the hermitage eight times with her shy little friend Marina, returning each time *only* after their task had been accomplished. Her face covered by a veil, barefoot, she *journeyed in faith*, across the countryside of Montefalco, extending her little hand from under her cloak. She offered thanks on her knees, accepting humbly and good-naturedly *all* that was handed her, which more often than not, were hurting, wounding words that were not uncommon in those times.

The Sisters, who loved Clare, had to stop her from begging after a while, as she was extremely beautiful (*"This is my embarrassment,"* she would say), and it was not uncommon for defenseless young people to become victims of violence in those days. Things don't change much do they? Her forty days of begging having come to an end, Clare was to spend the rest of her life as a cloistered Nun, inside the Convent, never to leave it again.

Clare would spend eight to ten hours a day, or more, in prayer, some nights falling down on her knees as many as one thousand times reciting the Lord's Prayer. As she walked with our Lord through His Passion, she pleaded to be allowed to help Him carry His Cross. She practiced such severe acts of penance that her sister Giovanna had to impose restrictions on Clare's practices of mortification.

"Lord, I am not worthy..."

We know a Priest who said God never takes back a gift. I believe that. But being the Good and Wise Father, I don't think He would hesitate, should He judge it had begun to do harm to our immortal souls. I believe, in the case of Clare, He did just that. Clare was constantly striving for a more ascetic form of prayer, that is the type of union with Christ that calls for self-denial and deep contemplation. It seemed as if she was beginning to reach that *Union of Complete Oneness*, when God put an end to it.

Clare was having a highly Spirit-filled, engaging conversation with Marina when the enemy of *pride* surfaced, and she gave into it. This is all we have been told, but let us conjecture for a moment. Was her sharing mixed with a little pride, in the form of bragging, at the Lord having chosen her, *specially*? There is such a fine line, such a narrow road to Heaven and Jesus. In any event, Clare was to go into the desert; besieged by all sorts of temptations, a victim of emotional highs plummeting into spiritual lows. Clare was alone. *She felt her God had left her.*

It was 1288; she was 20 years old. All the crosses she was to carry in the future, could not equal that of the pain she was suffering, not hearing or feeling her Lord. This torture went on for eleven years. I can't help wondering how she did it? We expect humans to betray us, and in the case of Clare and her Community, people had done a good job of that, but we always have God to turn to. In so many of the lives of the Saints, Clare's included, they were to know that loneliness that surpasses all other, that dreadful silence of God.

We had a Priest who, upon hearing confession, would humbly plead, "*You Saint of a woman (or man), pray for me!*" And so, it was with Clare. As Clare confessed her faults, seeking direction and penance for her faults, her confessors instead extolled her virtues.

I remember one time, when feeling pretty low about myself, I rushed to Church to confess my unworthiness to ever again receive our Lord Jesus in His Body and Blood, the Eucharist. As I was confessing, not hearing a reply, I looked up. The Priest had tears in his eyes. "*How close you are standing to Christ.*"

I thought, *he doesn't hear me.* So, looking up again, I began, "*Didn't you hear a word I said?*"

This Priest, not known for his sentimentality, gently came back with, "*Who can not consider himself the worst of sinners when he is standing close to our Lord, face to face? The closer you walk toward Jesus, the less worthy you will feel.*"

I never forgot his words. As they were so unlike anything he had ever said before or since, I have to believe the Holy Spirit sent me to this Priest, to have him say this to me, that I may share with you how very much Jesus loves us at this moment of our lives just as we are.

Without the spiritual assistance she so desperately sought, Clare carried the burden of her feelings of unworthiness in her *heart*. As she did not receive her desired penances, she imposed them on herself, to such physical harm that her sister had to step in again.

I remember one day, when our grandson was answering a non-Catholic about the importance of the Sacrament of Penance. He said, *"I need someone to tell me my sins are forgiven. I could never feel that God had forgiven me without hearing, 'Through the Ministry of the Church, may God give you pardon and peace, and I absolve you from your sins.'"*

Upon seeing the serious decline of her sister's health, which had resulted in all sorts of stomach problems as well as other maladies, Giovanna, along with the doctors, ordered Clare to moderate her *discipline*. As it would appear, Clare was all alone and misunderstood. *But I wonder if God wasn't saying to her what he said to a Priest when he felt abandoned and all alone, "Ricardo, how long I have waited for us to have this talk?"* God took this time with her in the desert, to toughen her, to prepare her for His Work, His Mission for her, which would continue even after her death.

The Hermitage becomes a Monastery

At last came recognition and peace. Or did it? According to one of the rulings instituted by the Council of Lyons (1274) and subsequently decreed by papal bull, the little band of hermits of *Santa Croce*, or Holy Cross, was required to adopt one of the established Rules of the Church. Their choice was the Rule of St. Augustine, that is to live a shared life, like that of the first Christian Community, with one mind, one spirit, one heart centered in God; in short, *to be what we are all called to be, One, Holy Catholic and Apostolic.* The Rule was granted to them by the Bishop of Spoleto on June 10, 1290.

They had started with a Community of two, Giovanna and Andreola. Clare joined and they became three. She was followed by Marina, and they became four. One by one, young women came and stayed. What began as a small raggedy remnant of hermits became a *Community* of Nuns. Their hermitage which had started very humbly, grew very slowly and painfully into what is today a Monastery. The life begun by those first Nuns of the Holy Cross, a life in common structured after that of the Rule of St. Augustine, has been faithfully followed for over 700 years to this day.

Although many people do fairly little to help and a great deal to harm, after all is established and time has justified a Community such as this, everyone wants to take credit for its inception, its survival, its very existence. And so, almost *two hundred years later*, during the fifteenth century, when there was need to be united behind the one, true Church of Christ, when our Church was being attacked from within as well as without, an argument ensued as to whether Clare and this Community of the *Santa Croce* had been Augustinian or Franciscan. *Sometimes, I wonder what is important when you're staring up at the ceiling, knowing the next person you'll be facing is the Father.* Some authors and historians say there is no documentation to justify, whatsoever, the claim by the Franciscans. Others say that the Community first lived a penitentially pious life in a hermitage, (under the direction of Giovanna, Clare's sister,) for nearly nineteen years prior to receiving the Rule of St. Augustine. This they claim would qualify them as Franciscan *secular tertiaries*[1].

---

[1]secular tertiaries - These are members of one of the three classes of associations of the *laity* recognized by the code of Canon Law (c.648ff) namely Third Orders. The associations promote Catholic life and action. The members are *not* religious in the strict sense of the term, and although they may make private vows, they merely submit to following a daily practice of religion in their lives.

After having listened and carefully considered all the testimonies passionately presented, the Holy See declared that Saint Clare was an *Augustinian.* Of the five Monasteries in Montefalco at the time of St. Clare, *three* followed the Rule of St. Augustine; *one*, that of St. Benedict and there is only conjecture which Rule the *fifth*, the Convent of St. Maria Magdalena, followed. This Convent had been the center of hostility, spearheading an all-out slanderous smear campaign against the little Community of Santa Croce during St. Clare's time. One historian writes it was known to be a Community of Poor Clares in 1239.

Clare is chosen to be Abbess and Mother

On November 22, 1291, Clare's sister Giovanna went to dwell with her Lord and Master, Jesus. People, soon after her death, began calling her *Blessed.* Many of our Saints before the twelfth century, were proclaimed Saints by popular demand of the townspeople, because of *the lives* the Saints had lived; and how they had been touched and changed by the Saints' example.

For Clare, the loss of her sister was to cause her pain unlike anything she had ever experienced before. Not even at the death of her father, had Clare cried. Not even when her mother died in Clare's Monastery, did Clare cry. She loved her mother and father very much, but she *had not* cried. Now she cried for three days and nights. Inconsolable, allowing no one inside of her, she grieved alone, privately. The Nuns were puzzled to see her cry at the death of her sister, as she had not cried for her parents. Concerned and troubled, they approached her asking her the reason for her tears.

She replied, "*How is it you do not understand? I weep neither for her (Giovanna) soul or her body, but only for myself.* Isn't that who we cry for? *Giovanna was to me an example and a mirror of life; everyday she spoke to me of God and of always new and profound and spiritual matters. For this I weep, for nothing else."*

The Bishop's representative arrived for the election of a new Abbess. The Nuns unanimously chose Clare. She wept, feeling totally unworthy, and begged them to choose someone else, someone who was holy and wise, claiming she was neither. She had been unsuccessful when she had requested to be allowed to be among the extern[1] sisters during her sister's lifetime, arguing that she was not holy enough to be part of the cloister. Now she was pleading again of her unworthiness, only to have her sister Nuns turn a deaf ear to her objections. She asked the Nuns to present her petition, to the Bishop, stating she was unqualified spiritually and totally lacking the necessary wisdom to be Abbess. To her dismay not only did they refuse, but her brother Francesco, to whom she then turned, refused as well. Her many friends from Spoleto, knowing first-hand her holiness and virtue, also denied her last ditch effort to have her unworthiness brought before the Bishop.

All the Saints teach one important lesson, from the Old Testament to today, God uses *who they are* to do His Work on earth. I can see this persistence of Clare, being molded for His Design. *(Author's note:* Whenever we wonder *"why us"* the answer we get is, *"Because I chose you, no other reason. Yes, there are others more worthy, but I have chosen you. Now just say 'Yes,' and get on with it!")*

"Call me Clare. I am simply Clare," she would plead. She continued to choose the most menial chores for herself, performing them humbly and joyfully. One Friday, when the chapter of the Community was held to discuss the matters of the Monastery, as a point of instruction (or possibly as an example), Clare knelt in the middle of the room and ordered

---

[1]extern - A Nun who is part of the Cloistered Community, but is excused from her life as a cloistered Nun to go outside of the Cloister.

the Sisters to give her the *discipline*[2] in memory of the Lord's Passion. Like so many before her, Clare had the over-riding desire to share in our Lord's Passion, praying she could take some of the Stripes of Jesus on herself, offering herself as a soothing balm for His Wounds.

Although she felt unworthy and suffered great inner turmoil, she accepted her responsibilities as Abbess and became Mother, teacher, and Spiritual Director to her charges. She helped them to offer to the Lord their *individual wants* that these might be molded into the *Community's needs*, thus forming them into one body, one shared, common life. By balancing prayer with the physical work necessary around the Monastery, *the lesson of Martha and Mary in the New Testament*, was to bring to this Community a joy, an everlasting love. Sensitive to those who felt called to more prayer, she allowed them to pursue it, but with the provision *everyone* did manual work! She, like another *powerful woman* we have written about, our Mother Angelica, *personally* directed each and every one of her Nuns, carefully, unceasingly, guiding them in their everyday spiritual and corporal needs.

She is quoted as saying, "*Who teaches the soul, if not God? There is no better instruction for the world than that which comes from God.*" That they might be more focused on the Holy Spirit, she instructed them to recognize His Voice, how to discern *Who* the Power was in their lives. But when the occasion presented itself, she did not hesitate, as well, to take them to task, counselling, reprimanding, and admonishing, making them cognizant of the dangers to their immortal souls. She looked over them, overseeing their concerns, their activities, often at the expense of her own health. One of the early followers of her sister Giovanna,

---

[2]Discipline - Name of the small whip or scourge used by some austere Religious orders in penitential practice as a means of bodily mortification.

Sister Tommasa stated, *"She kept late hours at night but was always up early in the morning."*

A voice from within the Cloister

It is said, we are tested so that, being found trustworthy in small things, we might be trusted in *great* things. (Matthew 25:21). And so it was with Clare. God wastes nothing, not a tear, not a doubt, not a hope, not a disappointment, nothing. As *she* had struggled with inner doubts, she was able to talk with authority to *others*, never talking down to them, having fought in a battlefield not unlike theirs. Through her own journey of doubts, she could relate and empathize with the inner warfare suffered by others.

Temptations and desires no strangers to her, she was able to minister to people outside the Community who came to her, calling upon the gifts of knowledge and wisdom given to her by our Lord. By her genuine love and care, Clare was able to attract, to the Monastery of Santa Croce, Priests, Friars and theologians, Bishops, judges and lawyers, the learned and the unlearned, lay people and Religious, Saints and sinners.

She never neglected her responsibilities to her Sisters within the walls of the Monastery, as she served in her apostolate to those *outside* the cloister. Cloistered, like St. Thérèse, the Little Flower, she was to be a *missionary* to the outside world. Whereas St. Thérèse was a missionary through prayer, with Clare, the *people came to her* and she, from the other side of the Grille, was able to lead many back to the life they had been called to by their Baptism, faithfulness to their vocation and Sacrament. A great deal of the treasures you will see when visiting the Monastery reflect the many she helped, from different walks of life, from Kings and Queens to their servants.

The Church as well as the world, was again in a state of extremes in Clare's time. The glaring contrast between good and evil were not only political and social, but religious as well. As we study the history of our beloved Church and that of the world, we discover frighteningly how much influence the world has on the Church. The time of Clare was filled with the mighty and the meek, the persecutors and the persecuted, the poor with much too little and the rich with much too much. Honesty was overshadowed by lies; wars were fought, treaties made and broken. Knowledge by the few and ignorance of the many, Life-giving mystical love and deadly crippling lust, Magisterium and heresy were all signs of the battle, the never-ending choice of Christ or Barabas. The restlessness we are suffering right now, they too thought they could not endure, and it's in those times God, in His Mercy, sends us a Clare.

From an early age, Clare had made the decision not to look at men or to allow them to look at her. Her Friar-brother Francesco was the only exception. This was an accepted practice in hermitages of her day. Her decision was as a result of her sincere desire to walk that narrow road to our Lord Jesus. We wonder if, in addition, it might have been she knew how easy it would be (remember how very beautiful she was), to be subtly suckered away from our Lord and their life together? Was it because there were (or are) those with a weakness for consecrated virgins, the devil using them to tempt our *fairest, the Religious* who have turned their lives over to the Lord? Did she know the devil wants to use the brides of the Bridegroom to hurt Jesus with their betrayal? Did she know only too well, the devil's lie that there is no harm in thinking or looking?

One thing we do know, like the *powerful women* before her and those who have followed after her, Clare knew herself. She said, "*If God does not protect me, I would be the worst woman in the world.*" I believe that Saints are given the gift to be the greatest Saints with their "yes" to the Lord or, like the rest of us, the most potent sinners by their "yes" to the *enemy*. Whatever her reasoning, Clare spoke to everyone who came to her for advice, *from behind the black curtained Grille*. This, however could not stifle the passion, the zeal with which she spoke to her visitors. Her words, so filled with the God she loved, were not above their heads, but so down-to-earth, the simplest of people could not fail to understand her. No matter who, the most learned theologians or most hardened sinners, Bishop or floundering Friar, the old or the young, all felt she was speaking directly, individually to each of them. Whether the problems brought to her were personal, spiritual, family or cultural, everyone left feeling they had received the answer to their particular predicament. We are told today we are crippled, not qualified to give advice, if we do not have a degree in Psychology or Theology. Well, be that as it may, Clare, without any *scholarly* knowledge, but with the never-ending wisdom of Scripture and the Faith of our Fathers, was able to counsel all who came to her, to such a degree, they came from far and wide for her Spirit-filled advice.

Though she loved all of the Father's children, Clare's favorites were the poor and the persecuted. She would send her extern sisters with food and medicine to the suffering in the surrounding areas. Whoever came to the Monastery in need, she gave all she had. Her brother Francesco, whom she had sent out hundreds of times with food and provisions for the poor, testified that Clare, although actually very poor, appeared at times very wealthy.

Writing about the *Powerful Women in the Church* can be a very humbling experience. I know Scripture says love your enemies, that even the Pagans loved their friends, but the living of that must be what makes Saints like *Saint Clare*. She gave to friends and enemies equally, if not *more* to enemies. It is reported she gave the most to those who had hurt her, who had spread malicious lies about her, like the Nuns of St. Maria Magdalena Convent. They were wealthy in things of

"How long
I have waited for
someone I could
trust with My
Cross."

Left:
*Jesus
Puts His Cross
in Clare's Heart*

Below:
Chapel of the Miracle

Above: *Crucified Christ
Found on Clare's Heart*

the world, but as their greed and avarice made them need *so much*, Clare gladly gave them what little she had. One of the words of advice from one of our *Powerful Men* in the Church, St. Anthony, "*Do something good for someone you like least, today,*" seems to have been a strong part of Clare's walk.

As she was loving, all-giving, generous and forgiving, she was also firm. She faced all her persecutors with these qualities, never backing down from slander with its merciless, unrelenting viciousness. She stood up to them, no matter who they were. She even showed her temper, one day, to lay people who had violently attacked the Monastery, in an attempt to kidnap a Nun who had entered without their permission. Although she had firmly sent away this relative who had done so much harm to the Monastery in his ill-advised attempt at retrieving his niece, soon after, when he became ill, she sent medicine and food to him, not once but several times.

She didn't show preference to those who bestowed favors on her over those who hurt her. Not one to flinch, or back away from unpleasantness, *she dared to be unpopular,* standing up against the popular thinking of the world as well as that of her own Nuns, if she believed it was wrong. The Christian friendships Clare did make, lasted a lifetime.

Mothers, wives, and sisters came to Clare asking for intercessory prayers for their menfolk who had left to go into the army. Sister Tommasa testified, "*When danger of war was threatening, she (Clare) suffered profoundly and enjoined on the Nuns' particular prayers for all that the danger might cease.*" Mothers came to her about their daughters or their wild sons. Cardinals asked her to pray for the needs of the Church. Priests who were about to leave the Priesthood came to her. And all these crosses she gladly carried, grieving with them as Jesus was surely doing.

Witnesses testified she was known to bi-locate[1]. Many from nearby Spoleto, in particular, would tell of her appearing at their home, sometimes in a bedroom, and of the miracles that followed. On the walls of the cloister in the Monastery of the Holy Cross in Montefalco, there are paintings depicting some of the thousands of miracles attributed to St. Clare's intercession: a child saved from a ferocious dog, a soldier surviving fatal wounds, a child living after falling out of a window, and on and on, too numerous to name. Though she was a Mystic, often deep in contemplation of Her Beloved Lord Jesus Christ (especially in His Passion), and in ecstatic adoration of God the Father, Christ the Son and the Holy Spirit in the Most Holy Trinity, she was nonetheless sharply aware of the world around her. She was not removed from it, but involved in it; praying and doing penance for its salvation.

"How long I have waited for someone I could trust with My Cross."

The year 1294 was to be a turning point for Clare. The Christmas of the past year had found her quite ill. This was compounded by a deep interior crisis. Judging herself lacking in gratitude for all God had given her, Clare attributed the spiritual dryness she felt as God withholding His Divine Presence from her because of her sinfulness.

On the Feast of the Epiphany, after making a general confession before all the Nuns, she went into ecstasy, remaining in that state for several weeks. The Nuns kept her alive with a little sugar water they would give her to sip. During that journey away from the world, Clare had a Vision in which she saw herself in *judgment* before God; she "saw"

---

[1]bilocate - Bilocation is the actual presence of one finite person in two places at the same time. *Many testified seeing Padre Pio in various countries throughout the world, including respected Cardinals, who saw Padre Pio in the Vatican, although he never left San Giovanni Rotondo.*

hell with all the suffering lost souls without hope, and Heaven with the Saints enjoying perfect happiness in the Presence of God. She saw God in all His Majesty; He revealed to her how very uncompromisingly faithful to Him a soul must live in order to be in Him.

When she recovered, she resolved never to think anything, never to say anything that would separate her from God. "*And by the grace of God,*" she confided to a friend years later, "*up to now I have been able to maintain this resolve.*"

In the year 1303, Clare was to realize her life-long dream to build a Church which would serve her Community as well as the Community outside of the cloister. On June 24, 1303, the first stone was blessed by the Bishop of Spoleto and set in place. On that day, the Church was dedicated to the *Holy Cross*.

In the Chapel of the Holy Cross there is a fresco depicting Christ, dressed as a poor *pilgrim*, His Face weary from the weight of the Cross, His Body showing the outward signs of the long, hard journey carrying His Cross. In the foreground we see Clare kneeling, trying to keep Him from going any further, pleading, "*Lord, where are You going?*"

To which, Christ responds, "*I have searched the whole world for a strong place to plant firmly this Cross, and I have not found one.*"

In the Nuns' Chapel, there is another small fresco. Clare is looking up to Jesus, her hands outstretched touching the Cross, expressing all the years of longing to share Jesus' Cross. Our Lord's Face is no longer gaunt with exhaustion, but beaming with love and joy. His Journey is over. He says to her, "*Yes, Clare, here I have found a place for My Cross, at last, someone I could trust with My Cross,*" and He thrust it in her heart.

Clare confided to her cousin Giovanna seven years later, this Vision which had occurred at the beginning of

1294. The excruciating pain she felt in her entire body, upon receiving the Cross Jesus Himself planted in her heart, remained with her. From that first moment, she was always keenly aware of the Cross she could not only feel but sense with every fiber of her being. He was part of her; her Love, Jesus and she were one in His Cross.

Apostle or devil

There was a Franciscan, Fra Bentivenga, whom everyone called the "apostle." He was renowned for his holiness, but in actuality was the head of a religious movement, whose doctrine was, diabolically, one of mysticism overtly intertwined with *lust and lechery.* The world looked upon him as a Saint. His Superiors and his brother Friars hung on his every word. He drew crowds every time and everywhere he spoke. His eloquence, his fervor, his persuasiveness, his look of feigned spirituality had every one fooled, and not only fooled, but *mesmerized.* He was learned and could twist and turn the Word of God to serve himself and his evil. Because he satisfied the hunger we, in the Church have always had, to hear more about our Faith, and because he spoke with the authority of those in the Church he had deceived, he began to gather a large following. He was not satisfied with the countless innocent, duped and deluded children of God he had poisoned with his lies; *he wanted Clare!*

He sought to convert Clare, Satan always going after the holiest, as her reputation for sanctity was well known throughout Umbria and the surrounding provinces. Having arrived in Montefalco one morning, Fra Bentivenga, went directly to see Clare at the Monastery. It was the year 1306; Clare was now 38. He smoothly engaged her in a very quiet, highly ethereal, yet exhilarating conversation, seemingly in agreement with all she believed. He shared how the soul enjoys such *freedom* when it rests in God. He continued speaking in this vein in an almost hypnotizing tone. Although sometimes she judged his language became a little *bold*, she thought he was trying to test her and did not grasp the devilish motivation behind his visit. *Nothing changes!* Today, in our time, heretics, many of them members of cults of the anti-Christ, use the language of the Church, the spirituality, espousing nine *accepted* tenets of our Faith, and lead us to hell with the tenth, a heresy undermining all the Church has taught for 2000 years. As in Clare's time, they are respected and very often in high places, in a position to influence.

The conversation ended that evening and he left. Clare spent the night in prayer. You can be sure, the Lord revealed the treachery behind the Friar's words because, the following morning, when the "*apostle*" returned, Clare spoke to him through the Grille, but not what he had expected to hear. Her firm, polite rejection of his philosophy was final! He was upset, but he did not give up easily. He persisted until evening, using all the guile, the ingenuity, the knowledge of Scripture and Theology at his finger tips, to persuade Clare, but to no avail. He finally left.

Clare wept for him and asked the Nuns to pray for him. *How had this happened to one of God's chosen ones!* Although she grieved for the state of the Friar's soul and prayed for his conversion, she could not keep silent. His heresy was so subtle, it was leading many of Christ's innocent lambs away from the Shepherd to the slaughter. The Friar was so careful in his argument that the Inquisitor who Clare had asked to investigate the matter, could not find a single point smacking of heresy with which to denounce him. All seemed against her. I'm sure she felt very much alone, except for that little voice inside that said, "*If they persecute you, remember they persecuted Me before you.*" And so, she sent a petition to the Cardinal. The Cardinal listened and through a Franciscan, Fra Ubertino da Casale, succeeded in exposing Fra Bentivenga and his fellow heretics. They were denounced, judged, and sentenced to prison.

"I have my Crucified Jesus in my heart"

"The life of a soul is the love of God," said Clare. She prayed that everyone she met would experience our Lord Jesus deep in their heart. She prayed, suffered and burned with passion, just as our Lord did; for, like our Lord, she had completely given up her spirit to God.

When she had had her encounter with Fra Bentivenga, she was already very weak from the many severe penances she had practiced over the years and the ecstasies which drained her almost to the point of death. In spite of her frail health, she continued to work as Abbess to her Sisters and missionary to those who came from outside the cloister. She did this unceasingly, never taking care of herself, until July of 1308 when she could no longer rise from bed (if you can call a few boards covered by a blanket, a bed).

Years before, her brother had summoned a prominent physician to visit her. We use the word *"visit"* because Clare would not even allow the other Nuns to see or touch her body, no less a doctor. The doctor had prescribed some medicine, but she never took any of it. Now, in 1308, another doctor offered his services to the Monastery. He differed from the previous doctor, in that he was more concerned about her ecstasies than by her physical ills. He told the Nuns that, unlike sicknesses caused by things of this world, there was no medicine that could remedy the weakness caused by her ecstasies. He told the Sisters to distract Clare; take her mind off her ecstasies; make a litter and carry her around the Monastery so she would not be able to experience any more of them (ecstasies). He meant well, but he did not know Clare. That determination that had brought them through all the persecution, was the same that would not allow anyone to keep her from her Lord.

Left:
***Community of
St. Clare
of Montefalco***

Below:
***Reliquary
of Her Heart***

Above:
***Cross Showing
Crucifixion,
Whip and Stones
Found in
her Body***

Right:
***Incorrupt Body
of St. Clare***

Like St. Francis before her, she never wanted to be called a *Saint*. When some of her Nuns could not help but blurt out, "*You are a Saint,*" she would sharply retort, "*Cast me away! Cast me away! Cast me out!*" As she cried out, they judged her humble. She was really in agony, fighting the "*enemy,*" sensing his strong presence. He attacked in his usual modus operandi, as with the Saints before her (like St. Thérèse of Lisieux), *that she was unworthy of God, that He did not find her pleasing; she had been wrong in all she had said and done, leading many astray, and on and on...* Her Shepherd beside her, with all the faith of those before her, she answered the devil, "*I do not want to give you what is yours nor do I want anything from you! You are accursed for thousands of years and I curse you still.*"

On the evening of August the 15th, she called the Nuns together and left them her spiritual last will and testament, "*I offer my soul and all of you, the death of Lord Jesus Christ. Be blessed by God and by me. And I pray, my daughters, that you behave well and that all the work God has had me do for you be blessed. Be humble, obedient; be such women that God may always be praised through you.*"

After speaking to all of the weeping Nuns, trying to leave them consoled and strengthened, she asked for the Sacrament of *Extreme Unction*[1].

When a Nun is dying, each of the Sisters make a sign of the Cross on her. As they attempted to do so to Clare, she gently but firmly protested over and over again, "*Why do you sign me, Sisters? I have the crucified Jesus in my heart.*"

Friday, late in the afternoon, she called for her brother Francesco, who was guardian of a Convent in Spoleto. That night, when he arrived, he found his sister very tired. But

---

[1]Extreme Unction - Now called Sacrament of Anointing of the Sick, this Sacrament is conferred on baptized Catholics who are ill, or "suffering" from old age, or in danger of death. The Sacrament may be conferred by a Priest or Bishop.

the following morning a very happy Dr. Simone greeted him with the good news that Clare had slept well and was resting comfortably. Francesco started to leave when he was called back by two of the Nuns. He followed them into the Chapel of the Holy Cross, her bedroom. She appeared completely recovered, was sitting up, the color back in her face, smiling, looking so well he suggested they give her something to eat. She gave her brother Spiritual Direction, as she was his Spiritual Director and teacher, talking at great length with him. As much joy and a mood of anticipated celebration began to spread among the Nuns and Francesco, Clare turned to Fra Tommaso, the Chaplain of the Monastery, *"I confess to God and to you my faults, all my offenses."* And a little later, turning to her Nuns, *"Now I have nothing more to say to you. You are with God because I am going to Him."* She remained like that, seated upright in her bed, her eyes turned toward Heaven, not moving, without even the smallest quiver. Several minutes passed. Clare was no longer speaking. Francesco took his sister's pulse; He turned to the Nuns circled about the bed and announced, tears running down his face, *"She is dead."* The doctor teased Francesco and the Nuns, believing Clare had gone into ecstasy. Nothing Francesco could say would satisfy him until he reluctantly took her pulse himself. Having done so, he agreed that she was gone, and he too, broke into tears. A friend was dead. The world would never be the same. It was 9 a.m. on a *Saturday* morning, the 17th of August. We're sure that Mary, the Mother of God, was there waiting to bring this faithful daughter to her Spouse, her Bridegroom Who had a place ready for her in His Father's Mansion.

Clare lives on, present among her Community.

As I write these words of Clare dying, I feel like crying too, because the story is over. But, is it? The Nuns immediately got the body ready for all the friends of Clare to view.   First they removed her heart and placed it in a flowered bowl made of wood.   Had they remembered her words, "*I have the Crucified Jesus in my heart?*"

The Funeral Mass was celebrated on Sunday, the 18th. The preacher, a Franciscan Priest from Bevagna, instead of giving the homily he had prepared, found himself delivering the most extraordinary eulogy, extolling Clare's sanctity and selfless giving to all who came, never counting the cost. As the words poured from his lips, they became his and he found himself realizing the gift the Father had given him; he was eulogizing a *Saint*.   His brother Franciscans meanwhile looked away, disapprovingly.   They were blinded and deafened by the anger they harbored at having been *ordered* to be here in the first place. It turned out, they were here only out of obedience to Clare's brother Francesco, their Chaplain.   And so, they, too, had been called to share in a gift, but their "*No!*" robbed them of it.

That evening, the Nuns opened her heart preparing it to place in a Reliquary. To their amazement, Clare's words came alive; there before them were the marks of Jesus Passion! Cradled inside the softness of her grand heart, was the Perfect Form of Jesus Crucified, even to the Crown of Thorns clearly evidenced on his Head, and the lance Wound in His Precious Side.   The Lord had not only planted His Crucified Body within the recesses of her heart, but the painful evidence of some of His Sufferings, the means of flagellation in a form of ligaments or tendons, the whip that was used to scourge our Beloved Lord, with the ends showing the metal balls and the jagged bones used to rip our Lord's Skin from His Bones.

The news of this miracle spread! As my husband says, "Tell an Italian and you tell the world." *(Author's note: I'm Italian.   Mother Angelica is Italian.   We're trying to tell the whole world.   Maybe that's what a Christian is supposed to do.)* The following Monday, an old adversary, Fra Pietro di

Salomone, made his way to the Vicar of the diocese of Spoleto, Msgr. Berengario. He *denounced* the Nuns, claiming their findings were willfully *misrepresented*. On Tuesday Monsignor left for Montefalco. Upon arriving there, he immediately called together theologians, lawyers and doctors. The heart was carefully investigated and they all *unanimously* concluded that the "*marks*" were not of an explainable scientific nature or of human understanding, in other words, a *phenomena*, or as we are so happy to say, God leaving another *miracle* in our midst. There was not only a document drawn by the Church and affirmed by science, but the civil authorities did their own investigation and issued their findings. *The heart of Clare did in fact contain this extraordinary sign and it was not the result of any false doings.*

Another phenomena or as we prefer to call it, *miraculous sign*, was the finding of three stones inside her bladder. When the Nuns further investigated they discovered in the gall bladder three gall stones the size of large hazel nuts perfectly equal in size, color, shape and weight. They were found to weigh all the same, one weighing as much as two, two as three, one as three. The Sisters at the Shrine tell us this *sign* was left to show the love Clare had for the Blessed Trinity. But we wonder if it was not also, possibly to explain the Blessed Trinity as much as The Triune God can be explained. *One Person equal to Each of the Other Two Persons, as well as equal to the Two Combined of the other Persons of the Trinity.* In the sign left by the Lord, in the body of St. Clare, the *three* weighed the same as *one*, the *two* as one, the *one* as two or as three, all equal. Coincidence?

God is speaking to His people. Yes, there is nothing new being said, *that is of the Lord*, outside of the Sacred Word; but when times are such, when we are getting confused as to *what* is His Word, He not only raises up Saints, but leaves teachings for all generations to see. Is this

His Way of saying, *"What you do or say today may, like the water that flows, either satisfy man's thirst for the Living God or contaminate his soul, leading him away for all eternity."*

St.Clare's body exuded such a sweet fragrance, the Nuns tell us that they never could bury her in the ground. Her body is still visible, nearly 700 years old, *never* having decomposed and is said to be supple (rigor mortis never set in). I think even more than the *physical* presence of her incorrupt body[1], of God choosing to leave Clare as a sign and a teaching in this world, is *her spirit that is still alive* as if she were there among them, teaching, spiritually directing. In this world, with a *crisis in vocations*, here is a Community of *cloistered* Nuns living the Rule of St. Augustine as adopted 700 years ago by their Foundress and upheld by their Saint, Saint Clare. They are the happiest, most loving group of women I have ever met. My vocation is the Sacrament of Matrimony, but if I were ever drawn to live the *Religious Life*, I believe I would be hard pressed to find one living more purely the Gospel, as this Community. We had need to ask them, in the light of the many Sisters who have left Religious Communities, if they had any Nuns leaving their Community. They answered that in their 700 years, *never* has a *professed Sister*, that is one who has taken her final vows, ever left.

You walk through the Monastery past a heavy wooden door which is locked by the same hand-made keys on the same bolted locks used 700 years ago to keep the world out, two huge beams further barring any unannounced and unwanted intruders. This began years ago to keep some very unscrupulous relatives, irrespective of the Nuns' wishes, from coming in and taking them home to use them for their own gains. Very often, it was to use them and their dowry, to gain more land or a higher social position by marrying them

---

[1]Incorrupt body - see footnote on Page 45

off to someone in high places. There were even relatives who, misguidedly judged the Nun should lead a more *normal life*, married, with a husband and children.

We walk past the many paintings dating back hundreds of years ago, to those of today, telling of the many miracles attributed to the Saint's intercession.

Before entering the garden, we come to the Grille through which the Nuns still talk to their families, who remain on the other side of the Grille in the parlor, and this only at specific times of the year. Because we are pilgrims interested in their Saint, we are privileged to talk to them face to face. I cannot help but stop and think of their *personal* families who are helping these Nuns to be faithful to their vocation. With only very few exceptions, these cloistered Nuns can *still* only receive from, and *give* to visitors on the other side, through a *Turn*, like a turn table.

As we enter the *garden*, there is a feeling of His Presence and that of the Saint that lingers here among the rose bushes, the other flowering plants and the *tree* Bob and I lovingly call the *Grandma Tree*. We have coined this name for the tree, as it dates back to the time of St. Clare. One of the frescoes on the wall as we approached the *garden*, depicts one of St. Clare's Visions. It shows Jesus handing Clare a stick, asking her to water it. Out of obedience, telling no one of her Vision, she watered the *lifeless stick*. It brought and continues to bring forth blossoms and little nuts, these 700 years, from which the Nuns make *rosaries*. At one time, they only sent the rosaries to other Augustinian Monasteries, but now they are available to visiting pilgrims, as long as there are nuts available for the Nuns to make the rosaries. As I said before, there is something about this Saint. Years after pilgrims have gone on pilgrimage with us, they still request additional rosaries for some needy member of their family. Clare is working through her Nuns and their faithfulness.

The ordinary process into the life of St. Clare, her virtues, her revelations and the miracles attested to her intervention *after she was dead*, began in 1309, less than a year after she died. The apostolic process went before the Pope in 1318, but the actual *Canonization* in St. Peter's was not to come about until December the 8th, *1881*, Feast of the Immaculate Conception. With more than 300 miracles attested to and accepted by the finish of the investigation in *1333*, with everything ready and in order for Canonization, nothing was done until *1881!* Clare lived in troubled times, with Satan trying to block her in every shape and form. Now, in death, he was still trying to keep her from being used for the Glory of God. Because of the troubled times, what with the Pope fleeing to Avignon, and the Great Western Schism which incurred when they returned to Rome, Clare's process was hindered and shelved. But we know and have an expression, *"When God wants something done, no matter how powerful the opposition, He will have His Way.* And so it was with St. Clare of Montefalco. *Alleluia!"*

St. Catherine of Siena

*"O Eternal God, accept the sacrifice of my life
for the mystical body of Thy holy Church."*

Catherine of Siena, what an impressive woman and Saint! As I start on our sister's story, like with the other *powerful women in the Church*, I can feel tears coming to my eyes, tears of joy. Thank You, Lord for the privilege of passing on what we have learned through our travels to the Shrines, as well as through the historians before us, who have felt this *lady* and her life so essential a part of the Story of our Church. As we write on the lives of these women we experience the same feelings we have had when we have walked on the cobblestone roads *they* walked, and touched the walls of the rooms *they* touched. If these walls and stones could talk, they would sing of the Glory and Love of Jesus and His Mother, as They spoke to and guided these Saints in their *journey of faith* to the Kingdom.

I'm so excited! Please stop a moment and pray with me that the words that flow on these pages be those of our Lord, the message He has for *you* today.

In 1347, Catherine was born into a large, wealthy family, the 23rd child of a family of 25 children. Catherine's parents built their huge home, which you can visit till today, in the heart of the city on Via dei Tintori (Street of the Dyers). Their home included their Dye Works on the *lower level* and rooms *above*, where most of their surviving twelve children (thirteen having died at infancy), with their spouses, the family servant and dye workers lived and ate. It was, all in all, a very impressive home, with its courtyard and beautiful gardens, but not a very peaceful one. The *hustle and bustle of the business*, right there in the house, drowned out whatever quiet family life they might have enjoyed. The choking, putrid fumes from the dyes below, permeated all the rooms of the house, clinging to everything; the stench on their clothes following them, lingering long after they had ventured out into the streets.

One day, Catherine and her brother were *slowly* returning from the country home of their married sister Buonaventura, as Catherine loved and preferred the peaceful countryside. She paused on the hillside to look over the valley. Her eyes travelled toward the great Basilica of San Domenico (St. Dominic). She saw a Vision which would affect and determine the rest of her life.

Catherine saw Jesus seated on a throne, dressed in the white, gold-embroidered vestments of the Pope. On His Head He wore the Papal Tiara which has been passed on for almost two thousand years from Pope to Pope. Standing beside Him were the Apostles St. Paul and St. John the Evangelist, but He was not looking at *them*. Instead His Eyes were on Catherine, His Love and Smiling Face filling her with a joy she had never known before. He stepped toward her and blessed her with the sign of the Cross. Her eyes fixed on Him, she felt herself rising out of her body, being removed from the world around her, losing consciousness of her very self. There was such a magnetism drawing Catherine to the Lord, that although only *six years old*, she knew her childhood was over. Catherine reminds us of the children, who after our Lady touched their lives at Fatima, their toys meant nothing to them.

Catherine's brother who had gone ahead, realizing she was not directly behind him, ran back to find her. Upon seeing her, as if in a trance, he called to her. Getting no response, he went over to her and shook her strongly. Her eyes were like someone who had been asleep, no, really more like someone who had seen something, or was it Someone, no one else had seen. Trying to share the experience, she turned toward him, saying, *"If only you could see what I see, you would never try to disturb me."*

She turned back to the Vision, but Jesus was no longer there. She was so upset with herself. Had He left her because she had turned away from Him, even for a moment? *She was to give her "yes" that day; and her commitment to say that "yes", day in and day out, for the rest of her life. We are sure that "yes" took all the strength she had at times; as she was tested, failing; as she was lifted up by our Lord, falling; as she was armed anew with His Love, going on to the next "yes." The life of a Saint is the story of a War, easy reading, but hard living.* Catherine and her brother, on returning home, shared nothing of what had occurred with the family.

We are told Catherine was a very healthy, happy child. But, Catherine, the beautiful child, was to grow into an exquisite young lady with golden hair, the pride of her family. She had an infectious, bubbly personality, her joy only surpassed by the love that she so generously poured out to everyone. Although she always made herself available to make the rounds of the sick with her neighbors, she preferred to be *alone*. You can still see the dark corner of the house, where she would go off, pretending it was a cave and she a hermit. The means of flagellation, or *the discipline*[1], a knotted rope she used on herself, is still there in the little room, beside an iron grate she used as a pillow.

She was not *easy* to play with as a child; being strong-willed, she insisted all the children play Saints or better yet, hermits. When she could convince them, she would play teacher; making them recite after her, the Lord's Prayer and the Hail Mary. She also taught them about fasting and penance, introducing them to the knotted rope *she* used for discipline, that they then proceeded to use on one another.

---

[1]*discipline* - Name of the small whip or scourge used by some austere Religious Orders in penitential practices as a means of bodily mortification. Voluntary use should only be undertaken on advise of a competent spiritual director.

This play-acting was good for *children*, but soon Catherine desired the *real thing*. She left the house one morning to seek out a cave where she could begin her life as a *hermit*. Well fortified, a loaf of bread under her arm, she walked to the outskirts of town, to a deserted area dotted with caves. She entered a cave where she would begin her new life. She fell on her knees and began to pray. She went into a state of *ecstasy*[1], feeling nothing around her, not even her own presence. When she came out of this trance, she didn't know where she was or why she was there. She began to worry. *It was getting quite dark out; she had been away from home a long time. Were her parents worried?* She feared the gates of the city would be closed. She hurried home, trying to run unsuccessfully, her legs feeling like lead, weakened as well by so much kneeling. *Lord, let me just get home and I promise never to worry my parents like this again,* she prayed, bargaining for all she was worth. How many times have we said this as children?

All her worries turned out to be unnecessary. But back in the safety of her home, the girl who had left that morning, had grown up. Something had happened to Catherine in that cave. She never tried to live as a hermit again, although I believe her parents might have preferred that to the life she was to later follow.

In this newly found, more mature relationship with the Lord, she recognized the importance of *virginity*, realizing how the world and its cares, could be very distracting in her search for the Lord. As she walked closer to Him, she knew with all she was or ever would be, she could not serve two

---

[1]ecstasy - an enraptured condition of the soul and body...entails a suspension of the activity of one's exterior senses...highest form of spiritual union...absorption of the soul in God...The end results are positive: holiness of life, deepened joy and love, patience, sorrow for sins, confirmation of one's belief, and the pursuit of perfection in one's state of life and in spiritual insight.

masters. She had begun to hate the world, as her love for the Lord grew. She thought about the words of St. Paul,

> "*The virgin - indeed any unmarried woman - is concerned with things of the Lord, in pursuit of holiness in body and spirit. The married woman, on the other hand, has the cares of this world to absorb her and is concerned with pleasing her husband.*" (1Cor 7:34)

Catherine, desiring virginity, turned to the Virgin of all virgins, our Blessed Mother, for guidance on how to put Her Son Jesus before all others. Who better than the Mother of God, whose "yes" brought her to the foot of the Cross, could intercede so powerfully with our Lord in Catherine's behalf! She knew the Lord would accept from His Mother, each act of death to self and to the world Catherine would make.

One day, she prayed,

> "*Most Blessed Virgin, overlook my unworthiness and my nothingness, and graciously grant me this favor - to give me as my Spouse the One I long for from my inmost heart, your own all Holy and only Son, our Lord Jesus Christ; and I promise Him and promise you that I will keep my virginity forever spotless for Him.*"

Mother Mary presents Catherine to her Son Jesus

As Catherine continued praying, Blessed Mother appeared with her Son. She took the Hand of her Son Jesus and presented Catherine to Him. Catherine considered herself *engaged* to Jesus from that day on.

Knowing Jesus deserved the very best, Catherine strove to become the best bride *she* could be. As one of her biographers, Blessed Raymond of Capua said, she "...*began to fight against the flesh before the flesh began to rebel.*" She gave up eating meat, passing it to her brother Stephen or that failing, dropping it under the table for the cats.

Her relatives were pious, spirit-filled people; so no one paid particular attention when Catherine, as a little girl,

preferred playing "*saint*" over "mother" or "king and queen."
God carefully chooses to whom He sends His chosen ones.
Catherine's father was not only a holy man, but he was
equally respected for his integrity and patience. There was
an incident in their lives which could have resulted in the
family losing everything they had, making them destitute. A
man *falsely* accused Catherine's father Giacomo of owing
him money. Most men of that time would have reacted
violently, starting a *vendetta*[1], a blood bath. Giacomo asked
his family, instead, to pray for the man. Giacomo consoled
them, reassuring them of God's mercy and justice; God
would show the man, who had falsely made that allegation,
the error of his ways; *God* would be their Defender. "*When
they take you before synagogues and magistrates and
authorities, do not worry about how to defend yourselves or
what to say, because when the time comes, the Holy Spirit will
teach you what you must say.*" And Giacomo was right! The
truth became known; Giacomo was exonerated, his good
name restored and his fortunes returned to him.

Catherine's family were people of great faith. They
prayed together. They attended Mass as a family, regularly.
They believed in *miracles* and passed that belief on to their
families. Their role models were the Saints. They instilled
faith in God and confidence in themselves, by teaching their
children, through the *lives* of the Saints; they provided them
role models, with particular emphasis on Saints of their
region, considering them part of their heritage.

Catherine never went to school. Women of those days
did not receive any formal education, not even those of
wealthy families like Catherine's. She loved to hear about
the Saints and study the stained glass windows and paintings
in the churches, using them, as many who had no formal

---

[1] *vendetta* - a feud in which the relatives of a murdered or wronged
person seek vengeance on the wrongdoer or (and) members of his
family.

education did, as textbooks from which to learn. She listened intently as the Priest at Mass would bring yet another *hero* or *heroine* into Catherine's life on that Saint's Feast Day. She would also pay strict attention to the Word, wanting, no, hungering to know more about Jesus.

Catherine was quiet, requiring solitude in order to grow in the Lord. The house in which she lived was crawling with people, a hub of activity and noise, not conducive to someone called to Catherine's special walk with Jesus. To compound her struggles, her mother, although a good woman, very often contributed to the madness with her very loud and incessant chattering.

Having turned twelve years of age, Catherine was no longer allowed to go outside the house *unchaperoned*[1], not even to attend Mass. She was a favorite with her mother, father and brothers. They all carefully set about choosing the very best *husband* for her. Her mother prodded her to bathe often and dress attractively. Sensing no interest on Catherine's part, her mother was completely confused. *After all, wasn't that why she had been born, why every woman is born, to love and serve a husband?*

Whereas the mother's interest was to provide for her daughter's welfare, the father and brothers were spurred on by the *added* incentive of possibly accruing more wealth and land for themselves. This was the custom of that time, to arrange a *good* marriage of one's daughter to a man of high social standing and great wealth. It helped no end if the girl, like Catherine, was beautiful with *golden hair*.

Catherine tirelessly resisted her mother and the other members of her family with their endless nagging and coaxing. As they made plans, choosing this suitor and that

---

[1]chaperoned - The custom of that day was for an older or married woman to accompany a young unmarried woman in public or to be present at any parties, dances, etc., to provide supervision over her behavior and that of others.

beau, Catherine kept faithful to the vow she had made to the Lord. Finally, to placate them, she started to fuss over her appearance, grooming her hair, almost taking her mother's foolish suggestion to dye her beautiful golden hair. She even agreed to go out *socially*, which she would regret the rest of her life, and was introduced to many eligible bachelors. Finally one was chosen! No sooner done, Raymond of Capua said later, it was as if the Hand of God struck her sister down; Buonaventura, who had encouraged her to take on things of the world, died suddenly and painfully.

Catherine gave up all ideas of marriage and resumed her life of prayer and penance. The family, not knowing of her vow of virginity, were more than a little confused and upset. They called on a cousin, who had had a great influence on Catherine's spiritual life, for *help*. He had told her many stories of the Saints and was now a Priest, someone to whom she would listen. Catherine confessed to her cousin, the promise of eternal love and faithfulness she had pledged to the Lord. Although knowing the ways of the family, her cousin gave her a piece of advice that was to blow the lid off the house. "*Shave your head!*" Cutting off her beautiful golden curls, her head shaved clean, was a clear sign that Catherine *intended* to become a Nun. Not only would Catherine's mother not accept this symbol of marriage to *the Bridegroom*, but on seeing Catherine's shaven head, she loudly moaned, calling upon all the colorful expletives of that day to curse their misfortune.

The family hatched a new plan! If she would not marry, well then she could be their servant! They dismissed their servant and took away Catherine's bedroom, so she wouldn't have a place where she could be alone and pray. Now, without her bedroom, where she had been able to come and go as she pleased, she formed a room within her *soul* that no one could take away from her, one she could enter and leave as her *Lord* dictated. She suffered the ridicule of her brothers, returning their jeers with love. As she served them, they treated her without even the common courtesy they had shown the *servant* she had replaced.

This went on for months, until one night she had a dream. All the founders of the different Orders in the Church were there. One stepped forward, St. Dominic, and said, *"Do not worry. You will wear this habit."* Having said this, he handed her the black and white habit of the Mantellate[1].

Taking on courage from this dream, she told her family of the promise she had made to the Lord, to be His and *only* His bride. She strongly, but lovingly told them marriage to anyone but the Lord, was out of the question, so they might as well stop looking for suitors for her. If they wished her to remain as their servant the rest of her life, she would try to do that to the best of her ability. Even if they were to throw her out of the house, she went on, she would not be afraid, for she knew her Lord would provide for her all that she would ever need.

When Catherine's father heard her speak of her commitment, his heart was moved. He assured her the family would no longer interfere with her keeping her vow, as he accepted it as the Will of the Holy Spirit. He now understood the Vision he'd had a couple of months before: *Thinking she was being disobedient, kneeling and praying against his wishes, he angrily stormed over to where she was. She was motionless, as if transfixed, a dove hovering over her head. In an instant it (the dove) was gone and so was Catherine's father's anger.*

Giacomo ordered his family not to interfere with Catherine's vow to the Lord. He hired a servant to do the work Catherine had been doing, and to her greatest delight,

---

[1]Mantellate - Third Order of St. Dominic, a lay or secular Order. Members were not required to make the vows Nuns of religious Orders made, that is, chastity, poverty and obedience.

gave her back her own room. It was a tiny room, very much like the cave she had desired, away from the rest of the household. She hung a Crucifix on the wall. Her room included some planks of wood on which she slept, a little bureau to hold her clothes, all in all, the barest of furnishings; it was *Heaven* to her.

Catherine was thirteen years old and as yet did not know how to read. As she could not study the Gospel to learn more about her Lord, she spent long hours kneeling before the Crucifix. Looking on the Wounds of our Savior, she prayed she might share in His Sufferings.

Catherine's self-denial, her intense fasting and penance, changed her from a robust, healthy girl to someone who would suffer the rest of her life. Now, before you judge her walk, please read on.

Although Giacomo had forbidden everyone from interfering with Catherine's call, her mother could not stand seeing her daughter destroying herself, physically. She would insist Catherine sleep with her, on her soft, down bed. When her mother fell asleep, Catherine would quietly leave and go to her own room. Catherine and her mother are not unlike mothers and daughters today. Her mother hoped that by giving Catherine a taste for luxury, she would change her mind and give her some grandchildren.

Her mother came up with a new plan. She asked Catherine to go to a spa with her. Catherine, being no fool, beat the mother at her own game; she insisted she bathe alone. She went into the hottest part of the spa, almost scalding herself. She explained to her mother,

"I thought about the pains of hell and purgatory, and I asked my Creator to accept the pain I felt in the water in exchange for the pain in the next world which I know I deserve for my many sins."

Here we have two strong-willed women. No amount of cajoling, manipulation, crying, bullying, screaming or yelling could dissuade Catherine from her chosen life.

Catherine longed to wear the habit of the Mantellate, as handed to her by St. Dominic in her dream. This was not possible: *first*, she was too young; *second*, she was a virgin and they only accepted widows; and *third*, (and you're out), she was too pretty. Catherine begged her mother to go to the Sisters with permission for her to enter. Her mother, reverting to type, at first refused, but then gave in.

Her mother returned from the Sisters, trying to hide her delight. They had held fast to their rules. Catherine became suddenly, dangerously ill with high fever, blisters covering her whole body. She was too weak to fight this monster which was taking away her life. Her mother, sure she was losing "the sunshine of her life," *made a deal* with the Lord, St. Dominic and all the Saints in Heaven. If they would only *save* her daughter she would do anything they asked of her. Catherine, on her part, close to death, warned her mother, that if she did not go speak to the Nuns and get her admitted into the Third Order, The Lord and St. Dominic would see to it that she would not have Catherine in *any* habit.

At first, the Sisters objected that Catherine was too pretty. But after the mother brought them to Catherine's bedside and the Sisters saw her in her emaciated state, they accepted her. At last, Catherine would receive her habit. Now, she had one more hurdle to clear, temptations of the flesh! Satan attacked her with the fact she would never know children of her own. She remembered the joy in her sister's face as she held her new-born baby. The excitement of young lovers, the friendship of marriage, a partner for life, a husband, the satisfaction of raising a family, none of these would be hers. Alone in her room, as she fought these thoughts, she heard a man's voice, *"Why did you cut off your golden curls?"* Frustrated at Catherine's silence, a very handsome young man appeared to her, coaxing, *"Why put a hair shirt next to that delicate white body and in a few days, a coarse, rough habit, when you can wear this instead?"* He held before her the most resplendent silk gown embroidered with pearls, gold and jewels. Catherine was just about to take the dress when, suddenly, she understood who this was and what *he* wanted. *"No,"* she shouted, pushing him and the gown away. And with that, he vanished.

She had been fighting so hard to be received into the Third Order of St. Dominic, to live as a bride of Christ, so busy fighting her mother and family, she never considered what they had been saying. *Sometimes we're so busy fighting, we get more involved in winning the battle, not taking into consideration whether we want the spoils.* And so, here is Catherine, about to begin her new life, the one she had fought so hard to have, and what was it, a life of loneliness and hardship, in a dark, little room away from all she loved? Catherine, with what little strength she could summon, threw herself to the foot of the Crucifix, crying,

" *O my only, my dearest Bridegroom, You know that I have never desired any but You! Come to my aid now, my Savior, strengthen and support me in this time of trial!"*

Her eyes fixed on her Lord on the Cross, oblivious to anyone or anything else in the room, she heard the gentle stirring of a silk gown gliding toward her. She turned; before her was the Mother of God, Mary Most Holy. She was holding out to Catherine a silken dress, shimmering from the golden thread, jewels and pearls adorning it. As Mary clothed Catherine in the heavenly gown she had chosen, she said gently, lovingly,

"My daughter, I have drawn this garment from the Heart of my Son. It lay hidden in the wound in His Side, as in a golden casket, and I have made it myself with my own holy hands."

Once more Catherine said "yes" to Jesus' call to an intimate life with Him. *It reminds me of Peter having to say "yes" to the Lord three times when asked, "Do you love Me, Peter?"* Was Jesus asking this of Catherine *once again* knowing the pain and the struggle connected to that life, how many times she would be tempted to run away to a more comfortable place? The next day found Catherine, with her mother and father, at the Basilica of San Domenico, receiving her black and white habit; at last, the bridal gown she had longed for!

Catherine becomes a Third Order Dominican

She privately took the vows of Nuns who belonged to *Religious Orders*, poverty, chastity and obedience, although as a Third Order Dominican, it was not required of her. She stayed in her room, a recluse, except to attend Mass. For three years she lived this solitary life, scourging herself three times a day, denying herself sleep and adequate nourishment, not seeing or hearing anything or anyone outside this little world of hers. Although she allowed no one in her cell, she was never alone. Jesus, sometimes accompanied by His Mother and other times by Saints and Angels, would come and instruct her about God His Father, the Truths of the Gospel, about salvation and sin.

But, Jesus and His Heavenly Companions were not her only spirited visitors. The *fallen angels*, with their lies and deceptions, never failed to take an opportunity to attack. Catherine turned to prayer; the demons only howled the louder making it impossible to pray. They appeared in all forms of lewd behavior, attacking her mind with all sorts of sexual thoughts and desires. Not even by closing her eyes, could she block out the filthy work of these demons. She scourged herself all through the night. Still, the barrage of offenses came crashing down on her head and soul. They let her have it again and again, with the *idiocy of this life*, how wonderful and natural it would be to be *a wife and a mother*. One night, drenched and drained from the battle that had been ruthlessly ensuing, *she had a thought* from the Holy Spirit. She remembered the day she had asked the Lord for the *gift of Fortitude. (Author's note: I have become more careful what gifts I ask from the Lord, based on whether I am prepared to accept the test).* The Lord's words came back to her, *"If you want to have the strength to overcome all the enemy's attacks, take the Cross as your refreshment."* Fortified by the Lord's words, she stood ground, to do battle with the little devils.

Finally giving up, the demons dispersed. The Lord appeared for the *first* time since the attacks had begun. Was Catherine upset! She asked the Lord where He had been during the onslaught. I wonder if He wasn't smiling a little, enjoying the little spitfire He had chosen for a bride, as He replied, *"I was in your heart."* Catherine, no different than the rest of us, could not understand how the enemy could be attacking her if her Lord was there, and she told Him so. He responded by asking her if her temptations brought her enjoyment or sorrow. She told Him of her feelings of repulsion and her intense trial. He told her it was He who planted those feelings of displeasure. If *He* had not been in the center of her heart, the thoughts and temptations of the enemy would have pleased her instead of displeasing her. She (or is it we) was to learn a hard lesson, one she was never to forget, God is always with us, even when we do not *feel* Him.

Catherine learns to read

Catherine wanted to be able to read, desiring to pray the Office along with the Priests, Brothers and Sisters in church during vespers. A friend of hers, from a noble family, lent her a book of alphabets. Hard as she tried, she could not learn how to read. Frustrated and upset, she turned to her Bridegroom with *"If You want me to read, You'll have to teach me, yourself. Otherwise, I'll remain the ignorant fool I am."* I wonder how many of us would dare to have that wonderfully intimate, *trusting* relationship with the Lord. Catherine had it and she paid for it with her flesh and blood. From that time on, reading came easier and easier to Catherine, until the day she was to master it completely. She never learned to write, however; *she dictated* all her marvelous writings, which later earned her the honorable title, *Doctor of the Church*.

Being able to read changed her life. Jesus would come into her room and they would say the Holy Office together; only when she said, *"Glory be to the Father,* she would change *and to the Son* to: *and to You, Lord, and to the Holy Spirit."* For three years, she lived this blissful life with her Bridegroom, until Shrove Tuesday[1] when she was to receive one of her greatest gifts from the Lord. It was the last night of the carnival in Siena; it was as if Satan was doing his last howling. It was like when Moses came down from the mountain and saw all the Jewish people worshiping a golden calf and reveling wildly. The partying was loud, wine overflowing, everyone misbehaving as the Lord must have seen them doing at Sodom and Gomorrah. It was this night, when all hell was breaking loose, that Jesus chose to wed His Catherine, making her His Bride.

The Mystical Marriage of Catherine to our Lord Jesus

As Jesus was speaking, His mother entered the room. With her were St. John the Apostle, St. Paul, Saint Dominic, and King David. We can see David dancing as he joyously accompanied them with his harp. Catherine's walk, as with

---

[1]Shrove Tuesday - Shrovetide is the collective name of the few days immediately preceding Lent. It was (and is, in places like New Orleans) customary to hold carnivals at this time in anticipation of the long fast of Lent. The feasting was climaxed on Shrove Tuesday, the day before Ash Wednesday, with a variously named festivity, such as Mardi Gras.

the other Saints we have studied, male and female, was *to Jesus through His mother.* Mother Mary took Catherine by the arm and gently placed the young virgin's hand into the Hand of her Son, our Lord Jesus, asking Him humbly, and ceremoniously, to take Catherine to Himself, in the Holiest of Matrimony. Jesus, the Most Handsome Bridegroom, smiling with only His Blinding Smile, took Catherine's hand and placed on her finger, a gold ring with the purest pearls surrounding a brilliant diamond, which danced and glittered like the Star in the East must have the night He was born.

"*There. I marry you to Me in faith, to Me, your Creator and Savior. Keep this faith unspotted until you come to Me in Heaven and celebrate the marriage that has no end. From this time forward, daughter, act firmly and decisively in everything that in My Providence I shall ask you to do. Armed as you are with the strength of faith, you will overcome all your enemies and be happy.*"

Having spoken, Jesus, with His Mother and the heavenly witnesses, left Catherine. With her ring as proof she had really been married to Her One True Love (although she was the only one who could see it), Catherine was strengthened to withstand all the persecution that lay ahead. She shamefully admitted that even *she* was not able to see the ring, when she had offended her Lord and needed to go to confession. *I wonder how many gifts we cannot see, because believing the evil one and his lie that there is no sin, we are in a state of sin and no longer have that gift of peace and joy, that comes from Reconciliation with the Lord.*

Catherine did as most newlyweds do, except the *faraway place,* she chose for their honeymoon, was not one of a romantic spot on some deserted island, but it was an island, quiet, with no one or nothing to distract her from learning from her Spouse. She listened and asked questions, her whole mind and heart intent on what wisdom the Master was

Right:
**Crown of Gold and
Crown of Thorns**

Below:
Mystical Marriage to Jesus

Below Left:
**St. Catherine and
the Beggar**

Below Right:
**Catherine appeals
to the Pope**

imparting to her, His Bride. She achieved her greatest moment of unity with Jesus after she received Him in the Eucharist. At that moment, when Jesus was *physically* Present to Catherine, she felt her soul soaring up to Heaven, experiencing all the exquisite wonders *there*, with the Lord as her Guide and Host.

But as we mortals know, honeymoons come to an end. *In Marriage Encounter¹, we learn first there is the courtship, then the honeymoon, then the disillusionment, then the living out of the Sacrament of Matrimony.* Catherine's honeymoon, not unlike ours, had to come to an end, so their new life could begin.

One afternoon, Jesus spoke to Catherine of the future, how He wanted her to live out the two most special commandments He had given us, to love God and to love *neighbor*. The second was the hard one. She had been so happy loving Him. There was one *fear* she had, which had always held her back from any human relationships; that was loving humans at the expense of being wholly faithful to her Lord. As we know, we can trust in God, but humans are only too willing to show us we cannot trust in *them*. This was probably another major stumbling block she envisioned, as He gently laid out His Plan, His Work for her. She thought of the possible rejection. She protested that she did not know how to love her neighbor. She had kept that love for her Lord safely tucked away, just for Him, from the first time He had appeared to her when she was six years old. She had forgotten her great capacity to love her brothers and sisters, how they and their souls had been a priority to her. He

¹Marriage Encounter - a retreat where married couples learn *sharing skills*, how to dialogue among themselves to enrich their Sacrament. In a spiritual atmosphere and context, the couple reflects on the dignity and meaning of married life. There is a chapter on Bob and Penny Lord's Marriage Encounter experience in their book, "We Came Back To Jesus."

playfully reminded her of her desire "*of disguising yourself as a man so you could become a Friar Preacher and go off to teach My truth.*"

Like Mother Mary before her, she was not doubting our Lord, but asking as a woman, how could this come about. "*I am a woman and ignorant.*"

Her question, logical in the eyes of the world, was answered by the super logic of the Lord, "*In My Eyes there is neither male nor female, rich or poor, but all are equal, for I can do all things with equal ease. I spread abroad the grace of My Spirit where I will.*"

It wasn't lack of faith that He could do it, but, *how.* After all, she was a woman, and women could not walk alone on the streets; she, like other women had not been formally educated, except in household duties; who would listen to her, a *woman*, especially in matters men have reserved as *their* business.

I wonder if the Lord was not smiling more than a little *lovingly* at this gentle dove that was to become a *powerful woman in the Church*; and more than a little *sadly*, at the words he was about to say,

"*I realize that you do not speak from lack of faith but from humility. Therefore you must know that in these latter days there has been such a surge of pride, especially in the case of men who imagine themselves to be learned or wise, that My justice cannot endure them any longer. To confound their arrogance, I will raise up women, ignorant and frail by nature, but endowed with strength and wisdom. For it is only just that those who try to exalt themselves should be humbled. Therefore be brave and obedient when I send you out among people. Wherever you go I will not forsake you, I will be with you, as is My custom, and will guide you in all that you are to do.*"

Catherine started to obey the Lord's command by *eating with the family.* As she had not eaten in years, real food repulsed her and she ended up *serving* them instead. After so many years of solitude, the normal noise of family eating, talking, laughing and arguing would have been almost unbearable, had it not been for the Lord.

Communicating with her family was a little intimidating at first, especially with her brothers who had mocked her. But she could not keep the love and knowledge she had been given by our Lord to herself, so she started to inadvertently *teach* her family. The dinner table started to collect first relatives and then friends of relatives, until throngs of people came just to hear Catherine's teachings. Her favorites, like ours, were the young, enthusiastically seeking the Lord. They got caught up in her obvious love and excitement for the Lord and became like *holy sponges*, sopping up all that poured forth from her. A little group started to form around Catherine. Her cell or room was no longer a refuge where she could be alone with her Lord. It seemed, *alone* was something she was not to be anymore. The little group of Dominican Priests, some of the Mantellate, and her sister-in-law, congregated not only to hear Catherine teach, but they prayed together, sang and shared together, their dreams and disappointments; they became *friends*.

Catherine and the lepers

Catherine's apostolate, with some of her Mantellate, began with visiting and caring for the sick. Catherine worked in the hospital ministering to the worst cases, people who were scarred physically and emotionally. They returned kindness and love with the worst physical and mental abuse. Catherine always came back for more, seeing Jesus Crucified in all their *wounds*.

One of Catherine's patients was a leper named Cecca, whose condition was so bad the hospital wanted to send her to a leprosarium[1]. Because of Catherine's insistence, Cecca was allowed to remain in the hospital. Cecca was grateful at first, but then when the pain became unbearable, she had to lash out at someone. Who was the *someone* she could trust not to turn against her, no matter what she said or did? You're right, Catherine! As in all small communities, Cecca's abuse of Catherine became town gossip, and finally fell on Catherine's mother's ears. She was furious! She did everything in her power to try to dissuade Catherine from continuing her care of this *ungrateful wretch.* To her mother's pleading, *"If you keep up with this woman you will end up a leper yourself and that I could not stand,"* Catherine's reply was, *"Have no fear about that, Mother. What I do for this woman I do for God. He would never let me suffer for it."*

Famous last words, for soon white sores began to appear on Catherine's hands. She had begun to show the first signs of the dreaded illness. Trusting in her God, she nevertheless continued to care for Cecca, even to washing her body and preparing her for burial, when she died. When the last act of faith was completed, Catherine's hands returned to their clear, white state, unscarred and more exquisite than ever.

Another patient, a bristly, angry Mantellata named Andrea, had a rancid-smelling, festering, open wound on her breast. Here we go again, another one who returned the ongoing, loving, considerate, compassionate care Catherine gave her, with the spreading of vile, vicious and totally untrue rumors about Catherine which delighted those who were jealous of her and angered those, like her mother, who loved her. Again, her mother begged Catherine to stop, for her sake, but to no avail. Her Lord came to the rescue

---

[1]leprosarium - a sanitarium, a hospital or a colony for lepers

again, for He showed Catherine *in her glorified state* to Andrea and she became one of her strongest allies.

One day, having removed the bandage from Andrea's chest, the smell and the sight so turned Catherine's stomach, she had all to do to keep from throwing up on the poor soul. Catherine was so angry with her body, for being so weak, that after cleaning and dressing the wound, she drank down the liquid that had poured forth from her chest. As she did so, all her former revulsion passed, and as she later shared, *"Never since the day I was born did any food or drink afford me such sweetness and delight."* She confided that she pressed her face close to the wound that had so repulsed her; instead of the nauseating stench of before, she was greeted with a fragrance sweeter than that of any flower she'd ever smelled.

Later, her Adoring Spouse came to her, as she prayed in thanksgiving for another day to serve Him. Our Lord praised her for overcoming her instinctive revulsion, out of love for Him. To reward her, He invited her to drink from His Side, from the Wound inflicted by Longinus the Centurion[1]. He called it the *fountain of life* itself. *In (Lanciano) the town where Longinus came from, a miracle of the Eucharist was manifested by the Host turning into a Human Heart and the consecrated wine turning into Human Blood.* So, isn't it natural the Lord would reward Catherine, whose *love* dictated her actions over the weakness of her flesh, with this sign of *His Love*, Blood from His Side[2], from the tip of His Heart?

According to the Life of St. Catherine, written by Blessed Raymond of Capua, her confessor and confidant, in an

---

[1]Longinus -Pierced the Side of Jesus, striking the Tip of our Savior's Heart. He is mentioned in "This is My Body...This is My Blood.

[2]"Jesus says to them that it is not in some kind of cannibalistic way you are going to eat My Flesh and drink My Blood because I am going to ascend to Heaven. It is in a way you cannot conceive. (Fr. Harold Cohen, SJ)

Apparition which took place about the year 1372 she was given a special gift, one which would stay with her for the rest of her life. She was allowed to drink of the Blood of Jesus, from His Side. She shared with Blessed Raymond that after drinking the Blood of Jesus, she couldn't eat anymore. She was neither hungry, nor could she hold anything in her stomach, other than the Sacred Species, the Body and Blood of Jesus.[1]

We have a Priest whom we love very much. One day, as part of his homily, he said,

"Worse than cancer; worse than heart trouble, is the wounds inflicted on the human heart, the hurts that no medicine can heal. As humans break each others' hearts, as one betrays another's trust, robbing that person of his or her illusions, it is hard to accept, at that moment, that Jesus is going to not only heal, but give you one hundred-fold for accepting this Cross He is trusting you with." This is the making of Saints.

There was another patient, another Mantellata, whose name was Palmerina. I mention this *Mantellata* because the ones who disillusion us and jade us, wounding us irreparably at times, are the ones we consider the *"good guys."* Very often they are those who love the Lord, one of us; they are Priests, Sisters in our Community, family, friends.

Palmerina had come from a wealthy and well-known family, and had given all her money to the hospital where she was now seriously ill. She had done many charitable works, but the enemy of jealousy and envy was one area of her life she had not allowed the Lord to heal. She manifested all these feelings against Catherine, who infuriated her the more with her ongoing kindness and concern. She refused to see Catherine, hoping that would discourage her and she would stop trying; but I guess, she didn't know Catherine. When all else failed, she, being well thought of, successfully

---

[1]excerpt from "This is My Body...."

spread her poisonous innuendos and false gossip about Catherine around Siena. Catherine repaid her slander with prayers. Our Lord revealed to Catherine the precious goodness of Palmerina's soul and how this cancerous malignancy of jealousy was contaminating her, fatally sentencing her to eternal damnation. The Vision inspired Catherine to pray all the harder. Palmerina was on the brink of death. Catherine prayed, "*O my Lord, if You will not grant me the mercy I have asked for my sister, I shall not leave this spot alive.*" As Palmerina lay dying for three days, at one end of town, Catherine prayed endlessly at the other end, until the Lord (probably exhausted from Catherine's persistent prayers, or perhaps *was it pestering prayers*), enlightened Palmerina's soul. She repented the wrong she had done and, with all her heart, welcomed Catherine. She later died in peace.

After Palmerina's death, Jesus told Catherine He had shown her the beauty of a human soul so she would pray even more passionately for the salvation of *all* souls. He then gave her another gift, to see into all the souls that came to her, the light and darkness of each soul, even extending to those souls she had not *seen* but for which she was praying.

Catherine's father became seriously ill. She rushed to his side. Although her father had been a good and virtuous man, Jesus revealed to her he would need to spend some time in Purgatory for some of the "*rust spots his soul had contracted.*" Catherine went back on her knees, pleading to her Lord to inflict on her, instead of her father, any pains he would have to suffer in Purgatory. The Lord granted her plea. *Do you sort of get the idea Jesus can't resist this little lady?* Catherine had a Vision of her father in Paradise; this was to sustain her as she carried the *added pain* to the excruciating suffering she already had. If you would like to be proclaimed a Saint someday, how does the price sound? Do you still wish you could have been Catherine? Well,

Catherine, along with other powerful women in the Church, would not have traded the life they knew with Jesus as a result of their suffering.

Catherine has no sooner said good by to her father, then she was faced with her mother, gravely ill, in bed. As Catherine prayed for a happy death, her mother, never as far along spiritually as her husband and daughter, complained, *"Why are you praying I die, instead of praying for me to live?"* God had revealed to Catherine the many tragedies her mother would suffer if she lived, but her mother was insistent. She lived, but to regret every day she had not died, seeing children and grandchildren die before her eyes.

Catherine softened the hearts of the hardhearted

There had been an election and a new faction had taken over the government. The *victors* were running wild in the streets, drunk with power, seeking members of the defeated party and *those* who had supported it. Friends came to Catherine's home to warn her brothers (as they had been supporters of the ousted party), that the mob was heading their way. Over the friends' objections and their pleas for the brothers to come with them to the *safety* of the church, Catherine instructed her brothers to walk *through* the mob; walking *toward* them, not *away* from them. She warned, *"My brothers will not go to the church and I feel sorry for anyone who does."* She told her brothers she would walk with them, in the middle, with one of them on her right and the other on her left. *"Do not be afraid now. Come with me, and walk bravely, like manly men."* With their sister's words and her presence to enforce them, her arms linked with theirs, they walked right into the mob, heads held high, *manly men.* The mob made way for Catherine and her brothers, not touching a hair on their heads. When the mob saw the *Mantellata* who had ministered to them and their families, they could not raise a hand against her brothers. As she had prophesied, many of the men who had gone to hide in the church, were massacred that night.

Again, Catherine was to hear the rumbling of a mob, only now it was at the home of her friend Alessia. People were on the side lines, watching and taunting two criminals who were being paraded through the streets. The criminals would scream in pain, cursing God, as the townspeople pinched them with red hot prongs. As they had committed unspeakably cruel crimes, there was no sympathy for them as they passed on their way to be executed.

No, no one but Catherine! She began to intercede with her Lord, pleading for them, reminding the Lord of the *good thief* that hung to the right of Him. She begged Him *to have mercy on these two, as He'd had mercy on that thief, when He promised him he would be with Him in Paradise; soften their hearts so they will repent and not know the everlasting pains of hell.* God allowed Catherine, *in spirit,* to walk beside the two criminals, praying and mourning for them and their sins, as if they were her *flesh and blood* brothers.

The devils were also parading beside the two, laughing and rejoicing as they would have two more to keep them company in the *pit of darkness*; all the while throwing menacing looks at Catherine, frustrated they could not stop her unconditional love pleading for the two.

When the two criminals came to the place of execution, Jesus appeared to them, bloody and beaten, covered with *spit.* He raised His Head; His Beautiful Eyes, blood and tears spilling from Them, looked at them with so much love and compassion, they saw themselves as He saw them, as He had created them to be, and as they were. They were sorry for their sins, called for a Priest and after confessing, went to their execution in peace.

When the Priest shared with Catherine, who had not been present *physically* at the execution, what happened, she smiled; for at the moment of death, she had known *"this day they were with the Lord in Paradise."* And so, Catherine got the reputation of softening the hearts of the hardest-hearted criminals.

Catherine's reputation began to grow in Siena
Mothers and wives asked her to pray for their loved ones. When they wanted to be sure God would listen to their prayers, people would come to Catherine and ask her to intercede with the Lord. *"God listens to her!"*
But not everyone admired Catherine. There was a professor of philosophy, a Franciscan named Fr. Lazzarino, who although he had never heard her speak, criticized her teaching to any and everyone who would listen. A fellow Priest suspected Fr. Lazzarino's criticism was more out of jealousy and the sin of pride *"Why her!"* than anything else. He was excited when Fr. Lazzarino agreed to meet with Catherine, trusting she would win him over. The meeting took place, and much polite conversation passed back and forth. When it was time for the two Priests to leave, Catherine humbly knelt before Fr. Lazzarino and genuinely pleaded with him to bless and pray for her. As the whole evening had been one of politeness on both parts, and Catherine had acted so humbly, what could the Priest do, but ask Catherine to pray for him, too. He did not believe in her sanctity or power of intercessory prayer; but felt he would accommodate her. She seemed like a good woman, but special, *no!*
He never *imagined* the impact Catherine's prayers were to have on his life. The next night, not being able to sleep, he found himself weeping; confused as to why he was weeping, but not able to stop. The next day was to be a continuation of the night before, with Fr. Lazzarino crying unceasingly, weak and broken, not able to teach or go out. The Lord spoke to the interior of his heart, lovingly

chastising him for being prideful and polite, almost demeaning as he asked for Catherine's prayers.

Father Lazzarino rushed to Catherine's house and prostrated himself, humble for probably the first time in years, while Catherine prostrated herself beside *him* at the same time. They sat side by side, praying and talking, hours on end. Catherine directed him to shed himself of all the things of this world: wealth, acceptance, recognition and friendship; so he might trade them in for rejection, poverty, and humiliation, in imitation of Jesus Crucified and his holy father St. Francis. The Priest knowing it was not Catherine speaking, but God through her, did as she instructed and became a disciple of Jesus through Catherine. He became, as his friends said, *be-Catherined*. Catherine *be-Catherined* all the men who came to her, who the Lord touched through her. She became a brilliant light showing them what they could be, *"manly men,"* as her Jesus had been. The Famous as well as those of little fame, came to her and were touched, never to be the same, again. They loved her holiness and her wisdom; her astounding courage to say, without flinching what needed to be said. They looked upon her as a *giant*, taking *Jesus* as her *Role Model*, representing *The Giant*.

When Jesus had given the mandate to Catherine to go out to all the world and bring *My Word* to them, she wondered how it would be done, knowing of the restrictions put upon women at that time. *But as we know, first Jesus plants the idea, waits for our "yes," and then lays out the plan, making available the circumstances and the opportunities for us to fulfill our "yes" to Him.* Most of her calls at the hospital were at night, as that is the hardest, most frightening time for the elderly and the dying. The fact that *women just did not do this* and that it was dangerous, as well, did not deter her. The hospital, which is there till today, eventually reserved a room for Catherine; so that, when it became too late for her to return home, she could stay overnight.

Catherine's knowledge of God and Scripture is questioned

Many of the *intelligentsia* quarreled over Catherine's teaching of God and Scripture. *Who was she to teach!* They could not believe that she, an uneducated woman (not having been educated formally in a school), could have received *infused knowledge*[1]. They accused her of lying and of purposely deceiving the Church. *If* she had supernatural gifts, then they had to be of the devil!

Not only did she have to suffer the malicious gossip of the *intelligentsia, that* she could have handled if they were alone. But the simple everyday people she loved so, those she had always been available to help, were spreading rumors casting doubts on her *virginity. What went on, with her and all those men* (it didn't matter they were considered holy Monks and Priests) *coming in and out of her cell, day and night?* My problem with people delighting in scandal about someone who is trying to do God's Work, is why? What is there in some people that they would spread gossip about another? My grandmother always said if you know something that would damage someone's reputation, hide it under your apron.

These were not the only wounds Catherine had to endure. They did not believe she fasted long periods of time; *She was probably eating on the sly,* they said; even though *no one* had seen her eat. Then there were the Dominicans *(always your own)* who had problems with Catherine's frequent reception of Communion; how she wept, crying aloud as she approached the Priest, to receive her Lord in His Blessed Sacrament. *This outward display of*

---

[1]infused knowledge - Supernatural virtue or principles of action placed by God into our souls as a special gift. They are higher than acquired moral virtues, and they grow with the increase and exercise of habitual grace, (also called sanctifying or justifying grace, includes the virtues and gifts of the Holy Spirit,...infused into the very essence of the soul *as a habit* is habitual grace).

emotion offended the sensibilities of the other worshippers. Then to compound the problem, she would go into ecstasy; completely disruptive. To make matters worse, if that's possible, her ecstasies would last so long, the Dominicans threw her out of the Church, bodily, at the end of the day.

A General Chapter was called, in Florence, by the Dominicans, to *discuss* Catherine. As a result of the Chapter, she was given Blessed Raymond of Capua, a Priest well respected and seventeen years her senior, as Confessor and Spiritual Director. Raymond, because of his reputation and standing in the Church, was to give Catherine the authority that would make her influence felt not only in Siena, but in the Church at large. Catherine, who some had hoped to have denounced as a *heretic*[1], to silence once and for all, was, instead, raised up by the findings of the Chapter, and proclaimed truly holy, an instrument through which God performed great *miracles.*

The Black Plague spreads in Siena

The little group, returning from the Chapter in Florence, had no time to celebrate. Upon entering the gates of Siena, the bloated bodies and horrible stench of the dying and dead greeted them. The Black Plague had returned to their Siena. Catherine rolled up her sleeves and started to minister to the sick and dying. The rich had left the city; only the poor and those tending them remained, and they were dying. No one was being spared. Many of Catherine's family died. She tended them, all through their illnesses, speaking of God and the Kingdom, and dressed them readying them for burial.

---

[1]heretic - A baptized and professed person who denies or doubts a truth revealed by God or proposed for belief by the Catholic Church is a heretic. The term is usually reserved for one who is guilty of formal heresy. (see Apostasy) - It is a grievous sin since it is a denial of the truth of God and the Church. One who so acts is called an apostate.

Raymond of Capua came into town, and worked tirelessly beside Catherine day and night. Because he, as a Priest, was urgently needed to administer the Sacraments, Raymond got very little, sometimes *no* sleep. This went on until one day he felt a pain and a swelling in his groin; his head began to ache and burn with a raging fever. With what little strength he had left, he dragged himself to Catherine's home. When she returned from doing her rounds of patients in their homes and at the hospital, she found Raymond on a cot, *delirious*, more dead than alive. He had all the signs of the Plague. Catherine placed her hands on his head and as she prayed she could feel the heat leaving his body, his old vitality replacing the weakness left by the disease. He later wrote, *"It was as if something was being pulled out of me at the ends of all my limbs."* Catherine finished praying; Raymond was completely cured.

"Have something to eat now, and then rest for a while and then go out again and work for the salvation of souls and give thanks to the Highest Who has saved you." And with that, Catherine sent Raymond on his way.

Catherine found Friar Santi, her friend and disciple, more dead than alive in his hermitage, certain to be a fatality of the Plague. She moved him to the hospital, reassuring him, *"Do not be afraid no matter how bad you feel. You are not going to die, this time."* She returned later; now he was in a *coma*! She whispered in his ear, *"Do not be afraid; you are not going to die."* Days went by. His condition only grew worse. All his friends gave up hope on him. Catherine went up to him, and this time *shouted* in his ear, *"I command you, in the name of our Lord Jesus Christ, not to die!"* With *that*, he shot straight up in bed, asked for something to eat; his crisis over, he was well.

There are many instances, where Catherine interceded with our Lord and people were saved, too numerous to put down in this chapter. Finally, the Plague was at an end;

Catherine and her Spiritual Director would be able to talk. Catherine *trusted* Raymond. She had never met anyone like him, with his wisdom, intelligence, and ability to listen. She felt, at last, she had met her *mentor*. She talked to him endlessly, words pouring out of her, of the Visions she'd had of our Lord Jesus, of her thoughts on sin and sanctifying grace. He was having a problem absorbing all she said; it was too much, like a faucet running uncontrollably. He had never heard of revelations such as the young visionary was sharing. He was having trouble believing in them *and* her.

The next morning, he reluctantly returned to Catherine, *convinced* she was not reliable. Upon arriving, he found her too weak to move, but not, to his dismay, too weak to go on endlessly about her spiritual ideas and many gifts from her Bridegroom. He found himself getting *agitated*. All this endless talk of hers was very annoying and irritating. He bent down, disbelieving, anxious to get this over with. Instead of seeing Catherine's face, the Face looking back at him, was That of Jesus Christ. Startled, he blurted out, "Who is this looking at me?"

"*It is He who is,*" Catherine responded. Raymond, was *now* convinced she was *genuine*, a true follower and disciple of Jesus. He became one of her most zealous champions and strongest advocates.

Wherever she went, her holiness went before her, as well as her ecstasies and her levitations.[1] They'd heard of the many miracles that had come about through her intercession. The fact she was known to go into ecstasy and perform miracles, made her a much sought after speaker and teacher. In her time, as in Jesus and Paul's time, *miracles* drew a crowd. People sought miracles, as they do today.

---

[1]levitation -...raising and keeping a heavy body in the air with little or *no* physical support.

I believe miracles are a sign God is with us, that He is involved with us, not only in allowing them, but in allowing us to be a witness to them. As with our Retreats and Days of Recollections on the Miracles of the Eucharist, where the faithful lined up, all day long, to have their confessions heard, requiring as many as four Priests, so it was with Catherine. Everywhere she gave talks, Priests would hear confessions of the people from early dawn to sunset and on to dusk. The darkness of night did not deter the people from staying to be reconciled with their Lord and Savior. *This* was the energizing force that kept her going. Catherine did not seek fame and recognition. She never considered or promoted herself as a *miracle worker*; rather as a poor instrument God was using for the *salvation of souls.* That was her only priority, that and growing closer to her Lord.

Catherine chooses the Crown of Thorns

From her youngest years, Catherine was being called to a closer walk with Jesus. He always accompanied that call with a *sign* to strengthen her for the *gift* of that walk, and the *days ahead* with that gift. For example, one day Jesus appeared to Catherine with two crowns, one of thorns and one of gold, asking Catherine which she chose. Catherine pointed to the crown of thorns. Jesus replied,

"You have chosen well. That you have chosen the crown of thorns for your time on earth, you will wear this crown of gold for all eternity when you come to make your new life with Me."

Then, another time, Jesus took her heart and replaced it with His. We read the words, *"Jesus replaced her heart with His."* Do we think about what that might have cost Catherine. During this exchange of hearts, she later confessed to her Spiritual Director, she was without a heart for days; she waited for Jesus to replace her *"stony heart"* with His Unconditionally Loving, Compassionate, Merciful and Forgiving Heart, with Which she was then to love His children. This had to happen for her to be able to love unconditionally, returning hate with love, envy with generosity, abuse with mercy and patience, forgiving all for their malice and gossip. *(Author's note: One day, many years ago, we had a thought; it was to consecrate our whole bodies to the Lord, beginning with our minds down to our feet. We started by asking the Lord to take our minds and give us His to think and choose with. This has always taken the most time to exchange with the Lord, as we struggle to give up control. When we have asked Him for His Heart to love with, in exchange for our hearts, we have seen the pain in people, the wounds behind their often cruel and selfish behavior. And when we have loved them with His Heart, looking beyond their masks, He has shared wih us, the rejection He suffered, even to the Cross.)*

Catherine receives the Stigmata

Raymond was with her in Pisa, when he saw her transfigured into the Image of Jesus Christ. He had just finished celebrating Mass for Catherine and her companions when she went into ecstasy, *"her soul separating as much as it could from the body."* They saw her body, which had been prostrate on the floor, rise. Mid-air, she kneeled, her face aglow with the fire of Jesus' Love inside of her. Then with a tremor, her body fell in a heap onto the floor. Her companions waited for her words, as she came out of the rapture. It was her practice, always, to share what the Lord had told her or what had transpired during an ecstasy. This time, however, it was different. Catherine awoke after a few moments, and went directly to Raymond.

"Father, I must tell you, that by His Mercy, I now bear the stigmata of the Lord Jesus in my body," she said. *"I saw our Lord fastened to the Cross, coming down upon me in a blaze of light. With that, as my spirit leaped to meet its Creator, this poor body was pulled upright.*

Above:
Cross of the Stigmata

Above: *Catherine in Ecstasy*

Above:
St. Catherine's Home
Left:
St. Catherine's Cell

Then I saw, springing from the marks on His Most Sacred Wounds, five blood-red rays coming down upon me, directed towards my hands and feet and heart. Realizing the meaning of this mystery, I promptly cried out: 'Ah, Lord, my God, I implore You not to let the marks show outwardly on my body.[1]*' Whilst these words were still on my lips, before the rays had reached me, their blood-red color changed to radiant brightness, and it was in the form of clearest light they fell upon the five parts of my body - hands, feet and heart."*

Although Raymond continued asking her if she did not mean the wound was in her *side*, she insistently repeated over and over again, no, *it was in her heart.*

We are in awe of those whom the Lord has chosen to share His Sacred Wounds, from very possibly St. Paul, "*I bear the wounds of Christ*," down through the centuries to our St. Catherine. But we know by her words to Raymond, *some* of the excruciating pain she *suffered* bearing the Precious Wounds of our Lord Jesus. Although Catherine had known pain all her life, this so debilitated her, she was in a coma for a week. Fearing she was dying, all her friends, including Raymond of Capua, prayed night and day. Not able to stir from her bed, feeling all the torture of Christ's Wounds cruelly rubbing against the blunt hard nails, *she*, too, was sure she was dying. *(Author's Note: In the Holy Land we were told, they drove square spikes into our Beloved Savior's Hands. Using this type of nail, rather than a pointed one, was to inflict more pain on the criminal as it broke through his skin. This type of execution was reserved for the worst offenders. As our Lord took on all the sins of the world, they let our Lord have it with both barrels. He willingly and innocently, suffered for all*

---

[1]The members of her Company reported that the wounds of the stigmata, although invisible during her life, became *visible* upon Catherine's death.

the wrong that had been done or would ever be done). And our Catherine now suffered this with Him.

Nothing helped to alleviate the agony and exhaustion that were companions of the stigmata. Catherine returned home from Pisa but this did not improve her condition. Not even the sight of her beloved Siena could give her back the strength she had lost. Her mornings were pure hell for her, as she tried to get up from bed, having had barely an hour's sleep the night before. Only the loving support of her friends in the Mantellate, and the eyes of her heart focused solely on the *Eucharist*, gave Catherine the strength to painfully rise from bed.

Feeling some relief from the pain, Catherine consoled Raymond,

"The Lord has heard your prayers, and it is now my soul which is afflicted with suffering; but as for my body, these wounds no longer cause it pain, but rather lend it force and vigor. I can feel strength flowing into me from those wounds which at first only added to my sufferings."

St. Catherine, Eucharistic Faster

"For the seven year period prior to her death, she took no food into her body other than the Eucharist. Her fasting did not affect her energy, however. She maintained a very active life during those seven years. As a matter of fact, most of her great accomplishments occurred during that period. Her death had nothing to do with malnutrition, or anything connected with lack of food[1]."

Not only did her fasting not cause her to lose energy, but became a source of extraordinary strength, she becoming stronger in the afternoon, after having received our Lord in His Eucharist. One of the only sufferings she found almost intolerable, was to be denied Her Lord in the Eucharist.

---

[1]An excerpt from our book on Miracles of the Eucharist.

Neither the Priests at the Basilica of St. Dominic, nor Catherine's Superior in the Mantellate approved of her receiving the Eucharist daily. They tried to discourage Catherine, unsuccessfully. The Priests flatly refused, insisting she receive solely from her Confessor; it didn't matter if he was out of town. At that time, Catherine would seek comfort looking at the Priest during the Mass. After all, through his consecrated hands, he was bringing her Lord to her on the altar where she could adore Him, even if she could not receive Him. Catherine endured the worst anguish over this until Raymond came to Siena and she was able to receive Communion daily. When he was in town, he would only have to hear her plea, *"Father, I hunger,"* and, if at all possible, he would celebrate Holy Mass.

Pope Gregory XI, who Catherine convinced to return to Rome from Avignon, later decreed a papal bull allowing her to receive *daily*, her Lord in His *"Body and Blood, Soul and Divinity"*[1], the Eucharist.

Catherine had Visions during the consecration of the Mass, sometimes seeing Jesus dressed as a Priest, repeating the words He spoke at the Last Supper. Other times, when she gazed upon the raised Host, instead of seeing the Consecrated Host, she saw the Baby Jesus in the Priest's hands. When we hear some people say they do not *need* Miracles of the Eucharist to believe in the Lord truly Present in the Consecrated Host, I can't help recall Catherine, who was *strengthened* in her belief in Him when she saw the Host in this miraculous form. *She did not need the miracle to believe,* but she did not refuse the help it gave her when she needed *strength*, or maybe as Mother Angelica said, *the grace to believe.*

---

[1]"Body and Blood, Soul and Divinity" - The Angel of Peace when he appeared to the children in The Cova da Iria, in Fatima, prostrated himself before the Eucharist suspended mid-air, saying these words. (As written about in *Many Faces of Mary by Bob and Penny Lord*)

Like with Jesus, there are those always putting His chosen ones to the test, *possibly, as with Jesus to trick them?* One day, a Priest who did not believe in Catherine's Visions and her special relationship with the Eucharist, gave her an *unconsecrated host*, under the guise it was Holy Communion. Her angry words lashed out at the Priest for trying to cheat and delude someone who *hungered* for Jesus, in His Body and Blood.

Priests were touched by happenings during Holy Mass with Catherine. One reported he saw the Host go to her without him moving his arm. Other Priests said they saw the Host nod to her, almost as if in recognition. There were those who could feel their arms being pulled toward her, with the Host. Raymond of Capua reported he *saw* a Host travel clear across the church to Catherine. It was as if the Lord desired her as much as she longed for Him. There was a magnet between them and that Magnet was the Eucharist.

At the moment of receiving Communion, her face would become transfixed, as if glorified, surrounded by an aura. Catherine often went into *ecstasy* at that time, levitating. Her friends remained with her so they could assist her home, as even from childhood, Catherine was always left weakened after an ecstasy.

God is in the kitchen

Catherine continued to join the other women, delighting in them, cooking with them, bringing them together as a family, her priority always being *Community* with *unity* in mind. When we read of the exciting happenings the Community witnessed at Catherine's side, there is no wonder they followed her whenever and wherever they could, hanging onto each word, watching her every move, treasuring *the moment* with her. We are sad there is not time and space to tell all the stories her companions have shared about Catherine.

There was one instance, when one of her friends returned to the kitchen and found Catherine had swooned, and fallen into the fire. Overwrought, she quickly pulled her out; to her amazement, she was not only *not* burned, her *clothes* were not even scorched.

Then there was the time after the Plague, when *famine* broke out, and the grain, as well as all food, became extremely scarce. Catherine and her girls began baking bread for the *hungry* who could not get grain, as it was only available to the rich. Day after day they baked, toiling and praying they would be able to stretch what little flour they had left. *What little flour* they had, because of the generosity of Catherine's friends, was a year old or more and *it was moldy.* Using the same flour as everyone else in her Company, not only was the bread that *Catherine* made, sweet and delicious, but it seemed she was always able to bake *more* loaves with *less* flour.

Catherine addresses the needs of women

When Catherine addressed women, she answered *their* needs and concerns, most often answering questions centering on their families. With men, she wrote to them *man to man,* discussing freely and boldly the matters at hand whether they pertained to local government or consequences of the Church at large. Never one to flinch or compromise with either, she, nevertheless, always spoke with love and charity.

Whereas men admired Catherine and took her advice, she was not a favorite with *women.* Her own mother, who loved her very much, disagreed with her most vehemently on *what* she did and *how* she did it. As with most of the older women, her mother did not approve of her travelling so much. She was embarrassed when Catherine made all that *fuss* in church, her ecstasies and her crying aloud at the reception of Holy Communion. Her mother regarded her behavior unbefitting a young lady *with breeding* of that time. Catherine, on the other hand treated and regarded women as *sisters*, never talking down to them, loving and counselling them with patience, compassion and understanding.

Catherine was spiritual director and advisor to men

With the gifts that had been given Catherine, that of being able to see into the interior of a soul, to smell sin, to know when someone had need to go to confession, she could see God's children as they *were*, and as they had been *born to be* in His Sight. And because of the responsibility she felt towards their souls, she prayed for them incessantly.

Although she was able to read, Catherine was never able to write. Her book, *the Dialogue*, as well as all the letters she *wrote*, were *dictated* to several young men who sat beside her taking dictation. They tried desperately to keep up with her, as her words rushed from her, to them, to the page. She never wasted a word; never was she in any way frivolous, always blunt and to the point, not bothering with lengthy, flowery niceties of the day. Life and God's Work were too important to Catherine for her to waste a moment. Like other *powerful women in the Church*, she had an urgency, always the ongoing feeling *time was short*.

One time, when she had been going on for hours until sunrise, without stopping, she turned and spotted the young man, *asleep*, who was supposed to be taking down her words. She indignantly chastised him, saying, "*This is a fine state of affairs. Who am I talking to, myself? Wake up; there's no time for sleep.*" With that, adoring her all the while, the poor exhausted secretary struggled to keep up with her, battling sleep, to take down all his "*sweet Mother Catherine's*" words.

She never shrunk from anything or anyone, as we will continue to discover as we study Catherine. For example, a Priest once wrote her a letter telling her *the power to fast so long* was given to her by the devil. Without flinching, she wrote back to him, advising him in short order *by Whose authority* she was able to do *everything in her life.*

Her cell was always filled with people coming and going. They never knew the ongoing *decision* she had to make to love her Lord through *them.* Although she *never* found it easy to be around people, they felt *electrified* in her presence. Once having met her, they were never to be the same again. As her life was in *imitation of Christ,* theirs was in imitation of the Power of Christ and the Holy Spirit flowing through her. One of her followers said, *"She is here on earth, but she lives her life in Heaven."*

Catherine crusades for reform in the Church

There were two men of God who were going to expose *the ignorant woman from Siena;* Brother Gabriel, Master Provincial of the Order of Friars Minor and his friend, Fr. Tantucci, a prior of an Augustinian Hermitage were two very learned theologians, both masters of Sacred Theology. Any resemblance to the life of *poverty,* they had been called to, was sadly absent in their tastefully decorated apartments, adorned with antiques and priceless paintings. This sadly, was the state of much of the Church, and it was tearing *the Church* apart.

Word of Catherine and the miracles performed through her intercession, had travelled to these two and they were incensed! *"You would think the Dominicans would stop her,"* Brother Gabriel fumed. Does this sound familiar? *"It's a scandal! She presumes to teach others. Has the little woman ever studied theology? Of course not. Has she studied Sacred Scripture? Can she read? Who would have taught her? She could lead thousands astray."*

Convinced that the Dominicans did not know how to stop Catherine or see the danger in her continuing with her false and ignorant teachings, they set out, *for the good of Holy Church, of course,* to stop her. Let this not appear as criticism of these two men or their motives. These were the days of wholesale heresy being taught to the people, who for the most part, were illiterate and uneducated, consequently highly susceptible. Heresies, once begun, quickly spread throughout the whole Church and it brought about drastic, sometimes even *brutal* measures, like the Inquisition, in an effort to correct them. *They believed it was better to stop the heresies and Catherine, before too much damage was done, once started.*

The plan was for them to expose Catherine in front of all her followers, forever ending her career as *teacher*. With their knowledge, they were sure to trip her up. They had no intention of listening, just to trick her. It sounds vaguely familiar, like maybe the Pharisees with Jesus?

As the two of them were walking towards Siena, excitedly planning their strategy, Catherine was *in Siena,* teaching her friends, as usual, about God. One of those present later reported, she stopped abruptly, her face radiant with a blinding love, and began to pray. Turning to them, she said, *"Soon, you will see two great fish caught in a net."* Before anyone had a chance to inquire as to what she meant, a servant announced that a Brother Gabriel and Father Tantucci were asking to see and talk to Catherine.

Graciously inviting the two to join them, she sat at their feet, listening intently. They let her have it, firing questions at her, not allowing her to answer, obviously trying to discredit her and her authority.

She waited for them to finish. Then she lashed out at them, as only an angry Italian woman can,

"How can you begin to understand anything that pertains to the Kingdom of God? You who live only for the world, and seek to be honored by men. Your great learning is no help to you or to others. It only harms you because you seek the shell not the core!" Then turning, looking Brother Gabriel right in the eyes, she

continued, "*How can you, son of St. Francis, dare to live the way you do?   For the sake of Jesus Christ Crucified, do not live this way any longer!*"

There was a long silence. Brother Gabriel recognized *Jesus* speaking to him through Catherine. Not even wanting to *go back* to his elaborate apartment, he asked that someone go and sell everything he had; from this day forward he would live a life true to father Francis. He spent the rest of his life cooking and humbly serving his brother Friars.

As for Father Tantucci, the Lord had also touched *his* life. He not only *grieved* at what he had tried to do to Catherine, and the way he lived, but he, too, sold everything he had and *became one of Catherine's followers.*

Catherine did not stop at Priests who had forgotten why they had become Priests. She went to the head, the Vicar of Christ, Pope Gregory XI, writing to him to *reform* the Church.

"*Uproot in the garden of Holy Church,*" she wrote in her letter, "*the malodorous flowers, full of impurity and avarice, swollen with pride: that is, the bad Priests and rulers who poison and rot that garden.*" She went on to chastise these members of the Church who... "*lived in such luxury and state and pomp and worldly vanity, whereas they should be as mirrors of voluntary poverty, meek as lambs, distributing the possession of Holy Church to the poor.*"

The Pope was not really living a life of poverty *himself*, in Avignon. He and his advisors lived in unbelievable wealth and luxury, using their power for their own benefit and that of family and friends. The papal court, which had been moved from Rome to Avignon because of the great danger posed to the Pope, had become "*a fountain of affliction, a house of wrath, a school of error, a temple of heresy...,*" to quote the Italian poet Petrarch. Not only had *he* come out against the court, but Dante Alighieri *(Dante's Inferno)* and St. Bridget of Sweden did, as well.

Pope Gregory had entered a court already filled with the decadence of the other (royal) courts of that age, those of the world. Pope Gregory was a good man, not in need of or enamored by wealth and power, but those around him *insisted* this was *necessary* for the Church to survive. And that thinking permeated the whole Church down to the smallest Parish Priest. *(Author's Note: I believe, when reading the history of the Church, we are given proof positive that Christ meant it when He said hell would not prevail against it. Were powerful women, like Catherine and others there in His Mind's Eye when He made that promise? I believe so.)*

Catherine saw Mother Church differently, seeing *her* as *spiritual* rather than material. To Catherine, Jesus took the Church to Himself as His spotless bride, to live in loving *obedience* to Him as Savior and Lord. Mother Church was to be *"the Mystical Body of Christ, continuing His Work on earth: loving, teaching, healing, and serving His people."*

She wrote letters to Priests, Bishops, Cardinals, all the way to the Pope, telling them what they needed to do. In any age, this would take outstanding courage, but in Catherine's day it was unheard of. *But she made a difference!*

Catherine set for others the same high standards she set for herself, especially the Holy Father, calling him to be *"like Christ, manly, loving, forgiving and honest."*

She had a fierce loyalty to the Pope, teaching even if he was *"not acting like Christ on earth,"* we should love and respect him as *"sweet Christ on earth."* When the Florentines were rebelling against Pope Gregory XI, she wrote to them, scolding,

"He who rebels against our Father, Christ on earth, is condemned to death, for that which we do to him, we do to Christ in Heaven - we honor Christ if we honor the Pope; we dishonor Christ if we dishonor the Pope."

The Florentines did not heed Catherine. They decided to tax the clergy. The Papacy of Avignon reacted, sending a Nuncio to straighten them out. They dragged him into the street and beat him up. Avignon excommunicated Florence; Holy Mass could not be celebrated and as usual, the innocent, Catherine included, were made to suffer. Catherine continued to write letters pleading for loyalty to the Pope. Florence responded by raising up an army of *"Priest killers."* She had begged for mercy from the Pope for the Florentines; he *excommunicated* them. How the Heart of Jesus, with His Mother Mary's, combined with the heart of Catherine must have been bleeding. After all, we are all supposed to be on the same team!

Catherine goes to Avignon

Catherine wrote *many* letters to the Pope, pleading the case of Florence. It was always as if she were writing to an old friend, very personally, very lovingly, or as to a father, calling him *"Babbo Mio,"* (my daddy), never intimidated yet respectful of his position. And he, on his part, answered in kind, to a daughter. He *liked* Catherine.

Catherine wrote, as someone sent by the Lord, with authority, fully confident she was to bring His Will to His Vicar on earth. Does this sound a bit lofty on her part? Well, she was not the first woman to be a *Prophet* to the Pope. St. Bridget of Sweden, also a Mystic, had the courage of her convictions to speak out *strongly* on the need for *reform*, attacking boldly the corruption and politics in the Church. Whereas Pope Gregory XI called her a *Prophet*, he did not have the warm affection for her, that he had for Catherine with her gentleness. Whereas St. Bridget spoke of *doom*, Catherine called the Church a *garden* with beautiful flowers having been allowed to grow wild, with weeds in its midst *choking it.* She saw the Church, at large, as foolish, stubborn children in need of Daddy, *Babbo*, but too strong-willed and prideful to come home and say they were sorry.

She felt the answer to the solution was for her to go the Pope in Avignon. So, at the invitation of the Pope, and with the hopes of Florence, Catherine set out for Avignon as a *peacemaker*. Catherine and the Pope met, at last, face to face in the year 1376. She was twenty-nine years old!

Catherine remained in Avignon for four months, at the express wish of the Pope, not only advising him how to deal with the crisis in Florence but that of the whole Church. As they tirelessly worked toward an equitable settlement, the government in Florence, that had sent Catherine to the Pope, for peace and reconciliation, was overthrown. The new government turned on Catherine and the Pope *and* the proposal for peace. They demanded nothing short of revenge. They wanted blood!

It would seem these four months in her all too short life had been spent in vain, but again *God writes straight with crooked lines*. The love and friendship that developed between the Pope and Catherine was to change the Church as it was then. In their correspondence, they had been in *agreement* on the policies crucial to bring about the necessary changes; but it took this time together, in Avignon, to work out the *implementation* of these goals.

Catherine always spoke *Peace*. Christ's Will for *His Church* could not be accomplished with opposing factions warring among themselves; they were not French or Italian or English, but Catholic against Catholic. She and Pope Gregory had three main actions: *first* the urgency of reforming the clergy, *second* the priority of relocating the Papacy to its rightful place in Rome, and *third*, finally and equally important, to launch a crusade to reclaim the Shrines of the Holy Land for Christ and His Church.

The *third* was paramount not only to the Pope, but to Catherine who, in a Vision, had seen Christians *in one* with

Muslims entering the Wound in Christ's Side, having been washed of their sins by His Precious Blood. What the Pope and Catherine desired, was not only to save the Holy Places from *further* desecration at the hands of the *"infidels,"* but conversion of the Muslims, so that they be saved through the Grace of Jesus Christ. This hope gave Catherine the *will* and the extraordinary physical stamina she so sorely needed to continue her work, sick and weak as she was.

Catherine was a woman *who got a thought and forged ahead, barreling through all opposition.* The Pope, on the other hand, vacillated between the different *cliques* in his court; one day he was going to Rome, encouraged by those who agreed with Catherine; the next day he was remaining in France, swayed by those who insisted he and the Papacy belonged in Avignon.

Very troubled, he asked Catherine to pray for a sign from Heaven showing him what was best to do. She did as he asked and, after Communion, Catherine's body became taut. She was lost in prayer for about an hour. As she came out of her ecstasy, they heard her say, *"Praised be God, now and forever."*

A few days later, when talking together, the subject of the Will of the Lord, whether to remain in Avignon or to go to Rome, came up again. Catherine replied, *"Who knows what ought to be done better than your Holiness, who has long since made a vow to God to return to Rome?"* Pope Gregory *knew* it had to be the Lord who told Catherine to say this, because no one knew of this vow outside of himself and the Lord. There was the *sign!* He would act!

The Pope travelled secretly by boat to Genoa. Until the very last moment, the forces of hell were trying to dissuade him; even his aged father threw himself across the threshold, begging him not to leave. Upon arriving there, what was waiting for him, but news his life was in danger and he best return to Avignon. Catherine, who had travelled by land, was in Genoa waiting for him. He didn't want her to come to his hiding place, *afraid* she would be followed. At the same time, *he* was afraid to go to her. Finally, summoning all his courage, the Pope, dressed as a humble Priest, went to *Catherine*. Praying together with his Holiness, she said this prayer,

"O Eternal God, permit not that thy Vicar should yield to the counsels of the flesh, nor judge according to the senses and self-love, nor that he suffer himself to be terrified by any opposition. O Immortal Love! If Thou art offended by his hesitations and delays, punish them on my body which I offer to Thee to be tormented and destroyed according to Thy Will and Pleasure."

This was the last meeting between Catherine and her Pope, but the love and friendship between them, never died. Their correspondence continued until he drew his last breath.

The Pope went to Rome. He was received and accepted by everyone. Not only the Roman citizens, but the clergy, the Bishops, the Cardinals, the most influential and the humblest welcomed their Pope *back home*. He was their hope for peace; but the peace he and they sought was never to be realized in Pope Gregory's time. His attempts at reconciliation with Florence never came about. On the 27th of March, 1378, the Pope died, having failed at his God-given mission. The very *long* year and a half after his hope-filled trip from Avignon, was, at last, over. His one moment of victory, that of bringing the Papacy back to the rightful seat of Peter, Rome, would soon turn out, under the new Pope, to be one of promise *trampled* by division.

The Church divided against Itself

Catherine had gone to Florence from Genoa. This is where she heard the heartbreaking news her friend and *Pope, her "dear daddy"* was dead. He had been called Home to be with her Beloved Jesus, His Mother, His Saints and Angels. She grieved it was he who had departed and not she, for she desired so to join her Heavenly Family.

Catherine had a greater loss than her beloved Pope. She could not receive her Lord in the Eucharist. Florence had been excommunicated by papal order and all the churches were locked. The Priests could not celebrate Mass.

The Pope dead, it seemed all Rome had taken to the streets, rioting, yelling, shouting, pushing and killing. The law of the mob, like that at the time of Jesus, was one of revenge and murder. They no longer remembered *why* they had begun. The chanting demanding a Roman Pope, one who spoke their language, one who understood them was *long forgotten* in the fury and passion that had built up. They were like an erupting volcano with its lava spreading, destroying everything in its path. Nothing and no one was safe. What the French Cardinals had most feared was the nightmare before them. They knew they had to elect a new Pope and he better *not* be French!

On April the 18th, a new Pope was elected. The white smoke came puffing forth from the chimney of St. Peter's. *Long live the Pope!* The fury turned into *festa*, as Romans, always eager for an excuse to celebrate, *now* took to the streets. The *celebration* short-lived. Pope Urban VI, elected through confusion and anger, was to prove himself hard and uncompromising. He had many *good* attributes, such as wanting no part of living a life of wealth and power like the previous Popes. He won Catherine's heart in that he was interested in reforming the Church and restoring her to the life of the Gospel, to *new life* in the Church's Founder, Jesus Christ. But sadly lacking, was the mercy and gentleness of the Savior; so, attacking like a bull in a china shop, the Pope left many dead bodies in his wake.

The situation became so serious, the French Cardinals asked the Pope to meet with them. They were going to ask him to resign. *He flatly refused.* They, in turn started a campaign of maligning the Pope, spreading *false* rumors, not content the truth was bad enough.

Catherine was horrified that anyone would turn against the Pope. Although uncompromising and unforgiving, he was *still* the Pope. *"Even if he were the devil incarnate,"* she had always said, *"we should not raise our heads against him because he is sweet Christ on earth."*

Catherine spent her nights dictating letters to the Pope, pleading for a *peace treaty* with Florence. After what seemed an eternity, on the 28th of July, the treaty was signed; peace was established with Florence; the excommunication was lifted and Catherine went home, at last, to Siena.

Schism rips the Church apart

Catherine continued to write letters. The Pope elected twenty-six new Cardinals, friends of his, with all but two, Italian. The French Cardinals were furious! They called for a meeting. He *refused* to meet with them. They declared him an illegitimate Pope and calling him the *Anti-Christ*, they elected a *French* pope on the 20th of September. The French pope illegally took the name of Clement VII. He had been a soldier and one of the most bloodthirsty, at that. He and the French Cardinals, adept at things of state, wrote to all the heads of state in Europe, and were able to persuade many to follow Clement as the rightful Pope. The Church was *split in two.* The people did not know *who* to follow. For Catherine, although Urban VI would not have won any popularity contest, he had been *properly* elected and that was the end of the matter. The Great Western Schism, that Catherine had foreseen and *prophesied*, was here!

In- the midst of all this chaos, Catherine finished dictating *the Dialogue.* The situation now desperate, the Pope called Catherine to Rome. She left Siena, accompanied by her little band of disciples and arrived there on the 28th of November. This was truly a pilgrimage *for the Church*. She and her friends walked the long and hard trip, carrying no money, begging for what little food they needed. As she wearily journeyed toward Rome, she prayed to God to heal the schism that had split the Church. When, at last, they arrived, Catherine was received by his Holiness. He asked her to address his Curia. Pledging the loyalty of herself and all her followers, she spoke to them of faith in Jesus Christ, the Loyal God to a very often disloyal people. She reminded them of His Power to do anything He chose to do. She called them to *new* courage, to rely not on their *frail* power but in the *Power of Jesus Christ!* Catherine having touched the heart of the Pope, he addressed the Curia,

"*This little woman puts us all to shame. We are troubled and afraid, while she who belongs to the timid sex, is fearless; she even gives us consolation.*" After a thoughtful pause, he continued, "*What has the Vicar of Christ to fear with Christ the Almighty with him? Christ is stronger than the world, and it cannot be that He will fail His Holy Church!*"

At the insistence of her Pope, Catherine remained in Rome, meeting with him and writing to different heads of state, begging them to remain loyal to the Pope. Catherine was reunited with the "*only human who understood her,*" Raymond of Capua, only to say good-by to him. Pope Urban VI was sending Raymond to France, on a dangerous mission of peace and reconciliation, in an attempt to convince King Charles to support *him* rather than the anti-pope Clement VII. This trip, calling very possibly for a martyr's death, was what Catherine would have relished; to Raymond, who was conservative and very level-headed, it left much to be desired. Upon arriving in Genoa, en route to France, he heard through the grapevine he was going to be captured. Without need of too much deliberation, he decided the best course was to remain in Genoa; he did and soon became the head of that Province. Although upset with him at first, she resumed her letter writing to him with all her old love and friendly insights. One of the sorrows of Catherine's life was to spend her last days without her other self, Raymond, with whom she could share all her joys and sorrows, understanding her every thought even before she shared it.

Catherine and the Pope called for a *new* crusade, the forming of a *Spiritual Army* to combat the forces that would use *division* to destroy the Church. They called all the faithful to Rome, on pilgrimage, to pray and fast for the healing of the Church. And they came! Hundreds and hundreds came to Catherine's apartment and prayed with her for Mother Church and Her salvation.

Catherine gave her last ounce of blood for her Church. Near the end of her painful journey on earth, her friends heard her say,

"O Eternal God, accept the sacrifice of my life for the mystical body of Thy holy Church. I have nothing to give save that which Thou hast given to me. Take my heart then and press it out over the face of Thy Spouse!"

She saw God take her heart from her body and squeeze it out over the Church. As long as Catherine had a breath of life in her to give, she prayed and sacrificed for her love on earth, Mother Church. She instructed her companions she would continue to fight for her Church even after death.

"Father, into Thy Hands I commend my spirit."

She had had a Vision in the early part of 1380, in which the ship of the Church crushed her to the earth. At that moment, she offered herself as a willing sacrifice. She was to be ill from this time until April 21 of that year, when she suffered a paralytic stroke from the waist down. On April 29, she went to her reward.[1]

---

[1]excerpt from Eucharistic Fasters from "This My Body..."

Catherine, with her last faint breath of life, continued to gaze on her Spouse on the Cross, whispering over and over again, "*Blood, blood, blood.*" She was joining Christ on the Cross, for the last time on earth; *His* Last Great Act of Love becoming *her* last great act.   On Sunday, Catherine whispered for the last time, "*Father, into Thy Hands I commend my spirit,*" and she went Home.

As Mother Mary had always been such an involved part of Catherine's *life* with Jesus, I believe we can be sure Mother Mary was there to present her to Her Son in their *final union* in Paradise.

The miracles that had permeated her life, and the lives of others through her intercession, continued after her death.   As a last act of love, her friends, like Raymond of Capua, said she appeared to each of them to say good-by, to tell them she was leaving them to go to her Jesus.

As people lined up to say their last good-bys to their Saint and mother Catherine, miraculous cures began to occur immediately.

As was the custom of that day, parts of a holy person's body were placed in Shrines for the faithful to venerate. With the exception of some relics sent to Dominican Monasteries, the body of Catherine remains incorrupt, in the *church of Santa Maria sopra Minerva* in Rome. Siena begged for the head of Catherine. Her companions and her mother followed in solemn procession as the sacred relic of Catherine's head, carried by her beloved Raymond, was placed in the Church of St. Dominic. Catherine had *returned* to Siena for the faithful to venerate to this day.

What had been Catherine's mission on earth?

What had she said "yes" to? If I would choose one major love and work of Catherine on earth and in Heaven, it was and, I'm sure, still is, the salvation of our Church. *She was and is Church.*

She has been proclaimed co-Patron Saint of Italy with St. Francis of Assisi. Although considered a Saint during her lifetime, she was solemnly honored and declared a *canonized Saint* in 1461 by the Church she so loved and for whom she gave her life.

Pope Paul VI raised her to a Doctor of the Church[1], because of her invaluable letters (some 400) and her writings, which are used as teachings till today. Her best and most frequently used work is *The Dialogue*, originally called *The dialogue of Divine Providence*. She did not take credit for the title of this work or its contents, as well as that of any of her writings, because, as she said, she dictated them as she received them from her Lord during her ecstasies. She, as with each beat of her heart, each breath she took, gave glory to Jesus for everything in her life.

She was and is renown for the miracles received through her prayers. She was responsible for the spiritual and physical healings of many while she walked the earth, as well as the thousands of *Miracles* received through her intercession to our Lord now that she is with Him in Paradise. She had one of the most uniquely intimate relationships with God known in the chronicle of the Saints. But if we could hear Catherine right now, she would say she lived and died for the Church!

†

On October 4th, 1970, a lay woman, a woman without formal education, considered by some almost illiterate, our sister Catherine, a Saint, only one of two women to be so honored, was chosen as a Doctor of the Church.

---

[1]Doctor of the Church - a title conferred on eminent ecclesiastic writers because of their learning and holiness of life. They are always canonized Saints prior to receiving this title.

Left:
***Bees Encircling
Mouth of
Baby Rita***

Right:
***Rita Miraculously Taken to
Convent in Cascia***

Left:
***Death of
Rita's Husband***

St. Rita of Cascia

Daughter, Wife, Mother, Widow, Nun, Saint,
Woman of Faithfulness and Forgiveness
Saint of the Impossible

St. Rita of Cascia is one of the most *powerful women in the Church* we will write about. She is a role model for women of our generation. There is nothing that any woman has experienced that Rita has not known. She was an obedient daughter, a faithful wife, a battered wife, wife of an alcoholic and woman-chaser, a widow, a single parent who lost her children when they were young. She was a Nun who was unwanted by her Community. She was given the gift of the Stigmata[1], a thorn in her head. Her body is incorrupt, never having decomposed after 600 years. She is considered the Saint of the Impossible.

We never knew very much about St. Rita, but as we discovered, one by one, the multitude of Saints in Italy, her name kept coming up over and over again. Every time we went to Assisi, land of St. Francis, which was at least once or twice a year, we always felt drawn to the village of St. Rita, Cascia. Although it was only 40 miles away, it was all mountain road. Each time we inquired about going to Cascia, the villagers of Assisi would laugh a little nervously, make motions with their hands and say, "*corvo, corvo*", which means "curvy". That was enough to make us stay that day in Assisi, and leave Cascia for another time. Whenever we determined *we were going*, the sign on the highway, pictorially describing the curvy, winding mountainous road to Cascia,

---

[1]Stigmata - Wounds that appear on the flesh of individuals, corresponding to the wounds suffered by Jesus in the Passion. Usually very painful.

would further dissuade us and we would firmly, if not weakly, promise "*We'll do it next year.*"

We'd return to the United States and sure enough St. Rita would just conveniently have someone send us reading material about her life, or else someone would speak of this *Saint of the impossible* who lived over 600 years ago. We would become upset because we had not gone to Cascia and make new resolves to go the next year.

Finally, the time came. We made sure we were in a state of grace, having gone to confession and received Holy Communion, left a copy of our Last Will and Testament in the hotel room in Assisi and started the perilous journey to Cascia! However, all the Good Lord wanted was our "yes." The death-defying, hairpin roads depicted on the road-sign to be all one-car, hugging, sheer drop, cliffside roads, turned out to be fairly good mountain roads, curvy but not hairpin curvy, with *a few uncomfortable* stretches of road. Unfortunately, the first time we went to Cascia, we had our daughter Sister Clare, and our grandson Rob, in the back seat of a small car. Now, unless you're driving a Mercedes Benz, which we were not, it gets a bit upsetting in the back seat. We were audio-taping our reflections of the drive, which is absolutely breathtakingly beautiful. All you could hear in the background was our daughter moaning, "*I'm going to throw up.*" We judged she was really just trying to get to sit in the front seat. Upon reaching Cascia, we found that we had deprived ourselves of a most meaningful Shrine to a very special Saint for too many years. We also found, in the same Church, a *Miracle of the Eucharist!*[1]

Italy is most decidedly *the land of Saints.* For example, as you are driving along simply beautiful countryside on the

---

[1]Miracle of the Eucharist of Cascia - One of the miracles written about in Bob and Penny Lord's book, *This Is My Body, This Is My Blood, Miracles of the Eucharist.* This miracle can also be seen in their documentary video, which was taped on location.

way to Cascia, you will see a sign to Norcia, the birthplace of St. Benedict. And so it goes, all over the country. As you venture toward one Saint you pass villages with multitudes of other Saints who have had an impact on our Church. One day as Penny, more than a little proudly (being of Italian descent) boasted to a Franciscan Priest from Assisi, "Do you realize Father, that we have more than 20,000 Saints in the Umbrian valley alone!" he jokingly countered, *"That's because we have so many sinners!"*

As you ascend this summit of the Umbria, you feel a breathlessness, an awe of the majesty of God's creative artistry, the setting He so generously fashioned for this humble Saint. Just as you breathe a sigh of relief at having arrived, with "Now, that wasn't so bad," the custodian of the Shrine tells you that after you visit Cascia, you must go another six or seven kilometers farther up the mountain to the town of Roccaporena, where Rita was born. And you wouldn't want to miss that!

God never leaves us alone. When He feels it's time to bring one Saint home, He raises up another to take her place. Rita was born in the year 1381, the year after St. Catherine of Siena died. She began her life in a time of war, earthquakes, conquests and rebellion. Countries invaded countries, towns attacked nearby towns, neighbor fought neighbor, brother against brother. The problems of the world, at large, seemed greater than even politics and governments could resolve. If there ever was a time for reform of men's lives, for fasting, prayer and penance, it was in the 14th and 15th centuries.

The Church under the shepherding of a holy and righteous Pope, Urban VI, was being crucified *again* by schism. The Church was under attack from within and without. This new Pope was a very stern man, who managed within the first year of his Papacy, to alienate most of the Cardinals of France, and many of the Crown Princes of

Europe. As a result of his unbending nature, a false pope was elected by the French cardinals and heads of countries he had offended. This anti-pope took up residence in Avignon, France. Thus began the Great Western Schism.

The Muslims, taking advantage of the dissension and resulting weakness of the Christian leaders, were systematically crushing all of Europe, with a goal of destroying all Christianity.

In other times of doubts and *heresy,* when the belief in the Real Presence of Jesus in the Eucharist was under attack, Jesus gave us *Miracles of the Eucharist.* So at this time our generous and loving God gave us an army of Saints to keep His promise that Hell would not prevail against His Church. Rita was to become such a Saint!

Born of a very devout mother and father who, in times when families were feuding amongst themselves, were called by some, *"Jesus Christ's peacemakers,"* it would appear from the very moment of her birth, God had special designs on Rita. There is a tradition in Roccaporena that as an infant, while she slept in a basket, in the fields where her parents were working, white bees swarmed around Rita's open mouth. Not only did the bees *not* sting her, but it is said that they dropped honey into her mouth without her uttering a cry of warning to her parents. One of the farmers, seeing the swarm of bees, tried to disperse them with his arm that had been deeply wounded by a scythe. His arm stopped bleeding and he was immediately healed.

Almost two hundred years after she died, a strange thing began to happen. At the Monastery in Cascia, white bees came out of the walls of the Monastery during Holy Week of each year and remained until the feast day of St. Rita, May 22nd, when they returned to hibernation until Holy Week of the following year. Pope Urban VIII, learning of the mysterious bees which buzzed about the walls of the Monastery where St. Rita had lived, requested that one of the them be brought to him in Rome. After a careful examination of the bee, he tied a silk thread around it; then set it free, only to have it later discovered in its hive at the Monastery in Cascia, 138 kilometers away. And so the tradition of the bees began. The holes in the wall where the bees traditionally remain until the following year, are plainly in view for pilgrims journeying till today to the Monastery. Coincidence or miracle? We are believers in miracles! When we see the Lord's intervention in a physical way that would otherwise be considered unconventional or phenomenal, for us, it's just His way of letting us know that He is with us, watching over us. Since the very breath we breathe is a miracle, we think we can call the extraordinary *miraculous*.

Her parents, without ever having learned how to read or write, taught Rita from the time she was a child, all about Jesus, the Virgin Mary, and some of the better known Saints. Rita, much the same as her counterpart St. Catherine of Siena, was never schooled to read or write. Whereas St. Catherine was miraculously given the grace to read by Our Lord Jesus, St. Rita's only book was the Crucifix.

As Rita grew into a young girl, she dreamed of giving her life to Christ as an *Augustinian Nun* in the Monastery of Cascia. Her parents, much advanced in age, feared for her well-being. They felt she would be more secure *married* to a fine man. It never occurred to Rita to question their advice, or their command. Rita had consecrated her life to her Savior, but she could not cause pain to her aged parents who were so plainly worried about her future. Therefore, like with others in our Lord's plan, God would have to open the right doors and close the wrong ones. We don't really know why they picked the husband they did. By man's standards, the choice of Paolo Ferdinando as her husband was, at best, an *unwise* decision. Rita, the obedient daughter, married at twelve years of age, and began eighteen years of pure hell.

Rita had doubtlessly heard of St. Augustine's mother, St. Monica from the Augustinian hermits who lived in Cascia. As the dutiful wife of Paolo, she would need the same kind of persistent, *relentless prayer for conversion* of her husband, that St. Monica prayed for *her* sinning son, Augustine. Rita never prayed for her husband to love *her*, to treat her attentively, to be kind, to cease drinking or being abusive as the result of the drinking, or to remain at home with her and the two sons born of their marriage. She prayed for his soul, unconditionally, that he would give his life over to Jesus and be converted. As her children grew, she could see that they were greatly influenced by their father's behavior. Her heart broke for them. But, as in the case of St. Monica, she prayed for them as she prayed for her husband.

After many long years and many spilled tears of crying out for mercy for her husband, Rita's prayers were answered by the Lord. Paolo was converted. He repented his past, begged forgiveness from her and his God, and became a model husband, father and Christian. He gave up his old ways and old friends, spending his time now with Rita and their sons. He tried to convince his sons that his former life had been wicked. He begged them not to follow in his ways. But children have a way of protecting their minds. If a parent does something, whether the law or the Church deem it wrong, it must be right, because their parent is doing it. This was the case with Paolo and his boys. He had convinced them over the years, that his wild and adulterous behavior was acceptable; they had a problem with this new image he presented them.

With Rita, Paolo's life became one of prayer, a searching for this loving, forgiving God he had for so long blocked out of his life. Rita began to think that maybe the hell of eighteen years was over. She was so very happy! Perhaps God had really meant for her to be married. All those years she had been so torn. *Was God angry she had not followed her course to become a Nun? Had her parents guided her unwisely?* Now she had peace, at last! It was so wonderful, but so short-lived.

Although Paolo had changed his ways, his enemies had not. His drinking, quarrelsome, violent ex-friends, did not appreciate looking upon the change in him because it brought to light the darkness in their own souls. One night as the hours ticked away very late into the night, Rita began to really worry. Paolo had not come home. She would never have been concerned with the old Paolo. There were times when he had not come home for days at a time. But she knew the new Paolo had not turned his back on Jesus, nor on her and the boys, so although she tried her best, she could not overcome the fear that was to become a reality. Suddenly all the years of dreading a knock on the door, and the final, fatal words, *"Your husband has been murdered!"* came crashing down on her. Early in the morning, her husband's lifeless body was brought to her. She held the husband she had waited so long for, the *horrible* years no longer even a memory, and she sobbed as if her heart would break. *The prodigal son had returneth*, and he was dead!

Her only consolation was that she knew he was with the Lord; he had to be, didn't he? What little solace she had was quickly destroyed. Her sons had been more influenced by the father's *former* violent nature, than that of his brief conversion. Their mother and grandparents' holiness had not had any impact on them. And so they swore to avenge their father's death, a *vendetta*[1]. No amount of pleading on the part of Rita would dissuade them. *An eye for an eye*; the murderers had to die as their father had died! Rita got back down on her knees to her faithful and loving Lord; she

---

[1]vendetta - A feud in which the relatives of a murdered or wronged person seek vengeance on the wrongdoer or members of his family to the last of the blood-line.

prayed, "*Lord, please save their souls. If they are to lose their souls in the commission of this act, please take them.*" The Lord answered her prayer; they were stricken by a fatal illness. As Rita ministered to their fever-racked bodies, she spoke gently to them of Jesus. She repeated the prayer of Jesus on the cross, "*Father forgive them, they know not what they do.*" Their hearts of hate turned into hearts of love. They forgave their father's murderers before they died.

St. Rita, did our Lord give you the strength I did not have as I looked upon my nineteen year old son Richard lying so still in his coffin? Had I really been praying as you had for your sons, when I had pleaded, "*Oh Jesus, he's yours....You take care of him. Take him; he's yours.*" Even now, eighteen years later, sometimes it is difficult to die to my selfishness, wanting my son back with me, no matter the cost. I know I should be praising God for loving my son so much he took him to *live* with Him. I *do* praise Him. But it hurts so much!

We read a sentence in a book and we often wonder what is the untold story behind that one sentence. Bob and I often say you could write a book around one sentence. *Rita lost her husband.* He had become her friend; someone with whom she had given birth to two children; someone whom she had loved, although it had been unreturned for most of their eighteen years of marriage. He died, cruelly murdered!

She had never given up on her husband and he was gone! Next, her children are going to commit murder. She prays; they die. *Her children, your children, (let's enter her heart) is there anything your children could do that you could stop loving them! Can you feel the utter agony she suffered as she lost every earthly human being she had ever loved? Is there a helplessness in your life? Reach out to Rita. Do you fear for your children or grandchildren? Have they left the Church? Ask this Saint of the Impossible to intercede for you with our merciful Lord in Heaven. She has worn your shoes and is touchable. Can you pray unconditionally for a husband who is an alcoholic or an adulterer, someone you are separated from by divorce, as Rita did, for the salvation of his soul? Impossible? Turn to Rita, she'll help you. The Holy Spirit, through her intercession will pray for you.*

Rita is alone in the world

Now her husband is gone. Her children are gone. The fears her parents had voiced twenty years before have come to pass! Rita is alone in the world! She felt as if she had awakened from a bad dream. All the obstacles were gone, everything that had prevented her from her childhood dream of entering the Augustinian Monastery of Saint Mary Magdalene. Her heart pounded as she walked down the steep hill from Roccaporena to the Monastery. Her mind was filled with fantasies of how her life as a Nun would be. At long last, she would be able to embrace the Lord as one of His brides.

Her walk *back up the hill* to Roccaporena was not as happy and hopeful as the walk down. At the Monastery, she pleaded with the Mother Superior of the Augustinian Monastery, conveying the lifelong desire she had, to enter the Community. No amount of supplication could change the Mother Superior's objections. Theirs was an order of virgins; they had never accepted widows; all her pleading fell on deaf ears. So she left the Monastery and started the long walk back to Roccaporena, her back bent, her breathing hard, her heart broken.

I wonder how Satan must have tortured Rita during this time. *Was it because your husband was so mysteriously murdered that you are unacceptable, not holy enough?* Or could he have attacked with, *What kind of a mother do you think they judge you to have been? What kind of upbringing could your boys have had to contemplate committing so grave a mortal sin as a vendetta?* Have you ever judged you were rejected by the Church? It's almost like the Lord Himself does not want you! But Rita did not turn her back on her Church. She turned to the head of the Church, Jesus Christ. She knew He would never let her down. Although she did not always know or understand His ways, she knew He loved her and she trusted in that love.

And so again, the Lord came through with a *miracle*. After allowing St. Rita to be rejected *three times*, the Lord answered her prayers, intervening in a physical way, to prove to Rita (and maybe to us) that He was with her; that He had never left her side. Late one night, she awakened out of a deep sleep. She heard her name called.

"*Rita! Rita! Rita!*"

She got up, and looked all around her. It was still; nothing was moving. She peered through the dark of the night. There was no one there. Who could have called her in the middle of the night? Perhaps it was her imagination. She went back to bed, but not to sleep. Again she heard her name called.

"*Rita! Rita! Rita!*"

This time she shot up out of bed, and looked around her little cottage. She was alone. She knew something was going on, but she could not figure out who was calling her. She returned to her bed again, only this time she prayed fervently to Our Lord Jesus. For a third time she heard her name called.

"*Rita! Rita! Rita!*"

She jumped out of bed, ran to the door, and opened it. Standing outside was St. Augustine, founder of the Augustinian order, St. Nicholas of Tolentino, an Augustinian Saint from a town nearby, to whom she had also prayed for help, and St. John the Baptiser to whom she had been devoted since childhood. They motioned her to follow them. She ran through the streets of Roccaporena in her nightgown, in pursuit of the three Saints, up the hill to the

Scoglio, the highest peak in the town, where Rita always went to pray. Only this time it seemed as if she were floating to the top, rather than climbing the steep hill. All during this, her heart felt as if it would explode. She *knew* our Lord Jesus was answering her prayers, and His answer was *Yes!*

Having reached the top of Scoglio, she felt herself lifted into the air, high above all the mountain peaks, floating gently towards Cascia. She could feel the soft spring breezes caress her cheeks and face. It was as if all the Angels of Heaven were kissing her. She found herself high above the Monastery of Saint Mary Magdalene in Cascia. Then she went into ecstasy.

She came out of her ecstasy inside the choir of the Chapel of the Augustinian Monastery. It was quiet. She was all alone in the pre-dawn hours of that Spring day. She could hear the birds singing gaily outside. She knelt there in prayer, praising Our Lord Jesus and thanking Him for what He had done. When dawn came, she was greeted by the rustle of the habits of the Nuns of the Monastery coming down for morning prayer. She heard the sounds of the huge keys going into the locks of the door. The Mother Superior, who always kept the keys on her person, opened the heavy door with the help of several Nuns. They looked at Rita, kneeling inside in prayer, and gasped. *It was impossible for her to have gotten into the Chapel, unless. . . !*

The Mother Superior, trying to compose herself from her shock, and also in an effort to retain order among the other Nuns, said to Rita, "You don't think because the Lord has given you this special gift, that you're eligible to enter this order, do you?"

Rita replied, "*No, Mother Superior. I know I'm not worthy enough.*"

†

Rita enters the Monastery

The rule of the Augustinian Order was changed so that Rita Mancini, later to be proclaimed to all the world, *St. Rita of Cascia*, could enter the Monastery.

During that first year, Rita was put to the test, not only by her superiors, but by the Lord. She was given areas of her life to meditate on. She was given the Scripture passage of the rich young man who wanted more from the Lord. When finally asked to sell all he had, give it to the poor, and come back to follow Jesus, he walked away sadly, because he had too many possessions. We would not think of Rita as having too many possessions, but then again, do we ever think *we* have too many things to give up to follow the Lord? Rita kept hearing the words in her heart, *If you would be perfect!*

Do you wish not to possess things? Rita had very little possessions. But there were things she had treasured from her childhood, from her years of marriage to Paolo Ferdinando, memories of her children. Is that what you mean, Lord? Do you want my memories? The answer kept coming back to her, *If you would be perfect!*

Do you wish not to will? Rita never considered herself a strong-willed person. But she did have her opinions. There were things she liked, and dreams of how life would be. She had fantasized on how her life as a Religious would be. Is that what you mean, Lord? Are you talking about self-abandonment? Do I have to give up those things, too? The answer was always the same, *If you would be perfect!*

Do you wish to give up conjugal love? Rita had been a one-man woman. Her man had died. She had never had relations with another man. But she was still young. She had known that love. She was a widow; she could marry again. *But Lord, I only love you. I never wanted that kind of love.* But you have known it Rita. Can you give it up for the rest of your life? Will you think about it, hunger for it, maybe not now, but five or ten years from now? The answer echoed loudly in her soul, *If you would be perfect!*

At the end of that first year, she gave her answer, a resounding *"Yes!"* She offered as her dowry to Our Lord, the gift of Chastity, Poverty, and Obedience forever. She made her vow, *"I, Rita Mancini, do make profession of chastity, poverty, and promise obedience to God, the Blessed Virgin, St. Augustine and to you, Mother Abbess of this Convent of Santa Maria Maddalena, and I pledge myself to observe these vows till death. Amen."*

The Mother Superior answered this profession with *"And I, in the name of the Most Reverend Father General, accept your profession and hereby make you a daughter of this Convent, in the Name of the Father and of the Son and of the Holy Ghost, Amen."* Rita was home!

St. Rita had been allowed to make her solemn vows of poverty, chastity and obedience. All the suffering of her life was worth it to Rita for this moment in her life. Gaining entrance into a Community is just the beginning, as any Religious will recall. Although Rita soon demonstrated she was no stranger to piety or chastity, her vocation had to be tested to see if it was genuine. *This formation the novice has to go through is a test where she tests herself as well as being tested by the Community to see if she is capable of conforming to the life of a professed sister.* We can be sure Sister Rita, as she was to become known, had to stifle the independent thinking habits of eighteen years as wife and mother many times.

This *"late vocation,"* as she would be called today, had to face and forbear many trials she had never known, or possibly dreamed of, in her life outside the Convent. We must also take into consideration the fact that she was in her thirties, while her peers in the Monastery may have been in their teens. She had to adjust her thinking to taking orders, and being spoken to as if she were a teenager. The obedience she vowed to keep was not as easy as she might have thought. She had experienced a whole life, had married, borne children, been widowed by a violent death, and watched her boys die in her arms. She was a woman, not a child. But she had to say yes to being treated as a child. She always kept her eyes on the Savior and the Passion He endured, and no struggle was to become too great to overcome.

Rita was tested one day by the Mother Superior. As an act of obedience, Rita was ordered to water each day, a dead stump, a stick that had been stuck in the ground. Rita did this obediently, good-naturedly, morning and night, as she had been commanded, while most of the Nuns probably giggled and gossiped. Their laughter and conjecture turned to amazement, as one morning what should they see, but the brown, lifeless stick blossoming into a vine, bearing beautiful clumps of grapes to be turned into sacramental wine for the Lord's Supper, the Sacrifice of the Mass. To this day the vine, now over 600 years old, is still bearing grapes for the altar of the Lord.

One night, Rita had a Vision. She saw a tall ladder leading Heavenward with Jesus at the top. He was beckoning her forward. He was calling her to that perfect mystical union with Him, that could only be achieved by her, through her daily obedience to the life He had chosen for her, her life in Him, as an obedient Nun. *He would be her Teacher, her Strength in her weakness, her Companion, her Love in her otherwise loveless life. He would be her very Life!* With Jesus to sustain her, St. Rita chose the most mended and worn clothing for herself, barely eating enough to maintain her strength. Word of her holiness got out, outside of the Monastery and people started to talk of the Saint in their midst.

With the threat of heretics on one side and barbarians on the other, all the Christian world was experiencing a return to devotion to the Cross. The Saracens were invading, conquering and desecrating all that Christians held dear, not excluding the Shrines in the Holy Land sanctified by the Lord Himself by His Incarnation, His Crucifixion and His Resurrection. The wars fought to protect the Holy Places were called the Crusades.[1]

Like St. Francis of Assisi, 100 years before, St. Rita was to stage her own kind of crusade, the shedding of her own blood to stop the atrocities and abuses against our Loving and Suffering Lord. As with *the poverello*[2] St. Francis, St. Rita grieved that she had not been able to share in the Passion of our Lord Jesus Christ. She spent many hours meditating on all the insults, the rejections, the ingratitude, the apathy our Beloved Lord suffered as He walked to His Agony on the Cross. She built a small Calvary of stones on the floor of her cell (bedroom), and kneeling there, she would relive the beatings, the scourging, the thorns in the head, the horror of our Lord's Passion, and the sorrow of His mother as she watched her Son. In the process for her canonization, witnesses (fellow Religious) testified they would visit her in her cell at times, only to find her on the floor, having fainted with the shared pain of the Savior's Passion.

We could spend a whole library of books sharing the miracles and examples of our Lord's love and care in St. Rita's life, but since her life is only a part of this book on heroic women our Lord has called us to share with you, we

---

[1] Crusade - to be marked with a cross.

a. any of the military expeditions which Christians undertook from the end of the 11th to the end of the 13th century to recover land from the Muslims.

b. any church-sanctioned war or expedition like this.

c. vigorous, concerted action for some cause or idea, or against some abuse.

[2]poverello - Italian word for "the poor one," as St. Francis was called.

Above:
**Incorrupt Body
of St. Rita**

Left:
Rita Receives Stigmata

Above: **Pilgrimage to Rome**

Left: **Death of St. Rita**

would like to recall one of the most outstanding gifts He gave Rita, a miracle.

Rita receives the Stigmata

During Lent of the year 1443, in Cascia, St. James of Marches, a great preacher of his day, gave a very personal, passionate sermon on our Lord to the Nuns. Rita was so taken by the sermon that she returned to the Monastery and began to pray, with all her heart and soul, before a fresco of Jesus crucified. As she humbly asked for a part of His suffering on the Cross, admitting that she was unworthy to share His full Passion on Calvary, a thorn fell from the Beloved Head of our Savior and pierced the forehead of St. Rita. She immediately began to bleed profusely, and the wound that kept bleeding has been accepted by all as the gift of the Stigmata of our Lord.

In the case of most holy people who have been graced with the Stigmata, like St. Francis of Assisi, and the saintly Padre Pio, the fragrance exuded from the *holy wounds* smells like a beautiful perfume from Heaven, more pleasing even than that of flowers. With the wound of St. Rita, came humiliation, estrangement and isolation. The wound had such a pungent, putrid odor emanating from it that she had to suffer the ostracism and rejection of her fellow Nuns who, at best, feared it might be infectious and, at worst, could not bear the smell. She spent the next fifteen years alone, suffering more and more excruciating physical pain. But although she was isolated from her Community in a small cell far away from any of the consoling companionship of other Nuns, she had *the Consoler!* Instead of looking toward herself and her pain, she focused on Jesus and His Crucified Head of thorns and all the thorns in her life were turned into roses of love by her Lord as she offered them to Him.

Here we have a perfect case of *Redemptive Suffering.* Stated simply, redemptive suffering goes like this. You have suffering which will not go away. For some reason, the Lord allows you to have it. You can't pray it away; you can't wish it away. You can become angry, and turn away from God, or you can offer it up to God for the souls in Purgatory, the conversion of sinners, or to relieve the suffering of someone here on earth.

We believe that Redemptive Suffering is a powerful offering to Our Lord. It's a way of taking a terrible *negative*, the pain inflicted on us by the suffering, and turning it into a great *positive*, by offering it to Our Lord Jesus. We believe that St. Rita used this unusual twist of not receiving the fragrance of Heaven that accompanies the Stigmata, to glorify Our Lord Jesus. She offered up to him the isolation caused by the putrid odor of her wound.

In 1450, Pope Nicholas V declared the *first* Holy Year, proclaiming Rome, once and for all, the center of the Christian world, and of our Faith. The popes had been away from Rome for sixty seven years. Our Lord wanted to unite His Church, to end the scandal of division and dissension caused by self-interest and resultant *schism*, so He inspired the pope to institute this Holy Year. And unite He did! All the Religious of Italy, as well as pilgrims from all over the world converged on Rome.

The Nuns of Cascia were also planning a pilgrimage, which was *not* to include St. Rita. Knowing and understanding the reasoning behind her exclusion (her wound which continued to bleed, fester and emit unbearable odors), she nevertheless did not take it lying down. She went to the *Big Boss!* She prayed that her wound be temporarily healed, that there be no external signs, only the internal pain of the wound to remain. Her petition was almost immediately granted; the wound disappeared and St. Rita was on her way to Rome with the other Nuns.

The pilgrimage to and from Rome was one of hardship, deprivation, suffering and sacrifice; the walking and living on the road, at times, more than the little band of pilgrims from the Monastery of Cascia could bear. But the always patient, never complaining joy of the eldest Nun, St.Rita, now in her late sixties, encouraged and sustained them. The highlight of the trip was to be the canonization of St. Bernardine of Siena. Little did the Nuns present with St. Rita this Holy Year know, that four hundred years later this humble Nun in their midst, Rita, with similar pomp and ceremony, would likewise be recognized by Holy Mother Church, by being raised to the Communion of Saints.

The wound did not bleed or reveal any evidence it had ever existed during the entire pilgrimage, but upon their return to the Monastery, not five minutes passed when the wound opened, with all the accompanying signs. Rita was again quarantined into seclusion with her Beloved Lord.

The Rose and the Fig

All the years of fasting, subsisting at times on so little (the Nuns judged she lived solely on the Holy Eucharist), began to take a toll on St. Rita. After four years of intense suffering, she lay dying, her last winter on earth, the land she had so dearly loved covered with a blanket of snow.

We are told that although St. Rita had lived the life of an obedient Nun these last years, the *wife and mother* asked the Lord for a sign that her husband and sons were with Him in Heaven. One of Rita's relatives from Roccaporena came to see her and asked her if there was anything she could do for her. *"Yes,"* replied the dying Nun, *"I would like a rose from my garden, at home."* As the thick snow of winter would have killed any roses had they survived the bitter cold, her cousin was disheartened. Judging Rita was delirious and she would never see her alive again, the relative wearily returned to Roccaporena. Upon approaching St. Rita's garden, what should she discover but a rose shooting up from the soft, white mound of earth.

It is said in the Bible that Moses never realized his dream to reach the Promised Land because he struck the rock twice. Be that as it may, Rita asked the Lord for yet another sign. No sooner had the relative returned to Rita with the rose than Rita, showing not the least bit of surprise, asked for two figs from her fig tree at home, another impossible feat for the middle of winter. Now, no longer doubting, the relative rushed off and joyfully returned with the two figs.

I sometimes marvel at the relationship we dare to have with the Lord. One time, I had shared with Bob how amazed I was that this man, whose home I had visited, had placed a bag over the statue of the Sacred Heart of Jesus because he and Jesus had a fight, Bob said, "What a personal God, Jesus is to him. He trusts the Lord enough to argue with Him!"

Another time, when in Lourdes, we came upon an Italian Pilgrimage celebrating Mass at the outside Chapel of St. Bernadette. We could hear what sounded like "We forgive You, Lord." I thought I must have misunderstood; they could not be saying what I thought I heard them say, but there it was again, "We forgive You, Lord." Bob and I approached, moving up the steps, the area surrounding the altar in plain view. There were over one hundred litters of obviously dying children, waiting, dressed in white to receive their first Communion, possibly their last Communion. I cry till today when I remember the words and those who said them. Have I forgiven You, Lord? If not, please forgive me.

Three days before St. Rita died, she had a Vision of our Lord Jesus and our Lady. The room, so often Calvary for Rita, was now flooded with a beautiful, bright light. *"You will be with Me in Paradise, in three days,"* our Lord told her, and three days later, on May 22nd, 1457, Rita was to join the annals of those who have lived for God; she was with Him.

The ugly wound she had borne uncomplainingly over the years, healed as she breathed her last, only to be replaced by a ruby spot. A strong fragrance, sweet and heavenly, poured forth from where the wound had been, replacing the stench she had lived with those many years. This fragrance continued over many years, for *St. Rita was never buried!*

Originally, the plan had been to have the body of St. Rita laid out in a Chapel in the Monastery. There were so many of the faithful who wanted to say a last good-by to Rita, whom the townspeople had already proclaimed a Saint, that the Nuns placed St. Rita in the parish Church. All the townspeople processed past her body, paying their last respects. The fragrance continued to emanate from the body. The Nuns decided to place St. Rita in a glass urn (coffin) under the main altar for the faithful to venerate until such time as the body would show signs of decomposition and then they would bury it. There is only one problem. It has been in a glass urn, on view to the faithful, exposed to all the elements, for over six hundred years and it has never decayed or shown any of the ravages of death.

Veneration to this gentle lady who had experienced all that life can possibly throw at us, began almost immediately. Down through the centuries, the power of intercession to St. Rita has been confirmed by a multitude of miracles. Most of these have been granted to those on the brink of despair, who felt their petitions were impossible. St. Rita has been given the name, "*Saint of the Impossible*". While the favors granted have not been solely to women in distress, she has become known as "The Woman's Saint." There are those, ourselves included, who believe that St. Rita is one of the most touchable Saints for the women of today. Millions of pilgrims climb the mountain to Cascia every year, in petition or thanksgiving to this humble Saint, whose greatest asset has been obedience and faith in her God. Many more millions who cannot physically go to Cascia, pray to St. Rita for help.

Somewhere out there, many Ritas are searching for help, but don't know where to look. Help is there; it has always been there. We have just been looking in the wrong places. While we believe the Lord has given us marriage counselors and psychologists as a means to help us through the trials of life, the answer is not in the horizontal. It's in the vertical. The horizontal by itself is a minus (-). But when you put it with the vertical, looking up to Heaven for help, it becomes a plus (+). It is also the Sign of the Cross.

Till today when you visit St. Rita, there is a feeling of family; she's one of us. Here, in a glass urn, honored by God and her brothers and sisters in Christ, the mystical body of Christ, lies *a daughter,* an obedient daughter whose parents did not make the wisest of decisions by man's standards, but possibly by God's; *a wife* of an alcoholic, an abuser, a carouser, a man easily provoked whose deadly silence could erupt into rage; *a widow* who loved her husband before and after his conversion only to lose him by an act of violence; *a mother* who watched her children grow up taking on the violent, non-Christian personality of their father, afraid they might commit murder, only to lose them to death through illness; *a Nun* who was rejected, judged, ostracized, laughed at, tested and glorified. Here lies our sister, Rita, a Saint, a woman of our time. And I, Penny, love her and thank God for the gift of her to remind me what I can be.

St. Teresa of Avila

"At last, at last, a daughter of the Church"

Teresa of Avila, lovingly referred to as *Teresa la Grande*, is a radical sign in our Church. She is so *grand*, yet so simple in her walk toward the Lord. We believe the reason we shied away from her for so many years is that we were intimidated by her biographers. We were afraid she was high above us, intellectually and spiritually.

We tried to bypass her Shrines at Avila and Alba de Tormes. But the more we attempted to go round her, the more she drew us to her. We planned a pilgrimage to the Shrines of Europe. A beautiful lady, Sister Jane, was celebrating her 25th anniversary as a Religious. She and another Sister also celebrating *her* 25th anniversary, were given the money to go with us. When we met Sister Jane, she bowled us over with her excitement. We were going to the Holy Land, Rome, Assisi, Siena, Lourdes, Fatima, and as an *aside*, Avila. When she heard Avila, she almost went into ecstasy. This was her greatest dream, to walk where Teresa, had walked. Because of her, we too became excited.

Teresa touched us again on that pilgrimage, in Lourdes. We were honored to meet up with our Archbishop, the late Timothy Cardinal Manning. He was on a private pilgrimage of Lourdes and the Holy Land (Ireland), with another Priest. He asked us our itinerary. When we neglected to mention Alba de Tormes, he looked us in the eye, and suggested, no, commanded, *"If you don't visit any other Shrine, you must go to Alba de Tormes."* Cardinal Manning had the ability to burrow through to your soul with his eyes and his voice.

The Shrines were beautiful. The tribute given this great Saint by the Church was awe-inspiring. But we got to know Teresa through her *Carmelite Priests*, at the Shrines. At her birthplace in Avila, a young Priest explained who Teresa was and is. In Alba de Tormes, Fray Hernandez, spoke of her with such simplicity and love, we hungered to learn more.

Teresa, is that when you became a part of our lives? Was it the day we discovered you were reachable, so touchable, when the Priest spoke of you so lovingly that tears came to his and our eyes? We never knew. When our daughter had spoken of castles; when we started to realize what castle she meant, the *Interior Castle*[1], we became intimidated. We tried to read about the different mansions in the *Castle*; we felt we would never be able to go beyond the first mansion (room), if we had the courage to enter *it*, in the first place. But after sharing you with those beautiful Carmelites, we fell in love with you. We knew you were reaching out to us; we gulped a few times, and said *Yes!*

We knew it couldn't be *our* design, to write about Teresa, instead of a Saint we judged *easier*. As we studied her life and her spirituality, *we discovered a woman for all seasons*. Rather than a Saint, too spiritual and too deep to understand, we found a woman, with practical, good common sense, someone not superior to the simple mind nor too simple for the *superior* mind. We found a warm, loving mother with an ear and a heart always open to her sisters.

---

[1]*Interior Castle* - originally called "The Interior Castle and Mansions". Authors and biographers have insisted instead to call this great work "*The Interior Castle*" or "The Mansions." Teresa wrote this great work under obedience to her Spiritual Director, Fr. Gracian. Teresa said the title was given to her by the Lord Himself. She went on to say that a flash of light had penetrated her understanding, so that in a twinkling of an eye, she understood "*more truths about the highest things of God than if great Theologians had taught her for a thousand years*." She completed this marvelous work in five months time, although the actual writing time was barely more than four weeks. Never has a book so rapidly written, under such unusual circumstances, had such an impact on the Church. It has been compared to Dante's Divine Comedy. The main theme is the human soul is like a beautiful castle, containing many mansions with God in all His Majesty dwelling in the center.

Teresa, model, and heart of the Church

Although Teresa was and is truly *Catholic*, we found her to be a model for non-Catholics as well. Crashaw, the English Protestant poet, who converted to Catholicism and later became a Priest, was just one of the many whose lives were changed as a result of her writings.

Blessed Edith Stein, went from being born a *Jewess*, to a life of science with the *exclusion of God*, to *conversion* to the Roman Catholic Church after reading Saint Teresa's autobiography. She died a Carmelite Nun and *Martyr* in the gas chambers of Auschwitz.

Macauley, a historian, said Teresa did more to block the spread of Protestantism, by her life and writings, than even St. Ignatius Loyola. *"If St. Ignatius Loyola is the brain of the Catholic reaction, Teresa is its heart; if Ignatius is the head of a great band, Teresa of Jesus belongs to its humanity."*

Saints like Francis de Sales and Alphonsus Liguori, both Doctors of the Church, not only greatly admired her, but turned to her works for enlightenment and inspiration. Her autobiography, written reluctantly out of obedience to her Spiritual Director, has become known as one of the most important books on the *Christian Way of Life*.

Popes, over the centuries, have extolled St. Teresa and her writings. Pope St. Pius X said one need go no farther than her books to discover how to live a truly holy life; that in her works she very clearly directs one, from the very ordinary, everyday *living* of the Christian life, to the highest peaks of holiness. Very simply, she teaches that true progress in prayer is achieved by the *faithful fulfilling of our daily duties* with Christ as the center, and the living out of our belief in a holy and obedient manner.

Teresa was born into a time of upheaval, with protesters (Protestants) calling rebellion *"Reformation."* The fight to restore Christianity had not ended with the expulsion of the Moors. Not even the thick walls of Avila, raised between 1090 and 1097, forty feet high and thirteen feet thick, could keep out the conflict and confusion. Only now, it was between Christians and Jews, as well as with conversos, Jews who had converted to Christianity in name only. Some of these *conversos* were Priests, Bishops, and Cardinals and they were teaching heresy to the unsuspecting faithful. Much of this was to lead to the Inquisition[1], which would affect Teresa later on in life.

Teresa's family claimed they were of *pure blood*, that is, no mixture of Moorish or Jewish blood (reflecting the prejudice of the time instilled by the hundreds of years of Moor domination); but there are those authors who say that Teresa's grandfather was a *converso*. He was brought before the Inquisition, forced to accuse himself of *judaizing*[1] and, as punishment, had to process in the streets, seven Fridays in a row, wearing the humiliating *sanbenito*[2]. Reconciling with the Inquisition, out of expediency, Teresa's grandfather moved, with his family, to Avila.

---

[1]Inquisition (Spanish) - instituted by King Ferdinand and Queen Isabella, by special authorization of the Holy See in 1476. Purpose was primarily (1) to protect *conversos* and Jewish converts, from the retaliation of their fellow men and from relapse; (2) to seek out lapsed Jewish converts; (3) to prevent the relapse of Moorish converts and to keep them from forming harmful alliances with various heretical groups. It became abusive, a tool of the state, leading eventually to persecution and abuse of the Jewish people, but not in the exaggerated numbers historically reported.

[1]judaizing-Dates back to the 1st Century, to the early Church Community, where Judaizers were members who considered it necessary to observe the *Mosaic Law* in order to fulfill th Christian Faith...the first heretical reaction the Church had to face. The Council of Jerusalem in 40 A.D. (Acts 15) answered the Judaizers, making the way clear for Gentiles to be part of the Christian family. Ebionites, one of the sects formed by Judaizers taught that Christ was a *mere man*, and St. Paul, an apostate.

[2]sanbenito-A rope worn around the waist, symbolizing penance for sins.

In 1514, the year before Teresa was born, Pope Leo X granted an indulgence to those donating money toward the building of a new Basilica in Rome, St. Peter's. Although the indulgence called for the usual conditions of penance and contrition, it became highly controversial.

The year Teresa was born, 1515, Martin Luther was to attack the very Foundations of the Catholic Church using the *selling of indulgences* as a tool. As a result of this act, not only would the Catholic world never be the same, but the very essence of Christianity would change for all time. Opening the door to more conflicts to this very day, this one act of disobedience was to lead to the scandal of over 3000 splinters of the Cross of Jesus. What with disobedience building on disobedience, and dissension building on dissension, the unity Jesus commanded, *"as I am one with the Father,"* has *instead* become Christian against Christian, brother against brother. And how our Beloved Lord weeps.

Again, we come to Christ and how He defends His Church. We would be foolish to believe it was merely a coincidence that Teresa was born the very year Martin Luther came out with his dogma *of salvation through grace alone.* Whereas Luther, troubled by the conflict between the flesh and the Spirit, addressed his dilemma by embracing the good things of the world, Teresa was to live a *radical* life of obedience, often under the worst of conditions, choosing the *Lord* of all, rather than the *all.* Teresa, always calling herself a sinner, was to do penance throughout her life in reparation for what she considered this evil brought about by Luther.

Teresa was born on March 28, 1515, in Avila, in the Castillian region of Spain. She came from a large family, with three children by her father's first marriage and nine by his second to Teresa's mother whom he had married after the death of his first wife. St. Teresa spoke of her family in the following way, *"I had parents who were virtuous and feared God....I never saw my parents favor anything but virtue."*

Teresa sets out to gain Heaven

Although she was close to all her family, her brother Rodrigo, near her own age, and she spent most of their time together. From the early age of seven, she studied the lives of the Saints, admiring them, wanting to live the life they had lived. She believed by doing so, she would one day know the *Eternal Glory* they had earned; "*Forever they shall see God.*"

One day she and Rodrigo set out to gain Heaven by dying Martyrs' deaths, believing the torment and torture would be all too cheap a price to pay for eternal life. Telling no one, they began their journey to the land of the Moors, to die for their Faith. They had not ventured far when, at *the four posts*, they were apprehended by an uncle who quickly returned them to their mother. Their mother found her panic turn into anger which then *exploded* into punishment. Facing his mother's wrath, blame needing to be laid, Rodrigo did the normal thing; he pointed to Teresa.

This by no means stopped their quest for *holiness*. They gathered stones, starting hermitages of rocks, in their little garden, which they never quite finished. Teresa, from an early age, sought to be alone with Her Lord, so she made her *room* at home into a hermitage. She prayed and talked to a picture she had of our Savior conversing with the Samaritan woman at the well. Teresa pleaded over and over again, "*Lord, give me of that water that I may not thirst.*"

When her mother died, Teresa, fourteen years of age, turned tearfully to the Mother of God asking Her to be *her* Mother. However, without the watchful eye of their earthly mother for supervision, Teresa and Rodrigo became fascinated with reading books on romances. As Teresa writes in her autobiography, these books not only led her away from doing *good things* for the kingdom of God, but were leading her slowly, insidiously to small yes'es, that could have led her to big yes'es, that could have added up to some very serious sins. Although she later says she never committed serious sin, except for the grace of God in her life, she could have. In her own words, "*I could not wait for the next tale (romance) to be in my hands.*" She became enchanted by the latest styles, the newest perfumes, hair styles, anything and everything created to make herself more attractive. Her father became alarmed with this growing change in his daughter. At age fifteen, Teresa was sent away to a Convent of Augustinian Nuns in Avila where she would be educated with young women of her class.

Although she got off to a bad start, Teresa began to enjoy the Convent, finding herself attracted to the Nuns and their way of life. But after a year and a half, Teresa became seriously ill and had to be taken home by her father. Sometimes, and I have seen it in our own lives, God has to knock you on your back to get your undivided attention. Teresa began to consider *seriously* a life as a Religious. She had a huge battle going on, as if two suitors were after her. Part of her was drawn to the life of a Nun and part of her was repulsed by the thought of it. As books of the world had led her away from Her Lord, a book, *the Letters of St. Jerome*, was to lead her to understand and respond to His Call.

Now came the task of presenting her wish to become a Nun to her father. "*No, definitely no! Should you so desire after I am dead, so be it,*" was his answer. Against her father's wishes, afraid she might weaken in her resolve, she quickly ran to the Convent of the Incarnation of the Carmelite Nuns outside of Avila. She recalls,

"*while leaving my father's house, I knew I would not, even at the very moment and agony of my death, feel the anguish of separation more painfully than at that point in time.*" She went on to say, "*not even the love of God I had inside me could make up for the love I felt for my father and friends.*"

Her father did not contest her action, as she was twenty years old by this time. The following year she was professed, only to be removed from the Convent because of an illness that had begun before her profession and had progressively worsened. The countless doctors, failing to find a cure, diagnosed her illness as *hopeless*. Her father, refusing to give up hope, brought her to a place renowned for its cures. Instead of relief, her suffering grew worse. She had an interminable struggle with excruciating pain and inner turmoil, for almost a year. Teresa had a *feeling* of uneasiness about the place, the methods, and the *doctor*. She puts it this way, "*At this point, the devil began to trouble my soul.*"

She looked for the village Priest and asked him to hear her confession. Believing he was intelligent, she felt confident he would be able to direct her spiritually. She had had struggles with Confessors who had little education. She soon discovered he lacked the wisdom she, at first, judged he had. But as he was kind, gentle, and compassionate, she continued to go to him. He encouraged her to come often and she started to have that *uneasy feeling* again. Guardedly, she advised him she would never want to do anything to offend God. He assured her this was one of the reasons he liked her and that he, too, was committed to loving God.

Teresa began to notice how strangely the local people would look when anyone brought up the Priest's name. She could not put her finger on it, but she was troubled by something in his attitude toward her. When she spoke of the love she had for her God and He for her, Teresa's face became radiant. In later years, the older Teresa writes in her autobiography she believed the Priest was attracted to this *goodness*. This brought about a reversal of roles, making Teresa the Confessor and the Priest the penitent. *The Priest confessed that for almost seven years he had been having an affair with a woman.* To compound this serious sin, he had continued celebrating Mass with this sin on his soul. *So, this was the reason for the townspeople's strange behavior.* He had created a scandal for himself and for his Sacrament. People stopped going to confession, and no longer attended Mass.

Although the older Teresa, looking back, could see the naiveté and the harm that could have been done to *her* soul, by her lack of wisdom, the young Teresa was blinded by her desire to save *his* soul. *"My intention was good, but the act was wrong; for to accomplish a good, however great it may be, even a small evil is not to be done."*

She learned from members of his household that the woman had given the Priest a copper idol to wear around his neck. And although she did not believe in magic, Teresa later writes of knowing people who had been deceived by subtle forms of witchcraft.

She continued to speak to him of God. Finally, he turned the little copper idol over to Teresa. She believes change came about the day she threw the idol into the river. He ceased seeing the woman altogether; spending his last year of life before going to the Father, praising Him. *"At the end of a year exactly from the first day I saw him, he died."*

This was a hard year for Teresa, one of pain, both physical and spiritual. But it had given her time to reflect on her vocation. She came to the conclusion that the Purgatory she would suffer on earth as a Nun, was nothing compared to the eternal hell she might know, otherwise. Her goal was to go straight to Heaven and she knew, for her, it was only through the *Religious Life.* After three months of the most excruciatingly painful, unorthodox medical treatment, almost killing her, Teresa's father admitted the doctor was little more than a *quack* and brought her back to Avila.

Teresa's condition deteriorated, going from bad to worse, doctors diagnosing, now, she had tuberculosis as well as heart disease. She lay in bed, her tortured body finding no relief for what seemed a never-ending April dragging into August. God, she felt, had refused to call her home to Him. One day in August, she asked her father to call a Priest to hear her confession, wishing to prepare herself for the Feast of the Assumption. Her father refused, judging instead, she had given up all hope of living. If he granted her wish, he feared this would be a sign to her she *was* dying and she would stop fighting to live. Teresa lost consciousness that evening. All attempts to revive her were in vain. Every test of that time, including a mirror held up to her mouth and tickling her with a feather, showed no signs of life. Having proven to their satisfaction she was truly dead, the doctors left; the Priest anointed her with holy oils; people recited prayers for the dead; and her poor father was beside himself. *Why hadn't he listened to her plea for a Priest!*

A grave was prepared; the Nuns were waiting to escort the body to the Convent. There was only one stumbling block, *Teresa's father.* He insisted he could feel a *pulse!* No one believed him, pitying what they thought was a half-crazed old man. This battle raged on for four days. On the fourth night, Teresa's body was almost consumed by fire; a lit candle having fallen, igniting her bed clothes. Thank God, her brother, who had been keeping watch over the body, awoke just in time to put out the flames. During all the commotion, Teresa did not awaken. Then, as her father and brothers were crying by her bedside, she suddenly sat up and complained, "*Why did you call me back?*"

While all had been judging Teresa dead, she was having a Vision, seeing her family and communities of Nuns in Heaven through the intercession of her prayers and suffering. Attempting to describe her Vision of Heaven, like St. Paul, she found its splendor too *magnificent* for words.

Teresa recovered, if you can call being paralyzed, weak and disoriented, vomiting every morning, *recovery.* She felt as if her heart was being strangled by the pressure it had to endure. Her body was a pain-wracked network of crucified nerve-endings. She returned to the Incarnation Convent, her paralysis remaining with her for an *additional* three years. She turned to St. Joseph, trusting in his never-failing intercession with his Son Jesus; Teresa was completely cured of her paralysis at the end of the third year.

For twenty years, from age twenty four to forty four, Teresa was to know *Purgatory on Earth*. Her physical pains were to be joined by spiritual and mental ones, in the *metanoia*[1] from sinner (as she often called herself) into Saint. Teresa speaks of the need to walk through the "*dark night of the soul*," turning your back on all the pleasures of this world, if you would know that oneness with our Lord. Being put to the test, as our Lord is prone to do for those who ask for closer unity with Him, Teresa was to fail over and over again.

The walk away from Jesus was subtle

The Incarnation was a Convent of holy Nuns, but problems arose because of the never-ending stream of visitors coming and going. Although these callers were very often loving and good, they were bringing *their world* and its allure into *the world* of the Nuns and the Incarnation. Teresa was to painfully discover in her day, just as we will in ours, *either we, the Church evangelize*[2] *to the world or the world will evangelize to us.*

An example of the seriousness of the problem: one of the elder Nuns strongly cautioned Teresa to stop seeing one of her friends, that her talk, more like gossip, was a threat to Teresa's soul. The older Teresa, looking back over her life, could see the advisability and wisdom of following the Nun's admonishments; but the younger Teresa chose to ignore them, conveniently judging the Nun old and too worried about too little.

------

[1]conversion

[2]evangelize-(In a Christian sense), "...it is to preach the Gospel or to convert to Christianity." (In a secular context), "...it is any zealous effort in propandizing for a cause."

The Lord had been carefully planting flowers of perfection in the souls of the Nuns of the Incarnation, forming them into a Heavenly bouquet for Himself. But instead of living more fully this *new life with the Lord*, the Nuns, Teresa included, looked forward, more and more, to news of the *outside* world. Teresa was slowly, but surely, sacrificing her prayer life and eventually her Lord, by being unwittingly tempted by her friends, their world and its vanities. And so, the Gardener, pruning shears in Hand, appeared to Teresa one day, when she was entertaining a newly found friend and visitor. She became aware of the Lord's Presence. *"I saw Him with the eyes of my soul more clearly than I could see Him with those (eyes) of the body."* It made such an impression, that even twenty-six years later, she felt That Presence before her, just as she had that day. That was enough for her. She never saw that person again.

As she began to feel the pull of His Love again, she found it difficult to believe the Lord would want her back. After all, she had foolishly put the visitors and their world ahead of her commitment to Him. But He *was* calling her back to Him. The Lord never gives up on those he Loves; because those He loves, He chooses; and those He chooses, He glorifies. (Romans 8:28) The Lord enlightened Teresa, affirming her and the Nuns of the Incarnation, that the fault was not really theirs, or even the visitors, but that the Nuns were not cloistered. Through prayer and meditation, she began to realize that the soul never stands still; it either walks toward God or away from Him. You cannot have two masters. You will love the one and hate the other. At the Incarnation, they were trying to have the best of *both* worlds.

Teresa loses her father to her Heavenly Father

Teresa was to know a pain so intense, she would say, *"I thought my soul was wrenched from my body when I saw him finish his life, for I loved him so much."* She and her father had been praying together. As they reached the middle of the Credo, "*Who for us men, and for our salvation, came down from Heaven, and was incarnate by the Holy Ghost of the Virgin Mary, and was made man. He was crucified also for us...,*" his voice trailed off; he closed his eyes; and with a look of peace on his face, gave up his spirit to the Lord.

Teresa suffered an ongoing struggle, with God calling her on the one hand and her temptation to follow the world, on the other. For *twenty years* she was to go through the worst battles, falling twice and getting up three times, then falling all over again. When she would recall the Lord's many gifts to her, she grieved all the more for allowing herself to be drawn away from Him and their life together. She was never able to give herself wholly to the Lord as she longed to, as the pull of loved ones and friends, with their needs of compassion and sympathy, was always there. She struggled, *every day of her life*, for a closer and more intimate relationship with her Lord.

Speaking of her Visions of the Lord, she compared them, that is seeing the Lord without her eyes, to a blind man *knowing* someone is there with him although he cannot see him. He talks to that person he *feels*, he *knows* is there; so it was with Teresa. She loved to look at holy paintings and statues because they helped her to *imagine* this Lord Whose Presence she so keenly felt.

Teresa felt a kinship and closeness to Saints who had been sinners, always judging herself the *worst* of sinners. She often pleaded with them to intercede with her Lord and Savior to have pity on her for all the times He had forgiven her and she had fallen. She would become consoled only when she remembered the love and forgiveness the Lord had shown the woman at Bethany when all had wanted to stone her. Was this to be a prophecy of the Lord's intervention, when years later Teresa was to be brought before the Inquisition, and they wanted to burn her at the stake?

Around 1555, someone brought to the Convent, a painting of Our Lord and Savior in His Passion, bleeding, bruised and broken. She prostrated herself before Him, begging Him to release her from the bondage of *the liar and his lies*, with his false gifts of the world and the flesh. She asked His forgiveness for the many times she had foolishly been tempted by people and things of the world, "*My Lord and my God, I will not get up from here until you grant me this favor.*" This was to be the turning point in Teresa's life. She had passionately prayed with her heart and soul, and the Savior responded, as He did when walking the Earth. "*Your faith has saved you. Your sins are forgiven. Pick up your mat and walk.*" She had fought the good fight and she had won! She was free, free at last of the lure of the devil and his kingdom, the world.

In her autobiography, she describes four stages of mental prayer and her journey toward intimacy with the Lord. Trying to define her walk with the Lord, she said simply, "*Mental prayer is nothing else, in my opinion, but friendly conversation with Someone who loves us.*" She shared the danger of being alone, of not having had someone with knowledge of *mental prayer* to discuss these gifts from the Lord.

Teresa had never forgotten the Scripture passage she had treasured as a child, of the Samaritan woman at the well. Teresa, now asked for that water that she might never thirst again. And so, she presented her soul as a garden to the Lord, a place where He could come, be comfortable and make His home; where He would love and be loved. She went from the first step of pulling out all the weeds by the roots so they would not be able to surface again, to preparing the soil, to lastly but most importantly watering the soil without which (water) nothing beautiful could grow.

"*It seems to me that it (the soul) can be watered in four ways: first, with great effort, doing it ourselves, drawing water from a well; or second, by using a wheel or with* *buckets being hoisted by a windlass (*used to lift a bucket from a well*) to draw the water, with less effort and more water; or third, from a river, this irrigating (the ground) much better, for the ground retains the water, making it unnecessary to irrigate as often, requiring less work from the gardener than before; or fourth, by the outpouring of a good rain which the Lord provides, irrigating without any toil on our part, and infinitely better than all I have (previously) said.*"

Teresa advises us to begin by placing ourselves in the Presence of the Human Jesus, loving Him by sharing in a phase of His Passion. One step that will take all the strength and courage we have, is to walk with Jesus His Last Walk, to look upon His Bruised Face and into His loving Eyes, at the Precious Wounds He bore for us; to hear His silent cry, "*I hurt!*" We find ourselves grieving for our sins, for the times we returned His Selflessness with selfishness, for every time we failed to love in Jesus' Name. Let's walk together, with Teresa by our side and offer this *suffering* for our sins and those of the whole world. The world will feel this! This walk will begin as a small tremor, and grow into a giant rumbling that will shake the whole Earth and we will all be made new.

St. Teresa's words are easy to write and read, but so hard to live, "*All who wish to follow Christ must walk the way He went.*" They are not unlike those of Jesus, "*If any man will come after Me, let him deny himself, and take up his cross daily, and follow Me.*" What is my cross, my Savior, the one You ask me to carry *today*? And will I betray and deny You because I seek the Resurrection *without the cross*?

Teresa warns that in the beginning of our Spiritual Walk, we will experience loneliness, "dryness"[1], and disgust, judging that everything we are doing is of no avail, worthless.

---

[1]dryness - refers to that time when a soul doesn't feel or sense the Presence of the Lord...an emptiness...to be dry spiritually.

We can expect to be barraged by temptations; but in the end, the Lover who has been testing us, before granting us greater treasures, will give us the understanding that we have been helping Him to carry the Cross, drinking from the chalice from which He drank.

Teresa speaks of the four degrees of prayer, stressing we love Jesus in the first degree, without seeking the next degree of prayer. She urged that, for our own good, we not look beyond this degree for what *will* come, but for the precious *now* with Him. Having struggled for *twenty years* with the first degree of prayer, she was not to receive the *second degree* of prayer she called the *prayer of quiet*, until she cast herself before a painting of Jesus in His Passion. She was nearly *forty years old* before she reached the fourth degree of prayer, the *Prayer of Complete Union*[1].

The Inquisition

As Teresa was growing deeper and deeper in her journey with the Lord, she went about her everyday life, fully living out her commitment to her vocation as a Nun, as well as to her *immediate* family. But this was to become a time of struggle of the worst kind, a time when she was to suffer one of her most painful temptations. She was plagued with doubts she had never had before: that her mystical experiences might be the work and deception of the devil.

It was a time of fear! The Inquisition, established under King Ferdinand and Queen Isabella but long dormant under Charles the Fifth, was suddenly resurrected by an incident which was to ignite fires best left extinguished. There was a Nun whose reputation for holiness extended even to the Crown. People, faithful to the Church, came from far and near on pilgrimage, to ask for her prayers, taking back with them objects she had touched, as relics. Members of the

---

[1]fourth degree of prayer-the highest plateau a human can rise to with the Lord.

royal family held her holiness in such high regard, they would ask her to pray and intercede with our Lord Jesus for them. Her *reputation* of intense fasting and sacrifice was accompanied by a claim she had received the *Stigmata*[1] from Our Lord Jesus. The Nun, Magdalena de la Cruz, further let it be known she lived strictly on the Consecrated Host, requiring no other nourishment to sustain life.

The Inquisition, becoming suspicious, arrested and questioned Magdalena, whereupon she made a confession so diabolical that it lead to her imprisonment. She told the inquisitors in Cordoba that she was not a Catholic, but an *Alumbrada*, a secret sect exposed a generation before by the Inquisition. It was an anti-Christian secret society which had been crippling Europe by undermining Christ's teachings and His Call for unity under the one true Cross.

Today, as we are being insidiously attacked from within and without by a wide-spread, dangerous heresy, which has been given the name of New Age, the characteristics of the Alumbrados sound suspiciously familiar. The Alumbrados sect was likewise oriental in origin, stemming from Buddhism. As with today's sects, it advocated the soul escaping from all reality and involvement, delving into itself to the exclusion of everyone and everything about it, seeking and achieving a state of nothingness, the mind completely blank. Today, people who have escaped from modern-day cults, speak of the many who lost their minds as a result of this type of mind-bending meditation. Psychiatrists say to give up complete control of the mind is to very possibly flirt with madness. The result is annihilation of the individual conscience and one's individual personality, and ultimately death. Many of the heresies throughout the ages, although espousing they were Christian, were influenced by oriental philosophy, in that some denied the

---

[1]Stigmata - The five wounds of Our Lord's Passion, in the feet, hands and side.

True Presence of Jesus in the Eucharist, others His Divinity, yet others the Holy Trinity, advocating reliance on feelings and intuition, rather than the true teachings of the Catholic Church.

The *Alumbrados*, closely allied with the devil, used *his* devious tactics; they took Christian expressions and truths and distorted them using them against Christ and His followers. Following the pattern of other heretics, they taught that only God was to be obeyed, that Jesus had not delegated others to guide and lead the Church to Him and His Father. They advocated distrust and fear of everyone who did not believe in their false doctrines. They promoted disobedience and unfaithfulness. If an Alumbrada was *married*, she was to detest the Sacrament of Matrimony. If she was a *Religious*, she was to avoid other Religious who would not embrace the Alumbrado doctrine, lest they attempt to lead her back to Jesus and His Church.

Magdalena de la Cruz confessed to being a devil-worshiper. She had been induced by the devil, at seven years of age, to *feign* holiness and the wounds of the Stigmata. At eleven, with the help of two demons who visited her periodically, she had administered the wounds on her hands, feet and side, imitating the Wounds of Our Beloved Lord Jesus.[1] She recounted how she had become quite adept at affecting trances where she became impervious to the pricks of needles and other forms of testing. She had been able to deceive everyone into believing she lived only on the Sacred Host[2] for *twelve years*, until one day food was discovered hidden in her cell at the Convent.

---

[1] There have been genuine Stigmatists in our Church, like St. Francis of Assisi, and Padre Pio, who bore the wounds of Christ on their bodies.

[2] There have been many documented accounts of Eucharistic Fasters, people who lived on no food other than the Eucharist for periods of up to 35 years. See chapter on Eucharistic Saints and Fasters, *This Is My Body, This Is My Blood, Miracles of the Eucharist*

As incredulous as it may seem, although everyone who ever met Teresa could plainly see she was humble and sincere, *she* soon fell under suspicion. Townspeople began to whisper she was like Magdalena de la Cruz. The problem with false mystics like Magdalena is that they could very cleverly imitate the outward signs of a true mystic like Teresa. Although Teresa was long free from any need to receive approval from the world, she began to *doubt* her gifts, to believe the townspeople might be right. *Suppose she had been deceived by the evil one!* She brought this fear to a Priest she highly respected. This questioning of herself alone, should have been proof she was not an Alumbrada, as they were hardly known for any type of humility or sincerity.

Her friends, who *loved* her, began to conjecture on whether Teresa's gifts were from God or the devil. A person whose opinions she valued, suggested she seek spiritual advice from an exemplary Priest known for his love of the Blessed Sacrament and for bringing many back to the Church. He was reputed to be a truly dependable and holy Priest. Because of her humility, and always striving for perfection, she confessed what she called *her terrible imperfections*. The Priest, concluding the Lord would not give favors, such as she spoke of, to someone with all her faults, ordered her to give up all forms of *Mental Prayer*.[1]

She shared what the Priest had said, with her friend Maestro Daza, seeking his counsel while at the same time enjoining him to keep all she had confided *secret*. In an effort to help her, he asked advice of friends, recounting the Priest's verdict, inadvertently spreading doubts about Teresa. The Priest's evaluation of Teresa's Visions coming from diabolical sources, *spread* throughout Avila. The Priest,

----

[1]*Mental Prayer* - as Teresa states, "to shut myself within myself, ...without shutting in with me a thousand vanities. She advises it is important that those who practice *mental prayer*, be directed by a holy and intelligent spiritual Director experienced in this form of prayer.

along with another holy and learned man, confident her *Mental Prayer* was all the work of the devil, advised her to go and give an account of her whole life to a Priest of the Company of Jesus[1], *"as she was in much peril."*

"Those that sow in tears shall reap rejoicing." Psalm 126. Through her tears, Teresa was led to the *Word*, for comfort. Her eyes came to St. Paul's consoling words to the Corinthians, *"You can trust God not to let you be tried beyond your strength, and with any trial, He will give you a way out of it and the strength to bear it."* (1 Cor 10:13) Teresa asked that the Jesuit Priest be called. This had to be done in secrecy, as in those days, Nuns of the Incarnation were only allowed Confessors of their own Order.

Teresa always stressed the need of learned and *holy* Spiritual Directors to guide us in the quest of Our Lord Jesus. The young Jesuit Priest that was sent to her, half her age and twenty-three years young, was quite a shock to Teresa, at first. He was of poor health, barely three years a member of the Company, and his Superior said of him, "He is a mediocre preacher; he hears confessions and is fit for nothing more." Yet, this humble Priest, because of his experience with Mental Prayer, was able to discern and provide the Spiritual Direction Teresa had so desperately searched for, from more important and highly regarded clergymen. Deferring obediently to his authority, she knelt before him, confessing all that had gone on with reference to

---

[1]It is interesting to note that the Company of Jesus' founder, St. Ignatius who, with a band of nine companions set out for Rome to seek permission from the Pope to serve God and their fellow men, was once looked upon as a heretic and arrested by the Inquisition at Alcalá. Exonerated, he and his company went on to preach the Word and tend to the poor throughout Italy, Spain and France. The Jesuits have been attributed with the renewal of devotion to the Holy Eucharist. Pope St. Pius X declared they had been called to bring new life to The Catholic Church, through the faithful's frequent reception of the Sacraments of Confession and Communion.

the Visions, along with her *"many faults"*. He not only directed her to return to Mental Prayer, but to do so even more deeply, as it was *a gift from the Lord*. His words, that the Lord would use her to bring Mental Prayer to others, were to become a *prophecy*. To this day Teresa's writings and experiences with Mental Prayer are followed not only by Carmelites, but by many of the faithful seeking this special union with our Lord Jesus.

Teresa never gave up on Mental Prayer, to the day she died. The young Priest told her perhaps she had suffered excruciating *physical* pain all these past years because she had not done enough *penance*. Again, she obeyed, and although she found the forms of mortification she practiced unpleasant, she noticed that her health began to greatly improve as she diligently followed her young Confessor's direction. Because of the penance she did, Her Lord *took away* her morning sickness of twenty years, enabling her to receive Him in His Eucharist. But He *left her* with the evening sickness. As she took on more painful penances, she found herself growing closer and closer to our Lord.

Her consolation in this Priest was short-lived, as were most earthly gifts in Teresa's life. He was transferred, because the Nuns were suspicious of Teresa having a non-Carmelite hearing her confession. *I wonder if perhaps, it could have been the Lord. In our own walk, if we start to make anyone a god, be it a Priest, Nun, friend or family member, that person is always separated from us physically or emotionally.*

Teresa had the love and joy of having her sister Juana staying at the Incarnation. Even that, one of the last of her beloved ties with her family, was to be severed as her sister Juana left the Incarnation to be married. Through her Spiritual Director, Teresa learned she would have to give up even the smallest attachments if she wished to please her Lord Jesus. Protesting, she pleaded this would appear as ingratitude toward those who had been so kind to her. As she followed her Director's advice to pray to the Holy Spirit, *Veni Creator*, she went into a rapture where the Lord said to her, "*I desire you no longer converse with men, but with Angels.*" From then on, although she was warm and caring, joyful and present to her Sisters, she belonged only to her Lord Jesus.

Teresa felt Jesus beside her, in His Sacred Humanity. Again, she went to a Confessor. Being a new Confessor, she was to suffer much because he badgered her, barraging her relentlessly with the same question, "*How do you know it was Jesus?*" She replied, at the point of tears, "*Because He told me so, over and over again.*"

The Angel of the Lord

Two years later, she received, what she called, a terrifying caress, a *Transverberation of her heart.*[1] She saw an Angel to the left of her. He was small and very beautiful. He was so illuminated he had to be one of the very highest of the Angels, the Cherubim. He had a long golden dart in his hand, with what appeared to be fire at the end of it. She said he thrust it into her heart several times, piercing her down to her innermost organs, leaving her burning with a great love for God.

After St. Teresa's death, when they investigated her heart, it appeared to be pierced through the center as if by a dart. In 1872, at the request of the Prioress at Alba de Tormes, three physicians, professors of medicine and surgery at the University of Salamanca, examined Teresa's heart. They found the heart still incorrupt and untouched by the ravages of death, after almost *three hundred years*. The heart was punctured on both sides, leaving a perforation above the

---

[1]Transverberation - (a)Teresa's mystical experience of the piercing of her heart which occurred in 1559. (b)On May 25, 1726, Pope Benedict XIII appointed a festival and office for the Transverberation, which is observed on August 27th. It was first instituted by the Carmelites and then later celebrated throughout all Spain.

left and right auricles, verifying what Teresa had said. *(Author's note: When we visit Alba de Tormes, the Convent where she died and where she asked to be buried, we can still see and venerate the miraculously preserved heart of St. Teresa, with the stab wound of the Angel's dart.)*

After the Transverberation, Teresa's raptures became more and more frequent. She would see Christ in the Eucharist during Mass, especially after receiving Communion. She would go into ecstasy, no longer being able to feel her body, with a weightlessness that lifted her whole body into the air, called *Levitation*. Some of her Nuns testified that one day they saw her body rise high above the window from which she had received the Host from the Bishop of Avila. Teresa was thoroughly saddened when this occurred in front of others, not wanting to be judged *holy*. In response to her requests of anonymity, our Lord would gift her with such outward signs of radiant beauty, it was impossible not to see her gifts of sanctity. Jesus loves to be playful with His children. He enjoys them so, like Teresa, in their human simpleness, finding them forever *"precious."*

Teresa comes under suspicion once again

People who feigned loyalty to the Church, had been exposed as Lutherans![1] They read like a *"Who's Who of Spain,"* from amongst the clergy, including a nominee for Archbishop of Toledo, to many of the most influential citizens in the highest of places. Priests and Nuns considered holy, confessed that they spread dangerous heresies. King Philip took *drastic* measures to forestall a civil war.

And so, the Inquisition was once more resurrected. Everyone became suspect. Teresa was again deserted by friends, tested to the breaking point by holy Confessors, avoided and isolated. She was even denied the comfort and

[1]Lutherans, Calvinists, Unitarians, even Catholics who were not friendly to the Church were called *Lutherans* by Teresa

companionship of her books. Most books not written in
Latin were under suspicion, because of the *misuse* of books
to spread heresy. Teresa was to suffer the backlash of this,
as she had not been educated to read Latin; now forbidden
to read her favorite books written in the vernacular
(Spanish), she felt quite alone! Even a translation of *St.
Jerome's Epistles*, the *Confessions of St. Augustine*, and *The
Imitation of Christ*, her favorite reading, written in the
vernacular, were among the prohibited reading material.
One day in her painful aloneness, she heard the voice of
Christ, "*Never mind I will give you a living book.*"

As if being deprived of religious books was not enough
to bear, her Confessor made her stay away from her Precious
Lord in Holy Communion, day after day, for nearly three
agonizing weeks. Berated, accused, vilified, deprived of her
only consolation, Holy Communion, she felt deserted, even
by God. Kneeling all alone, trying to pray, she was made to
suffer, for nearly five hours, *the darkest night of the soul.*
*(Author's note: What is the dark night of the soul? As you read
the lives of the Saints, you share in the extraordinary pain of
aloneness they had to endure, feeling nothing; neither hearing
nor seeing any sign that the Lord was with them; negative
thoughts answering them as they cried out to Him for help; the
tormenting voices of their companions filling them with doubts.
Among other tortures, "temptations against faith," is right there
in the forefront, with, very often, "physical suffering" as an
added gift permitted by God.)*
Feeling totally empty and alone, no friends to console
her, Teresa summoned the last ounce of strength she had, *to
hold on. Finally*, nothing left, she felt Him; Jesus was beside
her. "*Have no fear, daughter, for I am here, and I will not
forsake you, have no fear.*" As I read this, I recall how many
times the Lord has sent that special love note to us when we
felt helpless and alone, not knowing where to turn.

The Confessor, now joined by his *respected* associates, continued to order Teresa to rebuke the Visions, calling them diabolically induced. Although suffering the worst anguish imaginable, obedient to his strict orders, she would *douse* the Vision of our Lord with Holy Water. She obeyed her Confessor even to the extremely painful extent of making some kind of vulgar, evil sign toward the Vision to see if it would vanish, proving it was diabolical.

She said, "*This gave me the greatest sorrow for I could not believe it was not God. And although they ordered me to send Him away, I could not bear Him leaving me.*" The Lord told her not to worry, that she did well to obey. One day, after suffering one of her worst trials, she felt the Presence of Jesus. Fighting back the tears, but too weak to do anything but obey her Confessor, she held up her Crucifix defensively, so that if, in truth, it was the devil, he would disappear. Instead, a beautiful Vision of our Lord came toward her, extended His Hand, took the Crucifix from her and returned it. "*When He gave it back to me, it was of four large stones, much more precious, beyond compare, than diamonds. It had the five wounds very exquisitely wrought.*" He told Teresa that was how she would see it from now on, but she alone.

Gifts of this nature have been granted to other Saints, like St. Catherine of Siena, our other woman Doctor of the Church, who received a ring of gold and pearls from our Lord Jesus which remained only for her to see.

Teresa's words speak so of the life of a Saint on earth, misunderstood, persecuted, accused, deserted, tortured, but always trusting in the Lord, glorifying His Name.

"*The devil! The devil! where we could say, 'God! God!' and make him tremble. Yes, for we know he cannot even move unless the Lord permits it. What is this? There is no doubt that I am more afraid of those who are so afraid of the devil than I am of him, for he can't do anything to me, and they, especially if they are*

Confessors, disturb me much, and I have spent several years in such great trouble, that now I wonder how I have been able to endure it. Blessed be the Lord, Who has so truly helped me."

The Lord had finally freed her from fear, but not from persecution. The Inquisition continued to hang ominously over her head.

Teresa came to know that her Visions were of the Lord by the way of the *heart*. But now she desired the complete synthesis of the Spirit by knowing with the *head* as well. Another very holy Priest was to come into her life, for this purpose, *Fray Pedro de Alcántara*. As God's designs are not necessarily ours, Teresa was to find the contemplative she needed for this purpose, not from her own Carmelite order, but from the Franciscans. The holy Doña Guiomar arranged for Teresa to spend eight days with her so that under *Fray Pedro's* direction, Teresa would find the peace she so desperately sought. This temporary reprieve would, as well, separate Teresa from the intense barrage of the well-meaning, but torturous scrupulosity of her Confessor and his advisors.

When *Fray Pedro* first came into Teresa's life, he was sixty-one years old, a sorry sight, barely a skeleton, walking barefoot, the poorest, most ragged tunic covering his emaciated body. But reminiscent of his founder St. Francis, he was joyously proclaiming that *"God is with us, rejoice!"* As Father Peter heard Teresa's confession, he could see, kneeling before him, a holy and courageous lover of the Lord who was attempting to do with Mental Prayer what he had already done. He guided her and affirmed her, sharing the different forms of penance he had used to die to any of the things in his life that would separate him from this ultimate intimacy with the Master. Some of the penances shared were:

*"For forty years, I think he told me, he had slept only
an hour and a half between night and day, and this was
the hardest penance he had at the beginning, this
overcoming of sleep, and to do it he stayed always on
his knees or on his feet."*

He lived in a Community for three years, depriving
himself of the companionship of his fellow Friars, never
allowing himself the friendship of any of them. With no
human company for his consolation, his joy was to come
from his Lord alone. And this is the man the Lord, in His
generosity, sent to Teresa.

Pedro told her this gift of Mental Prayer was also to be
an ongoing *affliction.* He kept his word to her and spoke to
her Confessor, admonishing him it would be a serious
mistake to interfere with the Heaven-sent prayer life of this
Saint.

St. Teresa again finds herself saying good-by to a human
sent to her in her time of trial. Instead of cursing the
darkness she knows will follow, she instead, rejoices, giving
thanks, once again, to Her Lord, the Power in her life. Then
she gives thanks to His Mother and Saint Joseph, for she
knows it was through their intercession she was granted *Fray
Pedro* and his counsel at this time in her life.

The devil never let go of St. Teresa

She told of how, when she was reading something
spiritual, like the life of a Saint, she might have to read it
over and over again, perhaps four or five times, because the
devil would put thoughts in her mind, blocking what the
Spirit wanted to teach her. When this happened, she
shamefully confessed later, she felt such anger she would
want to *"eat everyone in my path!"*

*I know it is not the fashion to speak of Heaven and hell in
some circles,* but Teresa, like many Saints before her and
since, saw the horrors of hell. In trying to describe hell, she

said that no pain on earth could be compared to it and she welcomed any suffering on earth rather than the never-ending torture of hell. She had this Vision after she had just received many gifts from the Lord, so she was shocked to find herself in what seemed like the middle of hell.

"I understood that the Lord wished me to see there the place which the demons had prepared for me, and which I merited by my sins. This lasted a very short time, but I think that if I live many years I could never forget it. The entrance seemed to me like an alley very long and straight, sort of an oven very low and dark and narrow. The ground seemed to me of a water-like mud, filthy and of pestilential odor, and many reptiles in it."

"The most unbearable bodily pains, and I have suffered very grievous ones in this life, and as the doctors say, the worst that can happen here - the shrinking of my sinews...and others caused by the devil - all is nothing in comparison with the agonizing of the soul, a sense of constraint, a stifling, an anguish so keen, and with a sorrow so abandoned and afflicted, that I don't know how to describe it...as if the soul was being always pulled up by the roots...I felt myself burn and crumble up into pieces...so helpless even to hope for consolation...everything was suffocating, there was no light...I don't know how it was (that I could see without light), but I understood it to be a great favor, and that the Lord wanted me to see with my own eyes the place from which His Mercy had saved me...And so I don't remember any times since that I have had trouble or pain, without thinking that everything that can be suffered here is nothing...From then on I had the greatest sorrow for the many souls that condemn themselves to hell."

This great Saint who had seen hell itself, did not, like her fellow countrymen, condemn the *heretics* who were burning Catholic churches, killing Priests and Nuns, desecrating the Body and Blood of Christ in His Blessed Sacrament. Because she so loved Jesus, she prayed for them, for as they had been baptized Catholics, she feared their souls might be lost. She looked on them as *victims* of a great lie, rather than as perpetrators.

The Beginning of the Reform

The problem Teresa had in the Incarnation Convent, of following the life of a contemplative, with the frequent visits of people from the outside world and their worldly influences, was to lead her to bring about *Reform*. She would restore her order to the *Primitive Rule* that dated back to the founding of the Carmelite Order. For example, the number in a Convent originally calling for between thirteen and sixteen Nuns, had problematically exploded into close to one hundred and eighty in St. Teresa's time.

The idea of the Reform started almost playfully, in jest. Some of the Nuns and some lay women were in Teresa's cell. Their favorite topic came up again; the need for more solitude and their desire to live a truly monastic life free from the outside influences of the many visitors who frequented the Incarnation. "Why don't we start a *reform* right here in the Incarnation?" It was a young Nun, Teresa's niece, Maria de Campo who started it all with the suggestion; but it was Teresa who said "*yes*." Having held this in her heart all those years, upon hearing the young Nun's words, she knew it was the Lord talking through her.

As with other movements in the Church, Christ took over from there. Teresa, I am sure, probably began the walk toward Christ's open door for this idea, forging ahead, trusting that if He didn't want it, He would close the door. Why not? Turning the whole affair to the Lord, the little band of women that had been praying together, all committed the idea to Our Lord and His Will!

One morning, after Teresa received her Beloved Lord in Holy Communion, she felt Him next to her. He let it be known that the Reform was *His Will* and that He would be at one door and His Mother at the other, protecting them. He even gave her the name of the Convent to be founded; it was to be named after His foster father on earth, St. Joseph. This was to be the *first* of the seventeen Carmels[1], of the Primitive Rule, she would spend the last fifteen years of her life founding. She set out, as Don Quixote said, *"to do battle, only in Godly fashion as she was a Saint, not as a sinner in human fashion."*

The Convent of San José, she was commissioned by our Lord to establish, would be the prototype of those to follow. If this had failed, the others probably never would have come about. This was to be the leaven, the mustard seed, the city on the mountain top that our Beloved Lord spoke of in Holy Scripture. Although He let her feel the joy of the days ahead doing His Will, He also shared with her the pain, the price she would pay for her "yes." Now forty-five years old, she began to plan and execute her dream. It took from 1560 to 1562 to realize it, with much blood, sweat and tears.

The money came; her Provincial said "yes"; and her Confessor, although a little cautious, felt he could not say anything but "yes," too. *And then it began, the persecution!* Although all the holy Priests consulted, including Teresa's Confessor, had, as one, agreed to the opening of the Reformed Convent, when word got out in Avila, all hell broke loose and they buckled under the pressure. Teresa suffered more for her friend, Doña Guiomar, who had volunteered to help her, than for herself. Teresa was in the Convent, but Doña, being a lay person, had to endure all that the townspeople, with their petty jealousies and gossiping, could dish out. *"The nerve of that Nun, why doesn't*

---

[1]Carmels - Foundations for Discalced Carmelite Nuns

she stay quietly in the Convent and do what she is supposed to do? And as for that Doña Guiomar, why doesn't she take care of her own home! Isn't that what good and holy widows do, not get involved with such an ambitious, obviously useless idea as another Convent, when the town already had one."

Whereas Teresa had the Lord and her revelations to sustain her, Doña only had her deep conviction that this was God's Work. As everyone turned against them, friends as well as enemies, the Lord persisted with Teresa, encouraging her, always consoling her with the company of Saints who, before her, had founded Religious Orders.

The storm had risen not only in the town but in the Incarnation, as well. The Father Provincial buckled under the anger and indignation of the Nuns. It was more than he could withstand. He called her formation of a new Convent a *scandal* and ordered her to cease bringing all this pain and discord into the Community. The worst hurt Teresa felt was when she received a letter from her Confessor, accusing her of going against his will. It was as if he had *never* been in accord with her idea. This really wounded Teresa and she couldn't understand why he had changed his mind so abruptly. Her Provincial and her Confessor having lost all faith in her mission, Teresa was to have one Priest, a Dominican, Father Ibañez, who not only affirmed the concept, but together with Doña Guiomar wrote to Rome for permission to open such a house in Avila.

In her cell, now near fifty years of age, she was alone, except for the visits of two friends. Friendless for the most part, hated, tormented by doubt that her Visions might have not been of the Lord, Her Shepherd came to the rescue. He told her to obey her Confessor and leave the rest up to Him.

She remained in the Incarnation, alone and silent, obedient. *Then, the approval came from Rome to open a Monastery.* But as her Provincial had withdrawn his approval, Teresa had to proceed in secrecy. Now, they had

Rome's approval and Doña Guiomar picked out the house, volunteering the necessary funds. But, as they were ready to proceed, she found she did not have the money *necessary* to build the Monastery. Teresa reached out to her family, asking her sister Juana and her husband to purchase the house and supervise the necessary changes to make it into a Convent. It was the summer of 1561. Things were moving rapidly. She could feel the Wind of the Holy Spirit blowing everything and everyone into place. The additional funds necessary to complete the Monastery arrived from Teresa's brother Lorenzo in America.

Everyone judged the first house too small for a Convent, but Teresa. I believe Teresa could *see* that Convent unfold, envisioning what no one else could. But although Teresa believed, *if this house was too small the Lord would have sent her enough money to buy a larger one*, the objections of everyone around her started to make her doubt herself. At the very inception of that thought, not wasting another minute; after all He had a lot of work to do; the Lord spoke to His Teresa. *"Enter it and you will see what I shall do."* Praise God! Now all that was left to do was sign the deed.

We say, in the ministry, we know when the Lord has something really important He is going to do because the attacks are so brutal from the evil one. And so it was with Teresa and the first little Convent. Her family, loving and supportive, suffered mercilessly. It began one day when Juana and her husband entered the house, only to see their tiny son pinned under part of a wall that had fallen on him. They carried their little boy's lifeless body over to Doña Guiomar, where Teresa was staying that day. Taking the child and placing him on her lap, Teresa ordered her sister, now screaming uncontrollably, to be silent. Teresa lifted her veil and lowered her face over the child's until their faces almost touched. She prayed, arguing, as the Prophets before her had, with her Lord; *He could not allow this to come to pass.* After a short while, the child lifted his hands, one by one, and began to play with her. Later, when people would try to sound her out about the incident, questioning her, probing with *the child had been dead, and now he was alive,* Teresa would only smile as if nothing had happened.

Walls continued to fall; money continued to run out. As if the fury of hell, attacking her on all sides, was not enough, her favorite nephew, Juana's second child, an infant barely three weeks old, died. When he was first born, Teresa had prayed, as she lovingly cradled this precious child in her arms, *"If he is to lose his immortal soul, please take him, Lord."* And now, he was dead! In her autobiography, she does not speak of the pain she suffered as she looked upon the lifeless form of her nephew. But I wonder if, for a moment she did not want to take back the words, *"Thy will be done?"* Do we really mean it when we place this trust in the Lord and His Wisdom and Mercy?

As even the most supportive of her friends began to have doubts, not only did the Lord come to fortify her, but St. Clare of Assisi, as well, along with the Blessed Mother on her right and St. Joseph on her left. They pledged to help, reassuring her of their intercession with the Lord. They made no secret of how delighted they were with her, their love radiating, warming her. As she saw the Angels carrying them Heavenward, she knew her Jesus had called out the heavenly artillery just in time. *Our eleventh hour God came to the rescue once again!*

Consolation for Teresa was to be short-lived. The townspeople began to suspect what was going on. One Sunday, Teresa was to hear the Priest deliver a homily accusing her (not by name but definitely leaving no doubt) of plotting against the Church and trying to destroy Christianity as a whole. Her sister began to cry, but Teresa just laughed it off. Her laughter soon turned to concern, when she considered the strong probability of the Provincial stopping the work when all this came to his attention.

The second shoe dropped! The Provincial ordered her to Toledo, away from Avila and her dream. *It would be a way to kill two birds with one stone*, he thought. By spiriting Teresa away, he could quiet the storm in Avila, and at the same time satisfy a very rich and persistent widow in Toledo, who believed, hearing of her holiness, that Teresa would be able to help her cope, spiritually, with her unbearable grief.

Our Lord, the Perfect Weaver of stories and of lives, has a profound and delightful sense of humor. Teresa was sent away from Avila to Toledo, to a *palace*, no less. This Nun, who was fighting to bring about Reform, to live as Jesus lived in true poverty, is sent by her Provincial to a palace! The palace and its visitors were, to Teresa, worse than the worst of penances. Teresa listened to the widow Doña Luisa, sharing *over and over again* the virtues of her late husband, all the sorrows in her life, the death of five of her children, the loneliness, the hurts and emptiness of her life. After a while, the Lord consoled Teresa by showing her how, by exercising all His Love and her patience, the despondency was *leaving* Doña Luisa. Doña Luisa, for her part, could not stop proclaiming Teresa's sanctity. This time, of pain and separation from her Community and *her dream*, gave Teresa an opportunity to think, to pray and to discern.

Away from her dream and maybe away from the doubts of others, what should she receive, but a letter from her friend, Fray Pedro de Alcántara, who had been responsible for bringing some peace into Teresa's life, in Avila. He wrote to her, reaffirming his counsel to hold fast to founding the Convent *without* endowment, as she had originally desired. *Now*, even those who had agreed with her initially, found this much too idealistic for the materialistic world, they argued, *everyone* had to live in. Teresa, with her *heart*, believed in Fray Pedro and his wisdom, but with her *head* she found herself agreeing with her other advisers. The Lord allows us to have some pretty rough meetings in our head and heart; but, bottom line, when He has a plan, He calls His People into *action*, in Heaven and on earth.

Enter a Carmelite Nun dressed in tattered clothes. She just *happened* to be visiting the palace. Originally from a very wealthy and influential family, Maria de Jesus had given it all up to become a Carmelite Nun, late in life. Maria de Jesus had had the same thought, that of founding a Convent of contemplatives, *the same month of the same year*, as had Teresa. Maria further confirmed Fray Pedro's advice when she showed Teresa a copy of the original Rule of St. Albert,[1] where it speaks of Carmelites *owning no property*.

Even after reading and rereading the Rule of Saint Albert, Teresa still had doubts about whether to found her Convent dependent solely on the donations of others. It didn't help much, either, to have her friends pursuing her with all the war stories of the contemplatives, who had become discouraged and distracted, by the poverty they had to endure, when the charitable donors grew cold.

Teresa must have felt like a ball being tossed back and forth. On the tail of all this, *should I, shouldn't I,* who should arrive at the palace, but Fray Pedro. By reiterating all he had formerly told her, he was at last able to bring peace and resolve into Teresa's life. She went no farther for advice, for if *that* was not enough, the Lord Himself told her it was *His* desire and that of *His Father* that she found this house of *poverty*, that she need not fear; He would take care of her.

I don't think one ever gets over the sadness of meeting God's people, touching and being touched by them, only to have to leave them. Teresa was sad, for it was time to leave Doña Luisa who had been so good to her. It further hurt Teresa to see Doña so upset over her leaving. Her feelings

---

[1]Founder of the Carmelite Order

were like a kite being tossed by the wind, only she had the consoling *knowledge* that the Wind was the Holy Spirit. She was not looking forward to her return to the Incarnation, but on the other hand, she was eager and excited to please Her Lord by doing His Will.

The very night Teresa arrived in Avila, written permission arrived from Pope Pius IV for her to found a Convent under the Carmelite order. Now let's look into the Incarnation, where Teresa had gone, obediently placing herself into the routine of being a Nun there. It isn't known how she found out about the long-awaited good news, but she was not able to share it with the Nuns. She could not do anything, say anything, lest she arouse suspicion. She remained a prisoner of the Incarnation. Her fears were that when the Bishop heard the Convent would have no income, as well as no endowment, possibly pulling away donations from him and his work, he would deny them permission. When they had drafted the original Rule, Teresa had not included living under the *Rule of Poverty* with no endowment, as she had not been sure this would be the best way to go. Consequently, the permission granted by the Pope did not include this.

The grant that had been given to Doña Guiomar and her mother were under the special conditions of the Church, one of these being, obedience to the Bishop. Teresa's fears and apprehensions had not been far-fetched, either, because the inevitable happened; the Bishop would have nothing to do with it. The little band of disciples, Doña Guiomar and the rest, knew that, although the Bishop never changed his mind, there was one holy man he so deeply loved and respected, *he* would be able to reason with him. And so, once again we call on *Fray Pedro de Alcántara*, now very ill in bed. The holy Friar wrote a brilliant plea to the Bishop to grant Teresa permission to open the Convent. Not only did the Bishop refuse, but rejected the Friar's request for a meeting, hastily leaving for his country home some thirty-two miles away. We know that all good things are possible with God; so it is to no surprise that Fray Pedro de Alcántara, more dead than alive, barely able to stand, journeyed to the Bishop and extracted from him a promise to talk with Teresa when he returned to Avila.

The Bishop's heart of stone melted when he met Teresa, as did most hearts. She was humble but definite in her resolve, spoke simply, never wavering; in all her humanness he found her warm and gentle, but *strong*. He pledged his protection of her and her Monastery. He remained her true and loyal friend till the day he died, requesting he be buried beside her. Fray Pedro having performed his last act for Teresa, retired to a Franciscan Monastery and *went to the Father*, two months later. I just know St. Francis was there to greet him and with the Blessed Mother, presented him to the Father, through the Son, in the presence of the Holy Spirit. All the Angels sang, giving glory to God, for another son, job well done, had come home.

Teresa prepared her Nuns for what was ahead of them. The Primitive Rule of Carmel, formed by St. Albert in 1209, which she was adopting, no, *returning* to the Church, was the *strictest* of all the Rules in the history of the Church. The Rule encompassed, in addition to the vows of poverty, chastity and obedience, *the Nuns were to maintain complete silence at certain hours; to remain in their cells meditating on their God when not busy with other tasks; to fast from September 14, the Exaltation of the Cross to Easter, unless physically unable; to eat no meat (unless it was required because of health reasons); be engaged in doing all sorts of physical work for the Community.*

The Rule was formulated and adopted by Teresa, to keep any and all distractions from their loving and serving their Lord. The Nuns could not be seen without their veils,

except by a father, mother or sister, and *then* there had to be
another Nun present. No one could enter or leave the
Convent, without the Prioress' consent. They were not to
own anything personally; in short, *complete abandonment.*
Considering this stringent way of life, Teresa chose her Nuns
with an eye on quality, never quantity, each Monastery to
have no more than thirteen or sixteen Nuns at the most.

She chose Nuns with healthy and cheerful dispositions,
speaking of the harm that can be done a Community when
even *one* of the members are prone to melancholy. She also
made the decision neither to choose Nuns from other Orders
nor from the Calced Carmelites. She knew they were being
called to a radical life and it would be better if they did not
enter with any pre-conceived ideas of contemplative life.

The sun had not risen on August the 24th, when the
first four Nuns to be received, accompanied by friends of
Teresa, Priests, two Nuns from the Incarnation, Doña
Guiomar, Teresa's sister Juana, her husband and their
children approached the little Convent. Teresa was waiting
to open the door, having remained the night before to get
the Chapel ready for their first Mass. The first Discalced
Carmelite Monastery was no longer a project, but a *reality.*

The first battle was won, but the war went on

The townspeople discovered what Teresa and her Nuns
had done and they were up in arms, ready to storm the little
Monastery of San José. They demanded it be closed down,
at once. The Mother Superior of the Incarnation called a
very weary and discouraged Teresa to report to her,
immediately! Before obeying, Teresa went to Her Lord in
the Tabernacle and pleaded for His Help, using St. Joseph,
namesake of the Monastery, as additional ammunition.
Teresa, now *Mother* Teresa, was tried for her supposed crime
against the City Council by the Nuns of the Incarnation and

threatened with monastic imprisonment if she persisted in this *nonsense.*

The Mother Superior, listening to Teresa humbly and serenely offering her an explanation, was satisfied that nothing had transpired that called for the closing of the new Monastery. But wanting to *play it safe,* she later changed her mind and called for Teresa to appear before the Father Provincial, Fray Angel de Salazar. He *humbled* her before all 180 Nuns of the Incarnation, leveling all forms of false accusations. Teresa later wrote that she recalled the judgment that had been passed on Christ and considered hers too small a trial. Teresa begged forgiveness, of Father Provincial and all the Nuns, for causing them this trouble. Later, listening to Teresa's recounting of the process she had gone through to bring about the opening of San José, he became satisfied and promised the Monastery could remain in operation, if the townspeople quieted down.

Knowing that Teresa was still in the Incarnation, the people of Avila, many with family in the other Monasteries who opposed this *new* Foundation, called a meeting and converged upon the little Community of San José, ordering the Nuns to disperse at once and return to their homes. They expected the Nuns to *blow away,* without Teresa there to strengthen them, but they were in for a surprise! The Nuns stood their ground, firmly informing them, *"We will leave only when the one who put us here tells us."* The men were livid with rage and would have thrown them out bodily, but upon pushing open the doors, they saw the Reason for the Nuns' strength, the Blessed Sacrament on the altar.

There was such an uproar, you would have thought foreign invaders were threatening the city. One lone voice was raised for Teresa and the new Foundation, and it was a *Dominican.* The Bishop ultimately stepped in and declared his support of the new Foundation, which, after all, had permission to open through the *Holy See!* He let everyone know, in no uncertain terms, he would not dare nor care to question that higher source.

Furious and incensed, determined to be victorious over this impending drain on their pocketbooks, the City Council waged war, threatening a never-ending lawsuit against them, *unless,* and here was the big temptation, "*Teresa would have it endowed, that is with financial support.*" The Lord appeared to her advising if she compromised now, she would never be able to have it without an endowment in the future. The lawsuit continued for months. But praise God, since all belongs to the Lord, this war finally ended; Teresa was, at last, accepted as *Foundress of San José Monastery.*

Teresa is very much alive today, in Avila!

Teresa awaits you in the Monastery of San José. She is ever-present here, in her *Cell,* austere and clean, simple with only a wooden bed for furniture and a cork mat for her carpet. She is present at the rough stone seat, in the corner, which she used for a desk; at which, seated on the floor, she wrote her *Life.* This masterpiece, in which she sings God's praises for the many mercies He bestowed on her, has been proclaimed on a par with *The Confessions of St. Augustine.* I remember thinking what a sense of humor our Lord has. You can hear the Young Mary echoing, "*He has deposed the mighty from their thrones and raised the lowly to high places.*" And her voice resounds loud and clear. In this simple, modest, austere room, a *Doctor of the Church* and a *Mother* was raised up for the children of God, for all time.

The *Recreation Room* reminds us of her admonishment to beware of "long-faced Saints," calling for a Community filled with laughter, with simple, friendly and sometimes, even humorous relationships.

We go on to the *Kitchen,* the comforting reminder to women that God is ever-present even "*among the pots and pans.*"

I need several volumes to go on about the gifts at the Monastery, but I would be remiss in telling her story if I did not point out the *Staircase* there, where the devil threw Teresa down repeatedly, God never permitting a bone of hers to be broken.

There is also the *Mule Chair* she once rode on. This could be the very one upon which she was mounted, as has been told to us by the Carmelites in Avila, where, when thrown from her mule into the mud, she cried out to the Lord, *"If this is the way You treat Your Friends, no wonder You do not have many."*

Teresa was to spend five of the happiest, most restful years of her life, here, as Prioress of the Monastery of San José, her first *child*. Not to be content with peace and quiet, what with her Lord calling her to open more Foundations, Teresa's life was to be one of acceptance usually followed by rejection, and hope followed by disappointment.

With a little borrowed money for capital, *"two Nuns from St. Joseph's and myself (Teresa), with four from the Incarnation, left Avila with our chaplain, Fr. Julian de Avila."*[1] As Jesus said, *"when the baby is born the labor is soon forgotten."* All the nightmarish conflicts they had endured with the founding of San José in Avila over, they looked forward excitedly to their second Foundation in Medina.

Teresa meets St. John of the Cross

As we have studied the lives of the Saints over the last fifteen years, there is one thread that ties them all together and that is their love for the Lord in His Body and Blood, His Holy Eucharist; and in going to Him through His and our Mother Mary. Teresa was called *"loca por la Eucaristía"* *(crazy over the Eucharist)*. If you asked us the reason we have chosen Medina to write about, we would have to say,

---

[1]Foundations 3,2

over the fact it was their *first founding expedition*, it was a *sign* of this Saint's Priority, her *Lord in His Blessed Sacrament*!

Although well known, both in the Americas as well as in Europe, as a formidable and successful commercial city, *Medina* was equally known for its *lack* of generosity to the Church. In spite of this, with the hard work of Teresa's friends, all the necessary permissions had been granted for the opening of the new Foundation.

They had been able to accomplish the impossible! But, the devil never sleeps! More than half way there, they received word to *turn back*. The Augustinians, upon hearing of the new Foundation, had objected to the house they had rented. The little raggedy band of Disciples, refusing to be deterred or discouraged, spent the night planning their strategy. Conclusion, "*Onward Christian soldiers!*"

The next day, when they arrived late at night, they were greeted by piles of garbage. They ploughed through dirt and cobwebs; they fought off insects and rodents. Not to be discouraged, they all pitched in and cleaned away the rubbish. That accomplished, Teresa did the most important work; she set up the Tabernacle for her Beloved Lord in His Blessed Sacrament. Delighted, her King enthroned, she said, "*To see another church where the Blessed Sacrament was reserved was always one of my greatest comforts.*"

Her Lord in His Tabernacle, with the rising of the sun, her delight and peace turned into anxiety and fear,

"*...because after Mass I looked out the window at the inner courtyard only to find the walls had actually fallen in places...When I saw that His Majesty had been placed on the side of the street, in the dangerous times we live in, ...my heart was troubled.*"

In the time of Teresa, heretics and unbelievers were stealing Consecrated Hosts and desecrating Them. Needless to say, she had a watch twenty four hours a day on the Tabernacle. She lived with this heaviness in her heart for a whole week, until our Lord was offered a *safe* refuge in a room on the second-story of a merchant's house. For two months our Lord and His Tabernacle remained securely sheltered, as Teresa made her Foundation fit for the Lord to live in. Soon after, a suitable church for the King of kings was added to the Foundation.

Even after the Lord was safely in His own Chapel in the Monastery, Teresa continued to keep watch, getting up during the night, to check on the watchman. Like the Prophets before and after her, Teresa believed God wants to speak to His children. But she knew that He tends to disguise Himself as a burning bush, at times in the wind, and Incarnate in Man. She was in love with This *God made Man*, but knew since the Ascension He could be found (physically) only in the Tabernacle. Teresa received her greatest graces after Communion and instructed her Nuns that the best time to spend with the Lord was right after Communion.

"The Lord had implanted such strong faith in her, that when she heard people saying they would like to have lived when Jesus was on earth, she used to smile to herself because she regarded Him as being just as Present in the Blessed Sacrament as He had been then; so what difference did it make?"[1]

It was in Medina that Teresa was to meet Father John of the Cross, the Priest destined to be the first Discalced Carmelite Friar, a Saint, a mystical poet, and a Doctor of the Church. Teresa had thought how good it would be if there could be a male branch of her Order so that they could administer the Sacraments and spiritual direction to her Nuns. After getting permission to start this male branch, who should come to the Foundation in Medina, but Fr. John of the Cross. *He* shared with Teresa his desire to go and join the Carthusians; *she* convinced him to wait *"until the Lord*

---

[1]Teresa's Way of Perfection - 34,6

gave us a Monastery." In addition to her many talents, no one could deny her anything. She had them spellbound, grown and important men, like boys in her hands.

(Author's note: Getting to know her, through her writings, through the Discalced Carmelites who continue to live the Rule of Saint Teresa, and in actually writing about her, I find myself with a heroine and I am proud to be a woman.)

Teresa wrote her Book of Foundations in Medina. Her ongoing, single biggest problem with writing was she did not think it was worth the time it took away from spinning wool, *which was really important.* She very often wrote hurriedly, taking snatches of time; she never edited; she humbly begged her Superiors to *do whatever they wanted* with her writings, correcting any error she might have inadvertently made. *I love Teresa!* I think the single greatest trait, outside of her passion for Jesus, was her sincere and consistent humility.

Malagón-the Foundation Teresa built from the ground up

Doña Luisa de la Cerda, the widow from Toledo Teresa had consoled, wanted Teresa to found a Monastery, in honor of her late husband, in *Malagón,* where he had been lord. Doña and her powers of persuasion, in union with the counselling of learned men and her Confessor, won out over all Teresa's objections to founding a house which *would be supported by endowments.* With their assurances that the authority and directives came from the Council of Trent, she conceded. Teresa was on her way, again!

Highly envied, much judged and condemned, she was to travel a very long and lonely road which would eventually earn her the title of *"God's wandering lady."* As we are writing about these *powerful women,* the thought that keeps running through our minds is, if there is no God or life hereafter, why would these Saints have suffered all they did? But, if, as we believe and as Jesus told us, there is eternal life, then what they did is all that *does* make sense. Certainly, their reward was not on this earth or in their lifetime.

Teresa always had time to help someone and especially to pay back a debt. On the way to Malagón, Teresa stopped at the Convent of the Imagen in Alcalá, at the request of her old friend, Maria de Jesus, the Nun who had helped her with her Rule originally. Maria de Jesus asked Teresa to take on the difficult task of removing, from her Community, all the excessive forms of penance and mortification, they had come to adopt. Teresa said a difficult "yes" and replaced the gloom of the Community with the joy and good cheer she so firmly believed in. Teresa stayed with them for two months, and mission accomplished, she was on her way.

The first house that had been chosen in Malagón, was not acceptable, as it was too close to the market. This, Teresa found, was definitely not *choice* for contemplatives seeking a life removed from the noises of the world; in addition, because of its proximity to the market there was more of a possible threat to the Eucharist. She refused another site offered her, as she (so rightly) prophesied there would be a Franciscan Monastery there someday. Finally, when she saw a white dove perched on an olive tree, she took this as a sign from the Lord, and chose this site for her Foundation.

What is most unique about Malagón is that this is the first Foundation that Teresa was to have full control over the design, building and furnishings. Until today, the original plans are in the Convent safe, to prove it. Work began immediately, but it was eleven years before Teresa could return for the solemn transfer of the Foundation from the old Monastery to the new. When she arrived, tired, sick, every bone in her body aching, too ill to get out of bed, what greeted her? The builders would need another six months to complete the work. She was up at the crack of dawn to see for herself. She inspected what had been done and what needed to be done, made a few calculations and announced the work would be completed for the Feast of the Immaculate Conception, just twelve days away.

Masons, carpenters, Nuns, friends, all in a state of shock, skeptically watched as Teresa barreled through the task ahead, working side by side with the workers, supervising day and night; her "yes" allowing the Lord to do in *twelve days* what man had not finished in *eleven years*. We believe that God can move mountains; we have seen the evidence of God moving a house (in the case of the Holy House of Loreto[1]). But, in this case, God moved a great heart, Teresa's, and that heart moved some very stubborn, *bull-headed* builders. On the *Feast of the Immaculate Conception,* Jesus handed this House to His Mother Mary. The new Monastery they had opened, received Jesus among them in the Blessed Sacrament. Alleluia !

To this day, Carmels request these plans to use as a model for new Monasteries being built. The Monastery of Malagón has been carefully and faithfully preserved as a living sign of the Power of Jesus through the *fiats* of His beloved Saints while still imperfect, on earth.

Valladolid-To save a soul

Four months before completing the Monastery of Malagón, Don Bernardino de Mendoza, a man well known in the area, approached Teresa and offered her a house, if she start a Foundation in *Valladolid*. Again, tired, not quite over this founding, she did not give him a very enthusiastic *"yes"*, but *"yes"*, reluctant or not, she said. Two months later, this young man suddenly contracted an illness which

---

[1]Holy House of Loreto - Scene of the Annunciation, where the Angel Gabriel appeared to Mother Mary; where the Holy Family lived for most of Jesus' thirty-three years...the house that was miraculously transported by the Angels, with Mother Mary and the Baby Jesus, from Nazareth to Italy, because of fear of the Saracens who were desecrating all the Holy Shrines of the Holy Land.

deprived him of all speech. He was not even able to make his confession, but did make signs pleading for God's forgiveness. Shortly after, he died.

The Lord came to Teresa and said that He had mercy on him because of the house he had given to Teresa which would do honor to *His Mother* through the Carmelite Order. But the Lord said the young man would not leave Purgatory until the first *Mass* was celebrated in that house. Talk of the Wind at her back! Teresa was so conscious of the terrible sufferings of that soul, she forestalled the opening of the Monastery in Toledo, which had been her heart's desire, and plunged into the founding of this one in Valladolid.

She left Malagón on the 19th of May, 1568, for Valladolid. She was delayed along the way, needing to handle problems in her already established Monasteries. Teresa never sacrificed the established houses for the new *baby* (Monastery). She struggled with the preoccupations that always seemed to be detaining her. She knew they were *good* things, but were they *God's* Things, *His* Will for that moment. We believe, the greatest struggle a Christian has is not deciding between good and evil but between one good and another good. But again, when the Lord wants something done. . .He came to Teresa in a dream, *"While I was praying one day, He told me to hurry: that the soul (of Don Bernardino) was suffering a lot."*[1] Needless to say, she went in much haste, laying everything else aside for another day.

The house, Don Bernardino left them in Valladolid, was a disaster! Nuns could not possibly live here! Still, Teresa hurriedly went about making the necessary adjustments for them to move in. Everything had to be done, again, with the utmost secrecy, as they had not received the required permission. God was in a hurry, so who do you think *just happened* to visit them, but the Vicar General of the City.

---

[1]Foundations, 10,3

Either he was terribly impressed or was it *a miracle*, but he issued the order for them to celebrate Mass immediately. Teresa had no idea the Lord's promise was being realized at this moment. Had she, in the rush of *doing good things*, of founding the house of Valladolid, forgotten the *reason* behind it in the first place? On the Feast of the Assumption, as Father Julian approached Teresa with Communion, she had a Vision of a young man beside the Priest. It was Don Bernardino; his face was *illuminated*, radiating joy. He thanked her for her "yes" that the Lord used to free him from Purgatory and welcome him into Heaven.

I think the greatest pain in Purgatory has to be, to *know* Jesus is just beyond and you cannot be with Him. It has to be like when a beloved has been left by the other spouse. You know he or she is alive, but not with you to love and to be loved. The only relief is, we are promised that in the case of Purgatory, through the prayers of those on earth, there will someday be that union with Jesus that we long for, as He welcomes us Home.

Teresa having written her Way of Perfection twice, the pride of this Monastery is that the second version was written here. In the 16th and 17th centuries, when few women could read or write, *this* Monastery produced Nuns who could read Latin, Greek and Hebrew. They had, as well, a profound knowledge of the Scriptures and were talented poets. All in a time when women were *not equal to men!* It's amazing how much the Lord thinks of women; how when He sees the traits of His Mother in them, He makes their *Yes'es* change the world!

Teresa's Dream of Discalced Carmelite Friars comes true

I cannot pass up a little, out of the way place called *Duruelo*. It was one of Teresa's *distractions*, I spoke of earlier, when she was on her way to found a Monastery in Valladolid. After many disappointments and laborious negotiations, permission came, in Duruelo, on the 28th of November, 1568. Teresa's dream of extending her Reform to the Carmelite *Friars* began, under Fathers Anthony of Jesus and John of the Cross. *(You remember John, the Priest who wanted to go to join the Carthusians!)*

What were Teresa's hopes and expectations for Discalced Friars, and what did she find among them? Teresa discovered a *new image* of the Almighty Father. She saw Him as a Friend involved in the affairs of men, as well as amongst the pots and pans. She discovered Him hidden, too, within the *castle* of each person's soul. She found Him so touchable, so approachable, so within reach that she described *prayer as talking to God.*

Teresa discovered her Church, *in* all her glory, *through* all her dignity, *as Bride of Christ.* But to her sadness, she found this Church she loved so very much, besieged by great evils, as well. What did she mean, at the end of her life, *"A daughter of the Church; at last a daughter of the Church?"* She never raised her voice against the hierarchy or rebel over the injustices she endured, but remained faithful and obedient, a daughter of the Church. She imparted this to her Nuns, as well. She said their call was to surround themselves with simplicity, to thirst for poverty, to be a reflection of *Christ among them* in their cheerfulness and joy. They were to pray for all defenders of the Church. *And by their life, to be the light, the salt, the leaven from which the world would rise from the depths to be lifted up on high with the Savior.*

I need to be brief about St. John of the Cross, since this is not his story, but it's so difficult to separate him from the life of Teresa. Let me say, St. John, this humble raggedy Friar half her age, *personified* all her dreams of the men who would go forth to foreign missions, to prevent so many souls from being lost. *She* taught him her ways. She made him his first habit. As she instructed him through the Grille, she grew more and more aware of how refined, how intelligent, how learned, but humble he was. With *who* St. John was, with *how* singularly focused he was, in search of his vocation as called by Christ, he won Teresa's heart completely. St. John *loved* his Order. That he was a man of prayer and a lover of solitude, that his poetry captures the beauty of our Lord, till today, are well known. But are you aware of how open he was, this great man and now great Saint, to the new brotherly style of life created by *Teresa*, and the fact that he had no problems learning it from a group of *women* already living that life?

Teresa, for her part, sought out the best, the holiest of Theologians and Confessors, people known for their sanctity, like St. John. She *thirsted* to know more, so that she and the Nuns in her charge, would grow closer to the Lord through knowledge of Him, in *heart* and *mind*. Ever humble, always considering herself an ignorant woman, she looked to these men of God not only for their teaching, but for discernment, security and support. When we hear the outcry against the injustices suffered by our *sisters* in the Church today, the question that runs through my mind is, have those who are championing these persecuted sisters, themselves taken the *first step*, following the lead of the great men of Teresa's time, affirming and accepting them as future possible Doctors of the Church?

Teresa was aware, *in her time,* of the attitudes of the men of the Church and she did not silently stand by. Although the censor erased this passage from her first version of the *Way of Perfection*, it has now been restored and we can read the truly prophetic statement launched by Teresa, *in defense of women.*

"*When you walked on this earth, Lord, you did not despise women; rather you always helped them and showed great compassion toward them. And you found as much love and more faith in them than you did in men. Among them was your Most Blessed Mother, and*

*through her merits we merit what, because of our
offenses, we do not deserve."*

Through no wish of mine, I find, because of the need to
go on to our other sisters, our other *powerful women in the
Church*, I must sadly, reluctantly walk toward the final pages
in this chapter on Teresa's great life. It aches, like saying
good-by to a dear and loving sister you just barely got to
know. Teresa has become a part of our life we never
expected to happen. With an *"Adios until we meet again,"* I
start Teresa's final journey.

Alba de Tormes: Teresa's Final Journey

Mother Teresa was feeling really tired. Deep inside,
she knew that she had founded her *last* house. She was
being called to Avila, where she was still Prioress, for the
profession of her niece Teresita, who was with her in Burgos.
Although looking very tired, she did not appear seriously ill.
As her presence in Burgos was not essential, Teresa, with
her nurse and her niece Teresita, set out toward Avila.

She stopped at Medina, where her acting Provincial
ordered her to make a detour through *Alba de Tormes*. The
Duchess of Alba wanted to meet her and have her pray for
her daughter-in-law. Everyone present on that occasion,
agreed that this was to be the most difficult act of obedience
Teresa would ever be asked to make, as she was now
showing clear signs of how ill she really was. This last battle
was one Teresa would not have the *physical* strength to win.

The journey from Medina, in her usual, covered wagon
proved to be a more of a risk to her life, than Teresa could
take. Her nurse, not able to find nourishing food on the
journey, would burst into tears every time she looked on her
beloved Mother Teresa. *"She looked like a corpse."* Seeing
the nurse's distress at only having figs to feed her, Mother
Teresa assured her lovingly not to be concerned, as the figs

were *delicious* and there were so many worse off, who did not have figs to eat.

At long last, they arrived in Alba de Tormes. The Nuns seeing how gravely ill she was, died to their desire to talk with her and carried her to her bedroom. On September the 29th, she went to bed never to rise again. As she lay dying, between bouts of total collapse and speech loss, her pulse rising and dropping rapidly, Teresa dictated her *last* Testament.

According to her nurse, "*She asked for the Blessed Sacrament. . . When they were taking It away she sat up in bed with a great surge of spirit and said joyfully: 'My Lord, it is time to be going. Very well, Your Will be done.'*"

It was the 4th of October, 1582. Teresa was 67 years old. She closed her eyes thanking the Lord she had lived and was now dying *a daughter of the Church.*

Teresa is dead. *Long live Teresa!* When we spoke of writing about Teresa, we heard, "*She's not of our time. What does she know of us and our unique problems.*" Teresa is a book unto herself, addressing *all* times, but *especially* these times. Let those who have eyes see; those who have ears hear; and those who have heart, take courage from the life of Teresa.

Teresa left us her books, her words of love and life. She left us her words on the many *mansions* in Heaven, the many roads. The legacy she left those of us, whose walk may be in our *everyday* life, is the consolation that sometimes *Jesus is in the pots and pans.* In no way did she teach that meditations on Jesus in His Sacred Passion were the *only* paths to Jesus and new life in Him. For some, the *way* could be by reflecting on and praising God for all His Creation. I think we only have to look around us, at our families, our friends, our lives, and our beloved country to recognize how very blessed we are. Of all the people in the world, we have been placed, at this time, in this place with these precious gifts. This may be our way to a closer walk with our Lord.

†

Lord, You took us to Yourself. You consoled us when we cried. You held us when we were afraid. You gave us new courage, sometimes, minute by minute. You showed us we could trust You. You filled us with hope through the ongoing message and lives of the Saints. Oh, my Jesus, how very much we love You. How wonderful it is to be loved by You. We have never known such happiness in our life. This has been *our* walk. *And, so it must have been with Teresa.*

†

In the writing of this book, when it seemed all the demons had been released from hell and were concentrating on us, during each attack when we thought we couldn't handle another, Teresa and this prayer, came to us.

†

As we now come to the last page of this journey with Teresa, our Saint and sister, we are consoled and committed
to live the rest of our lives
saying "Yes," to our Lord Jesus
through His Mother Mary
with Teresa's words on our hearts,

†

Let nothing disturb you
Let nothing frighten you
All things pass away:
God never changes.
Patience obtains all things.
He who has God
finds he lacks nothing
God alone suffices.

Teresa de Jesús

Above: ***Incorrupt Heart***
of St. Teresa

Above: ***Tomb of St. Teresa***
Alba de Tormes

Below: ***St. Teresa's Room at San José***

Above:
Convent of San José

Above: ***St. Teresa is Instructed by the Holy Spirit***
Below: ***Chapel where St. Teresa was Born***

Above:
Jesus at the Pillar

Above:
The Four Posts

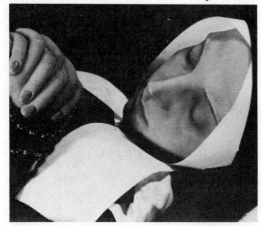

Left:
***Incorrupt Body of St.
Bernadette***

Right:
***Corroded Rosary Found
in Bernadette's Hands***

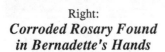

Left:
***Boly Mill
Birthplace
of
Bernadette***

St. Bernadette of Lourdes

"I cannot promise you happiness in this world,
but in the next."

There are Saints among us whose greatest virtues have been their lifelong battles against their human nature. Those of us who are privileged to study their lives, have a tendency to ignore what we believe to be their shortcomings, in an effort to go directly to their source of sanctification. When we do this, we miss the teaching the Lord has to give us by the example of His suffering servant. We go for the dream, and miss the journey. The sanctification is in the journey.

St. Bernadette used to complain about the accounts she read on the Lives of the Saints, in that they all seemed too sugar coated. She said of the Saints, *"They were human beings with faults and weaknesses, like all of us."* Mother Angelica once said, referring to the authors of lives of the Saints, *"They should all be given forty years each in purgatory, for making these Saints seem so perfect."* Bernadette probably felt the same way.

To the little Saint of Lourdes, the many gifts she was given during her lifetime: *one*, that of *beholding the presence* of Mary, the Mother of God, eighteen times in the year 1858; *another*, her *ecstasies* during those Apparitions, were just that, *gifts*. She believed that these were *aids* from the good God to help her get through a sacrificial life amidst a barrage of attacks, and to suppress her own fiery inclination to fight those attacks. She prayed the gifts would offset her imperfections, which included a strong will, a fierce temper, and a stinging tongue. What she may never have known is how Our Lord Jesus and His Mother Mary were able to use these traits for their glory.

We once wrote that Bernadette was a simple girl, an illiterate at the time that Our Lady appeared to her, but never did we consider her a *stupid* girl. Her behavior throughout the period of the Apparitions, her *inner strength* to hold up against great powers in the government and the Church, are a strong indicator of this. Her life after the Apparitions, and in the Convent of St. Gildard in Nevers, is proof of her strength.

We never knew much about Bernadette. As a young man, I became enraptured by the Apparitions of Our Lady to Bernadette, after reading *The Song of Bernadette*. I fell in love with Mary, but never thought much about Bernadette. Even the first time Penny and I visited Lourdes, we didn't see or hear much of the little visionary. This is as Bernadette wanted it. With the exception of the Cachot, where she lived during the time of the Apparitions, the Boly Mill, where she was born, and the Maison Paternelle, where the family lived after the Apparitions, Bernadette is not considered a major part of the Shrine. But Bernadette is very important, both as the intermediary for Mary during that period of time in 1858, and as a *role model*.

Once I got to *know* her, I came to *love* her. There is much in Bernadette which can be used in our everyday struggle to reach the kingdom, to be part of the Communion of Saints. We can learn from her. We can use her lifelong struggle for sanctity as a *teaching* in our own lives.

Bernadette at the time of the Apparitions

Bernadette once said, in reflecting on her life, that the reason Mary chose her was because she was the lowest of the low. *"What do you think of me? Don't I realize that the Blessed Virgin chose me because I was the most ignorant? If she had found anyone more ignorant than myself, she would have chosen her."*

She really underestimated her role in the Apparitions at the grotto of Massabiele in the little hamlet of Lourdes. Our Lady needed one such as she knew Bernadette *could* be. This was a very important message she was bringing the people of the world. She could not take a chance on trusting a weak person, who could be reduced to tears, or shot down at the first sign of adversity. She needed someone who would have the strength to stand up before the powers of hell, and *Bernadette was that person.*

Another time our Saint said, "*The Blessed Virgin used me like a broom. What do you do with a broom when you have finished sweeping? You put it back in its place, behind the door!*" referring to her much sought after life of seclusion at the cloistered Convent in Nevers. Without her being aware of it, she was exhibiting a great deal of depth of spirit, abandonment to the Lord, and humility. Penny and I call our ministry the Lord's balloon. We believe we are allowed to rise as high as He wants, for His Glory, but when He is finished with us, He will stick a pin in the balloon.

Everything in Bernadette's early life would agree that she was the bottom of the barrel, so to speak, if we were using the world's mentality. Her family was so poor that they brought the poverty level of the area down to a *new low.* Her father hired out for wages just under what was paid for a *work horse.* Between her mother and father, they could not earn enough money to bring them up to the poverty level. At the time of the first Apparition, they had been reduced to living in a former prison cell, *the Cachot,* which had been condemned for being below human standards.

Bernadette was a sickly girl from birth. She suffered from Asthma all her life. She was undernourished as a result of the family's living conditions. She was sent to a farm in Bartres, to live with the woman who had breast-fed her when she was an infant. Only this time it was because there was not enough room, or enough food to care for her in Lourdes.

She loved her family, especially her father, François. When she was sent away to Bartres during her childhood, he always found excuses to visit her there. She was the oldest, and for him, the most special. He grieved for his child, but could not see her being with the family under such austere conditions. So when Bernadette sent countless messages home to bring her back, they were unanswered. However, Our Lady had a plan.

Bernadette had been promised when she was sent to Bartres, that she would be able to study with the Priest there for her First Holy Communion. She was almost fourteen at this time, and the only girl of her age in Lourdes who had not received First Holy Communion. We have to believe that she was under the mantle of Mary all her life, but especially at this time. She was extremely good in her work, which turned out to be her downfall. She was given more and more responsibility as a shepherdess, which gave her no time to go to Catechism lessons. She found herself working in the fields all day long. The two children of the family she stayed with, left each morning for Catechism lessons, while Bernadette went out into the field. This hurt her terribly.

Shortly after she arrived at Bartres, the Priest left to enter a Monastery. When he left the village, the foster-parents of Bernadette felt guilty that they had not kept their promise to let her attend Catechism lessons. The foster-mother tried to teach her at home, but she could only read a little, and Bernadette not at all. In addition, the lessons took place after dinner was over, and all the chores had been completed. Under the best circumstances, it would have been difficult for the child to learn, but this was an *impossible* situation. She had a problem retaining information to begin with, and that, coupled with the fact that she was exhausted when they began, turned it into a disaster. Bernadette was extremely frustrated.

We see the first signs of her strong will crop up. She took the bull by the horns. She told her foster-mother she had to go into Lourdes one Sunday. When she arrived there, she confronted her family, insisting she be allowed to return home. She wanted to receive First Holy Communion, and would have to begin Catechism lessons *at once* if she were to receive in 1858. Her parents gave in. She returned to Lourdes on January 28, 1858, *just fourteen days before Our Lady came to her.*

Her insistence on going back to Lourdes to study her Catechism in order to receive First Holy Communion, shows her strength in the face of adult authority, and really the first inclination we see of the deep spirituality of Bernadette. Prior to this, she had never been considered a holy girl. She had always been good, very polite, and very lovable. But all the teachers, Priests, Sisters and neighbors of the Soubirous family interviewed after the Apparitions, maintained that she would never have been thought of as *holy*.

This brings to mind the Scripture passage regarding Jesus, when He returned to Nazareth after having begun His ministry. He spoke brilliantly in the synagogue, but the elders said to each other, "But isn't this Joseph the carpenter's son?"

The year 1858 had been declared by Pope Pius IX to be a *Holy Year*. He asked for solemn public and private prayer. Four years before, this same Pope, who had a great love and devotion to Mary, had proclaimed to all the world, the dogma of her *Immaculate Conception*, amid a furor that had not yet died down. Catholics were *required* to believe this. There had been a popular heresy spreading throughout Europe at this time, *Pantheism*, which claimed *that man was equal with God*. By this proclamation of our Lady's Immaculate Conception, Our Lord Jesus through His Pope, declared that with the exception of Jesus, *only* Mary was conceived without *Original Sin*. This proclamation caused more problems than it meant to solve. Rumbling went on *inside* the Church, and *outside* in Protestant circles. It was outrageous to give this singular honor to a *woman*, they argued. Shades of Lucifer!

On January 7th of this Holy Year of 1858, Bernadette had turned fourteen years old. On January 28, she returned to Lourdes from Bartres. On February 11, she went with her sister and a friend to pick up dry twigs at the grotto of Massabielle. The Bernadette who walked out the door of the jail that day would never return. She was to be touched by Our Lady, and would never be the same. Her life would be changed forever.

"We take you to a place high in the sky, so you can watch the drama of February 11, 1858, unfold, where Heaven and earth meet, the Divine touches the human, and the world is affected for all time. On earth, we see Bernadette and Toinette frolicking through the town, picking up a playmate, Jeanne Abadie. They don't even know where they are being directed. Their chore is to pick up firewood, wherever they can find it. At the other end of the spectrum, we see the clouds open, and a bright light appears from Paradise, moving slowly towards earth. The little girls wind their way through the town, then down the hill in the direction of the River Gave. From our vantage point, we can hear choirs of Angels singing joyous hymns in anticipation of the miracle that is to take place. If we could see into God's dimension, we would be able to witness these Angels surrounding and carrying the most magnificent creature the Lord has ever placed on the earth. Slowly, they descend from the Heavens, the drama building. We can feel our hearts pounding as the Angels and the Queen get closer and closer to earth.

The children approach the River Gave. They see a cave on the other side. It's the Grotto of Massabiele, a garbage dump. But it's dry inside. They can see sticks and twigs on the ground. Bernadette hesitates crossing the river, for fear she will catch cold. Her mother will kill her if she finds out that Bernadette even entertained the idea of crossing. The girls chide her. She feels a flush of anger and resentment rise up in her cheeks. She takes off her stockings and begins to wade across the water. At the same time a streak of light flashes across the sky at meteoric speed. We don't know if the other children see it. But as Bernadette walks out of the water, she is thrown to her knees by an unknown force. Before her is a brilliance that is indescribable. It's dazzling, yet there is a softness, a warmth, a shimmering, but oh, so much more. She looks to an alcove at the right of the grotto. She is speechless. The choir of Angels reaches its highest pitch as the eyes of Bernadette and the Lady meet. An electric beam rivets the gaze of the two together. Bernadette feels her heart swelling. She is afraid it will burst. She cannot breathe. She trembles; her fear turning into excitement, wonderment. She can't take her eyes off the Lady. It has begun. The Queen of Heaven comes to speak to her people. God puts aside the laws of nature, and creates MIRACLE!" The Many Faces of Mary, a Love Story Pgs 87-88

From the very beginning, qualities in Bernadette which would be criticized throughout her life as shortcomings, had to be put into play in order to convince the world of the *authenticity* of the Apparitions. This little girl had to be wise, firm, discerning, and extremely brave to stand up to all the people who would try to dissuade her, including Priests, Bishops, police chiefs, prosecutors, and on and on.

†

To give you some idea of the inner strength of the child, and the quickness of her wit, we would like to share some quotations of Bernadette during the various interrogations she was required to undergo.

After the sixth Apparition, on leaving the office of Jacomet, the superintendent of police, she was asked:
"What are you laughing at?"
Bernadette said: *"He (Jacomet) was shaking with anger. The tassel on his cap was jingling up and down like a bell."*

†

During subsequent interrogations, she was accused:
"You are certainly making everyone run after you!"
Bernadette: *"But what are they all coming here for?   I certainly didn't go to fetch them!"*

†

In what language did she (Our Lady) speak to you?   In French or in dialect?"
Bernadette: *"Oh!   Why do you think she spoke to me in French?   Can I speak French?"*

†

At his office, the Imperial Prosecutor, Dutour, threatened to imprison Bernadette. She said to her mother, who was in tears:
"You are really too honest to cry because we are going to be imprisoned. We haven't done anything wrong."

†

After making Bernadette and her mother stand for a long time, Dutour said (condescendingly): "There are chairs. You may sit down."
Bernadette: *"No, we might dirty them!"*

†

Dutour: "Mind what you are about, Bernadette. There is a certain gentleman who is on the porch, and who gives you advice. But perhaps he won't prevent you from going to prison."
Bernadette: *"You must remain standing when you speak to that gentleman."* (The man was the presiding judge, who was advising the family)

†

Again, being interrogated as to what language Our Lady spoke, Bernadette replied:

"She spoke dialect."

"The Blessed Virgin could not have spoken in dialect. God and the Blessed Virgin do not speak dialect."

Bernadette: *"How could we know dialect if they didn't?"*

†

As if Bernadette's bouts with the authorities were not enough, she had to defend herself as much if not more to the members of the Church.

During the 12th Apparition, Bernadette held her rosary out to Mary. A Priest questioned her afterwards:

"So you even bless rosaries now?"

Bernadette laughed: *"I am not wearing a stole, am I?"*

†

"I can't believe that it was the Virgin Mary who spoke to you. You must have heard the song of some bird which had taken refuge there, and you imagined that it was the Virgin Mary speaking to you."

Bernadette: *"But if it were a bird it wouldn't have spoken."*

†

To another Priest who questioned her, Bernadette said:

"I don't oblige you to believe me: but I can only answer by telling what I saw and heard."

†

"So, Bernadette, since the Blessed Virgin has promised you to go to Heaven, you don't need to worry about the care of your soul?"

Bernadette: *"But, oh Father! I shall only go to Heaven if I behave properly."*

†

Another Priest insisted she tell him the secrets.

Priest: "You must tell me your secrets. I am a Priest and I have a right to know, but I will keep them to myself, like in the confessional".

Bernadette: *"Silence is not a sin."*

†

During an interrogation before the Bishop of Tarbes, she was asked:

"The fact that you were asked to eat the grass does not seem worthy of the Blessed Virgin?"

Bernadette: *"But we eat lettuce, don't we?"*

†

Regarding the flock of pilgrims around her and the Cachot, she cried out:

"Lock the door."

"You're very tired, aren't you?"

To which she answered: *"Oh yes!   Especially after all these hugs and kisses!"*

†

When asked to sell pilgrims some medals, she replied:

"But I am not a shop-keeper."

†

In pain with a fit of Athma, she cried out,

"I had rather suffer (Asthma) than receive visits."

†

In response to a pilgrim who said, "If I could only cut off a small piece of her dress,"

Bernadette turned around: *"How very stupid you are!"*

†

Another pilgrim: "Touch these rosaries, these medals."

Bernadette: *"Go and have these objects blessed at the grotto, and leave me alone."*

†

And yet another pilgrim: "Cure me!"

Bernadette: *"Who do you take me for?   I am like you.   I have no power.   All I can do is pray for you."*

†

The above are just some random quotations attributed to Bernadette. They only represent the tip of the iceberg.

Her interrogations would go on for hours, sometimes full days. Her interrogators constantly tried to trick her into contradicting her statements. The interviews were invariably high-pitched, full of tension. She was always on her guard, knowing they did not want the truth, but to trip her up.

She had an encounter with the Pastor of the parish church, Abbé Peyramale. He had a reputation far and wide for his explosive temper. He could make people shake as far as 10 kilometers away. Our Lady told Bernadette to go to the Priests, and ask for a Chapel to be built. She assumed the Lady meant her Parish Priest, so she went to Abbé Peyramale. The first time she endeavored to speak to him, he received her politely until he heard her request, after which he flew into a rage, accusing her of lying, of being a lunatic, of trying to disrupt the peaceful hamlet. When Bernadette left him, she was very shaken.

But when our Lady asked her again to go to the Priests, to ask for a Chapel to be built, and especially for people to come in procession, our little Saint knew she had to confront the same Priest again. This time, she brought back-up with her, her aunts Basile and Bernarde. She did not want to be alone with the Priest, but her fear of him was not as strong as her desire to do what the Lady had asked.

She just about got to deliver the first part of her message when he went through the ceiling again. The barrage was so great that she stood, riveted to the floor, petrified. After he finished his tirade, she and her aunts left. But after they had walked about a block away from the rectory, she told them she had to go back. She had not delivered the second part of the message. The aunts thought she was crazy for wanting to go back, and refused to accompany her. They wanted nothing to do with his anger!

Let's think for a minute on the strength of this little fourteen year old girl. Two adults were afraid to go back, and be subjected again to his uncontrollable anger. One of them, Bernadette's aunt Bernarde, was a shopkeeper. She was used to confrontation, and dealing with all sorts of people. Yet, she lacked the *courage* to go back. Bernadette, on the other hand, *had* to return. She was not on the same level as either of her aunts. She was not an adult; she was the poorest child from the poorest family in Lourdes. Was it her overwhelming desire to please the Lady, her Aquero[1], or had the Lady chosen this special girl because she knew how Bernadette would react in this situation and the many other trials to which she would be subjected?

Bernadette had to get another lady, Mrs. Cazenave, to bring her back later that evening, to deliver the second part of the message, about building a Chapel. In an effort to calm the priest down, she said, "*It doesn't have to be a big Chapel.*"

The turning point for Abbé Peyramale came after the scheduled fortnight (two weeks) of Apparitions had ended. He had given the Lady certain requirements, one of which was to tell Bernadette what her name was. The other was to make the rose bush in the grotto bloom, which was just about impossible in the winter. While he wanted to believe in the child with all his heart, his humanity demanded a sign. *Mary gave him his sign.*

On March 25, the Feast of the Annunciation, Bernadette felt a calling from Our Lady to go to the grotto. It was in the wee hours of the morning. When she could not wait any longer, she got up, dressed, and went quickly to the grotto, only to find that there were quite a few people praying there already. As she approached, she could see Mary waiting for her in the alcove.

Bernadette went through the same custom she had always gone through with Our Lady. She kept asking her who she was. The Abbé insisted the lady identify herself. When Bernadette asked this time, the response was the

---

[1]Local patois term of endearment, meaning *That One*

same. *The Lady smiled lovingly.* But Bernadette persisted. She asked three times. The third time, the Lady lifted her eyes to Heaven, raised her hands to her breast, and said the words,

"I Am The Immaculate Conception."

"The sky opened up. The clouds disappeared, and the Heavenly Hosts of Angels shone as they had on that Blessed Day in Bethlehem. Choirs of Angels sang in praise of the Glory of God. A beam of light shot down from Heaven to the alcove, surrounding the magnificent creation God had made. Cherubim and Seraphim floated down and positioned themselves around Mary. A soft breeze enveloped the child and the Lady. Bernadette could feel the tingly flush of warmth that emanated from Our Lady.

The cycle was complete. A miracle that had occurred before the beginning of time, the Immaculate Conception of Mary, passed down through the years as tradition, proclaimed on earth by Pope Pius IX in 1854, was confirmed by Heaven in 1858, in this little grotto nestled deep in the Pyrenees, in a hamlet of no consequence, to this chosen Saint, who had no idea what the words of the Lady meant." The Many Faces of Mary, a Love Story, Pg 97

Bernadette rushed to the Parish Church after the Lady left her, repeating the words over and over again so she wouldn't forget them. When she arrived, a huge crowd followed closely behind her, waiting outside the door of the Priest's house, as she went in. Abbé Peyramale stared at the child, who was completely out of breath.

She repeated the words,

"I am the Immaculate Conception"

"What do you mean?" he asked.

"That's who she is. She told me, 'I am the Immaculate Conception'"

The Priest could feel a lump form in his throat. His eyes began to well up in tears. He tried desperately to control himself. "Do you know what that means?" he asked.

"*No, mon curé,*" she answered, her eyes as big as saucers.

He was convinced. This man, who struck the greatest fear into Bernadette's heart, became her greatest defender and supporter, using the same fiery temper against her *attackers*, he had leveled against her.

We have to take a moment out here to really dwell on Bernadette's situation throughout this time, and the years to come. She was illiterate, but had wisdom beyond her years. She was all alone. She had no support system.

In studying the other Apparitions of Mary down through the centuries, with the exception of St. Catherine Labouré, who could retreat behind a cloister to avoid all the attention her Apparition was given, and a little girl in Banneux, Belgium, Mariette Beco, Bernadette was the only visionary who saw Mary by herself. She didn't have friends who were also seeing the Apparitions of Mary, who could corroborate her story, to whom she could go for comfort and support, as in the case of the visionaries of La Salette, Pontmain, Fatima, Knock, Beauraing and the latest reported Apparition in Medjugorje. Nor did she have the visible sign given Juan Diego on his tilma in Mexico in 1531. Her *only* source of strength was that given to her by *Mary*. But it was enough for her.

A time was to come in her life when these traits, her inner strength, her quick tongue, all used in defense of the Apparition of Our Lady, would be used against her. To her supporters, they were considered her greatest *virtues*. To her critics, they were to be called her greatest *drawbacks*. Her inner strength became labeled as *stubbornness*. Her quick tongue became labeled as *sharp-edged repartee*. Self-love was a term used against Bernadette. St. Francis de Sales once said of self-love, *"Self-love dies only with our body."* At one time in the Convent of St. Gildard, in Nevers, when she was accused of having self-love, she drew a circle and put her forefinger in the center of it. *"Let the one who has no self-love put his finger in there."*

Bernadette in the Convent

As time passed, and the grotto and the Apparitions came to be more accepted by the Church and the government, it became increasingly clear to Bernadette and the local church, including the Bishop, that she could not remain in Lourdes much longer. She was the center of attention to all pilgrims who came to the Shrine. She did not want it that way. She knew Our Lady did not want it that way, either. We're reminded of the words of St. John the Baptist, when Jesus began His public ministry.

"He must increase, while I must decrease."

Bernadette felt the same way. The focus would never be completely on Our Lady and the message of Jesus, through her, as long as Bernadette remained. This was one of the greatest sacrifices this simple peasant girl had to make. The words of Mary resounded in her heart,

"I cannot promise you happiness in this world, but in the next."

Bernadette had decided that hers was to be the life of a Religious. Or had it had been decided by Our Lady *for* her. Some believe that one of the three secrets Mary gave her, which she carried to her grave, was that she was to live the life of a Nun. Just about every Order in France wanted the little seer to join them. But she had found happiness in a hospice in Lourdes which was run by a Community of the Sisters of Charity of Nevers, France. She decided to join that Community.

Bishop Forcade, the Bishop of Tarbes, went in person to present her petition to the head of the Order. The response he received quite clearly shocked him, as it would

have anyone. *They were not that anxious to have Bernadette.*
At least, that is what they gave him to believe. The
conversation went like this,

"Bernadette doesn't have the necessary health. She
will be in and out of the infirmary all the time. Besides,
there's not much she can do."

The Bishop replied: "You are aware that most every
Convent is trying to get her."

To which the Superior General replied: "Oh, well,
we'll take her if she asks."

So even this, Bernadette's greatest sacrifice, that of
leaving her home and family, her beloved grotto, the scene
of her greatest joy, was not accepted by those who received
the gift, in the way in which she *unconditionally* gave it. But
the gift was not to them or for them. *It was to Bernadette's
Aquero that she gave her life.*

The Superior General was half right, and half wrong.
Bernadette did spend most of her life as a Nun in and out of
the infirmary.   But on the other hand, she learned to
embroider well.   She made a beautiful alb for Bishop
Forcade. But this was of a physical nature. She also brought
with her a *spirituality* which spread throughout the Convent.
She lifted the morale of the Sisters at St. Gildard. She was
loved by all, and treated like one of them by all, *save one.*

Mother Thérèse Vazou was Bernadette's Mistress of
Novices when she entered the Convent of St. Gildard's in
Nevers, and later became Superior of the Community. She
was the cause of most of Bernadette's spiritual suffering over
the thirteen years that our little Saint was in the Convent.
This Nun mistreated her almost from the day she arrived.
After the death of the little seer, Mother Thérèse blocked
the process of beatification from being opened until after her
own death.

Mother Thérèse is a paradox. The authors of the
written research we have read on her are mixed as to

whether she was an angel or a devil. The Sisters at Nevers, where she was stationed, consider her close to being a Saint. It is very obvious when we go there that they can't accept that she did anything to cause Bernadette pain during her lifetime. When we submit instances for their explanation, they shrug them off by saying that we don't understand the disciplines of *Religious Life,* especially during Bernadette's and Mother Thérèse's time, even though it was not much more than a hundred years ago.

Franz Werfel, the author of the world famous "*The Song of Bernadette,*" depicts Mother Thérèse as a *torturer.* He makes constant references to her background as the child of a military man, and compares her methods of training her novices to a military man with his troops. He also makes mention of a time when Bernadette was still in Lourdes that she had an encounter with Mother Thérèse at the hospital run by the Sisters of Nevers, where Bernadette stayed for a time. Mother Thérèse was a teacher and supervisor at that time. The author talks of a night the two spent together in the same room. Bernadette was deathly afraid of this woman, who had an obvious open animosity toward the child, and bluntly declared her disbelief in the Apparitions. We've never found a reference to this in the other research we've read, so we don't know how true it is. Werfel believes that Mother Thérèse's great weapon against her novices was making them completely dependent on her for love, and then taking it away at will, as a form of punishment.

Another author on the life of St. Bernadette, Abbé François Trochu, tries not to be judgmental about the Novice Mistress' feelings for Bernadette, or her intentions, regarding her particularly rough treatment of the future Saint. He maintains that Mother Thérèse had a need to break her novices spiritually when they entered. He contends she insisted they confide everything to her, but that which they revealed to a Priest in the confessional. He admits at times there was a fine line drawn between the two, and there may have been times when she went over the line, however, probably not intentionally.

When our little Bernadette first came to Nevers, there are those who believed that Mother Thérèse actually liked her. The Church had accepted the Apparitions as authentic; the Shrine at Lourdes was becoming well known, and many miracles were attributed to Our Lady's intercession there. If Mother Thérèse had not believed Bernadette initially, she was able to believe in the truth of the Apparitions now. However, throughout her life, the Mistress of Novices could never fathom *why* Our Lady would have chosen one such as this illiterate peasant from the Pyrenees to come to.

Whatever warmth Mother Thérèse felt for the child at the outset, was quickly diminished when Bernadette did not follow the pattern of other novices, and confide completely in the Mistress of Novices. This might have been an understandable feeling on the part of Mother Thérèse, had it not been for the very nature of Bernadette, and the fact that she had been the seer of Lourdes. We have to keep in mind that this girl literally fought a single-handed battle against family, police, government and Church. No one on earth in a position of authority had believed in her. She'd had no one to confide in. She was not used to confiding in anyone, but the Lady. Turning her around to open up to anyone, even her Mistress of Novices, was an enormous task. It was not wise for Mother Thérèse to believe that this special child of Mary would *just fall into the pattern of other novices.*

Mother Thérèse also had a preconceived, possibly romantic concept of what a visionary was. She looked for an air of mysticism, for *visible* signs of a high level of piety, which Bernadette would *not* project. Bernadette spent her entire life trying to convince the whole world of her *unworthiness* to be the recipient of the gift given her by Our Lady. What Mother Thérèse saw as one of Bernadette's greatest weaknesses, was what Bernadette *fought* to be. *She was ordinary, an ordinary Nun.*

The easiest trap for Bernadette to have fallen into would have been that of pride. Remember, at one time, as a teenager, she was the most famous woman in France. A newspaper reporter from Paris, interviewed her in the early days, in Lourdes. He said to her, "Listen, Bernadette. Come with me to Paris, and in three weeks you will be rich. I will make your fortune."

"Oh no!" Bernadette replied. *"I want to stay poor."*

Another aspect of Bernadette's life that Mother Thérèse may have overlooked, or not considered valid, is the nature of Bernadette's relationship with Mother Mary. She had been given secrets, which she unashamedly stated, she would not even divulge to the *Pope.* She had been given special prayers, which she never shared. She had been given messages from Mary which were for her *alone.* How could she possibly be expected to share these with Mother Thérèse, if she were not willing to share them with His Holiness, to whom she professed total obedience? In order to keep these things to herself, not to allow herself to be tricked into revealing them to anyone, she had to have built up a guard, a wall of defense. She couldn't possibly drop this wall, and allow anyone into this inner place that was hers and her Lady's *exclusively.*

Mother Thérèse spent most of Bernadette's life cutting her down, ridiculing her, humiliating her. And this dear child put up with it. There were times when she fell, when her strong will and Pyrenean tongue lashed out in defense, but by and large, she put up with all of it silently. At one time, she even credited Mother Thérèse with being the source of her salvation and purification. *A whole book could be written about that one statement!*

Though her life was filled with emotional and spiritual suffering, as well as physical suffering, she maintained a most unusual sense of humor. She was one of the girls. The sooner that incoming novices got to know her, she had the freedom to joke and cut up better than the rest of them. She was not beyond childish pranks, which very often caused her grief at the hands of her Superiors. While she was the infirmarian, she had the kindest heart towards her patients, always giving them reason to smile or laugh in the midst of their pain. She brought *joy* wherever she went. She never took herself too seriously. She took her *journey* seriously, the special gift she had been given by Heaven, to be the recipient of a visit from Mary, the most *famous woman* the world has ever known. She knew she was specially chosen, and that called for a certain action on her part. She spent her entire life trying to live up to that calling.

When the statue of Our Lady was to be crowned at Lourdes in solemn ceremony, Bernadette was invited by the Bishop to attend. She refused, using her illness as an excuse. Her fellow Nuns could not believe that she didn't want to be there. One conversation went something like this:

"Would you be happy to see it (the grotto) again?"

"My mission at Lourdes is over. What should I do there now?"

"They are preparing great celebrations at Lourdes, with several Bishops taking part. Wouldn't you like to go?"

"Oh! I prefer a thousand times more my small corner in the sick room than to be present at Lourdes for this solemnity, which however, gives me pleasure."

Then she thought for a moment, and said:

"If I could be transported to the grotto in a balloon and pray there all alone for a short time, I would go with pleasure, but if I have to travel like everyone else and find myself in the midst of the crowds, I had rather remain here."

Bernadette was given a very special gift at the beginning of 1874. She had been the assistant infirmarian, a job she loved very much, but her strength was waning badly. After an unusual bout with bronchitis in the fall of 1873, in which she had to be sent away to a hospital, it was determined that she was too weak to keep up her post at the infirmary. She was given the least *physical* job in the Convent, which was also the most important, and which she loved even more than being in the infirmary. She became *assistant sacristan.*

Her new position gave her the opportunity to spend all her time in the Chapel, near the Blessed Sacrament. She was virtually without supervision, which allowed her to speak to Our Lord Jesus in the Tabernacle, without anyone thinking she was strange. She made beautiful embroidered holy cards. She was able to pray for long periods of time. There are those who claimed she became completely engrossed in her prayer to the point of being gone, spiritually somewhere else. We can just imagine where that Somewhere else was.

She handled all the items that touched Our Lord Jesus in the Eucharist with such reverence. The corporal, the purificators, the albs, everything was touched as if Jesus in the Flesh had touched them, which of course, He had, during the Sacrifice of the Mass. Bernadette became very possessive of her position. There were certain areas of her job that she would not allow anyone to help her with, such as handling the holy objects that had touched Jesus.

It's been said that Bernadette always had a great love for Jesus in the Eucharist. She had a hunger to receive her First Holy Communion. When she had received it, she was asked which had given her more joy, the Apparitions of Mary, or her First Holy Communion. Her reply was *"They are two things that go together, but which cannot be compared. I was very happy on both occasions."*

A cousin of Bernadette's, Sister Cassou, joined her at the Convent of St. Gildard. Sister Cassou shared her impressions of Bernadette during and after reception of the Eucharist,

"Nothing could distract her. Once she had received Holy Communion, she became so deeply absorbed that everybody left the Chapel without her seeming to notice it. I stayed beside her. . . . I watched her for a long time without her noticing. Her face was radiant and heavenly, just as it was during the ecstasy at Massabielle. When the Sister came to close the doors she rattled the bolts vigorously. Then Bernadette came out of her ecstasy, as it were."

If it was possible, she developed an even greater love for Jesus in the Eucharist during this 22 month period, when she was allowed to spend most of her time with Him. It was fitting that this was the *last* position she would hold in the Convent. She became too weak to do any kind of work towards the end of 1875. We're reminded of the prediction made to Bishop Forcade by the Superior General in 1866. *"She will be in and out of the infirmary all the time. And there's not much she can do."* This prediction was to come about, *according to the world's standards.*

Bernadette's Dark Night

Bernadette suffered physical pain all her life, so she was used to it. But nothing compared with that which she suffered in the last days. Her body was wracked with pain. The back side of her body was almost raw from bed sores. Her tubercular leg blew up. It was so huge, it was grotesque. She developed abscesses in her ears, which made her partially deaf for a time. If it had not been so obvious that she were suffering, no one would ever have suspected she were ill from her cheerful attitude.

But her greatest source of suffering was in her *soul*. She was *attacked* unrelentlessly by the evil one. Sisters who kept watch over her through the night, shared about the battles they could hear her waging with the *devil*. Her dark night was not a lack of faith in her *God*, as much as it was guilt on her part for not having *given back* to God in proportion to the gifts she had been given during her life.

She believed she had been specially chosen, but she was tortured because she judged (with a little help from the *enemy*) that she had not lived up to that honor. She prayed desperately for forgiveness. The worse the physical pain became, the greater the spiritual attacks. During her final walk to the Father, she carried a heavy burden, *and walked alone*.

After many false alarms, going as far back as 1866, when she was thought to be at death's door, finally, the little Saint of Lourdes, strong stock of the Pyrenees, gave up her body to Jesus and His Mother Mary on April 16, 1879. She had fought the good battle. She was being called Home. Mary had told her, "*I can't promise you happiness in this world, but in the next world.*" It was time for the *next world*.

While Bernadette's trial on earth was over, her Mistress of Novices, Mother Thérèse's was not. She suffered for the next 28 years in her soul, fighting the *struggle within herself* as to whether she had been right or wrong about the way she had treated Bernadette. Even in the light of the sanctification of the girl which surfaced after Bernadette died, Mother Thérèse would not allow the process of beatification to be opened during her lifetime. She threatened to be "*Devil's Advocate*," in which she would do everything in her power to discredit Bernadette.

The Lord has this ironic sense of humor, however. When Mother Thérèse was forced to retire, she found herself spending the last days of her life at Lourdes, in the same hospice where Bernadette had stayed. She still had not reconciled with the little Saint-to-be. When she heard the crowds singing, she closed the shutters of her windows. She became easily agitated during the processions. But finally, she asked "*Our Lady of Lourdes to protect me in my agony*."

The Superior General who attended the funeral of Mother Thérèse, prayed at her tomb,

> "Mother, things do not always look the same in Heaven as they do on earth. Now that you are, I trust, illuminated by the pure light above, be so good as to take Bernadette's cause in hand. I leave the initiative[2] in this matter to you. I shall not take any steps myself. I shall wait for a sign from Heaven."

Within three weeks, the Superior General was told by Rome to gather information immediately for the process of Beatification.

We always find ourselves going back to a Scripture Passage of St. Paul to the Romans, 8:28.

> *We know that God makes all things work together for the good of those who love Him, who have been called according to His decree. Those whom He foreknew He predestined to share the image of His Son, that the Son might be the first-born of many brothers. Those He predestined, He likewise called; those He called He also justified; and those He justified, He in turn glorified.*

This passage fits Bernadette, the little shepherdess of Lourdes, highly favored of the Lord through His Mother, our Mary. Less than sixty years after her death, less than forty years after the Process of Beatification was opened, Bernadette was raised to the Communion of Saints on December 8, 1933, to be called for all time, St. Bernadette.

Bernadette has been glorified for all to see

But that's not the end of the story. When her body was taken up from the grave for identification, at the beginning

---

[2]Cause for Bernadette's Canonization

of the process of Beatification, it was discovered that it had not suffered decay. When she was first lifted out of the ground, her rosary, held between her fingers, had corroded. Her habit was mildewed. But her body was perfect. To this day, the incorrupt body of the little shepherdess of Lourdes is laid out in a glass case at the chapel of the Convent of St. Gildard, in Nevers, France, quiet, unassuming, as was Bernadette in life.

There is a museum attached to the Convent, which shows the corroded rosary found in Bernadette's hands, when her body was taken out of the ground the first time. There is a photo of the Saint when she was laid in state. Everyone agrees that this holy lady is more beautiful today, than when she was alive. There is also a small book available at the museum at Nevers. It is called *The Body of Saint Bernadette*, by Fr. Andre Ravier. It is a compilation of documents in the Archives of the Convent of St. Gildard, of the Diocese and the City of Nevers. It authenticates that her body was never embalmed or preserved in any way, nor did it contain chemicals which could cause natural preservation.

Why did we choose Bernadette? How did she show the strength necessary to call her a *Powerful Woman in the Church?* How is her life a parallel to women in our Church today? If a 14 year old illiterate, from the poorest family in the worst section of town, could stand up against the whole world, and make them take notice, what can't our women of today do? What is her single greatest attribute that can be embraced by women 130 years later?

A Franciscan Priest for whom we have great respect, Fr. Richard Rohr, once said of Our Lady, "*She did nothing. She just stood there.*" She allowed the Lord to fill her, and then He did the rest. We believe the same holds true of the little boy on the Mount of the Beatitudes who gave Jesus two fish and five barley loaves. Jesus was able to use everything the little boy had, bless it, work with it and feed anywhere from five to fifteen thousand people. We believe Bernadette did the same. Like Mother Mary before her, she said *"Yes!"*

Bernadette's life was focused. She had one thing that the Lord asked her to do. She said "Yes" to that, and gave her whole life to that "Yes". In order for her to carry out her "Yes", she had to fight every institution in her world from 1858 to 1879. She used everything the Lord had given her, to convince them of the truth of her Apparition, *all the while, being obedient to the Church and State.*

The Lord gave her a fiery personality to use for His Glory, and when that task had been accomplished, He asked her to suppress and submerge that *gift* that He had given her. Her *strong points* had to become her *shortcomings*, and she had to say "Yes" to that. She spent the rest of her life trying to do what the Lord was asking of her at any given *moment*. It was probably easier during those earlier years, when she had to fight with all she was worth, to stand up to those who would destroy her, and the message Mary was trying to give them through her. There was battle. There was adrenalin flowing. There was challenge.

But the later years, the last 13 out of 35, which called for total obedience, total submersion of will, not questioning seemingly illogical orders that grated against her logical mind, those were probably the hardest. Did her sanctification come from those 8 years of fame, or from the 13 years of obscurity? Was her Fiat, her "Yes" to Jesus and Mary, one that we can imitate? Is Bernadette a role model that touches your heart? *Pray on it!*

Above:
Curé Peyramale

Above:
Bernadette - Age 20

Below:
*Grotto of Massabielle
at Time of Apparition*

Above:
*Le Cachot
Former Prison
where Bernadette
Lived*

Above:
The Little Flower (1896)

Above:
***Sister Thérèse
of the Child Jesus
(1895)***

Below:
Tomb of St. Thérèse

Above:
***Convent of Carmel
Lisieux***

St. Thérèse of Lisieux

"If God grants my desires, my Heaven will be spent on earth until the end of time. Yes, I will spend my Heaven doing good on earth....I will return! I will come down!"

St. Thérèse is one of the most powerful Saints of the Twentieth Century. We have never prayed for the intercession of another Saint who lived so close to our time. She died in 1897 at the age of twenty four, and was canonized in 1925. When she died, she was virtually unknown, *even in her own Community.*

Within two years of her death, the power of her intercession began to be felt all over Europe. Prayers and novenas were made to her for favors, which were answered in abundance, usually preceded by the reception of a *flower.* She called herself the Little Flower of Jesus, a name which has remained with her until today. The swiftness of time in which devotion to this Saint grew, would be called in secular terms, a phenomena. We call it a *Miracle.*

On March 15, 1907, Pope St. Pius X, in a private conversation, called her *"The greatest Saint of modern times".* This statement, made ten years after her death, from a man who would himself be raised to the Communion of Saints, is a great tribute to the little Carmelite that no one had known at the time of her death.

A year later in the Vatican, the Prefect of the Congregation of Rites, Cardinal Vico, stated, *"We must lose no time in crowning the little Saint with glory, if we do not want the voice of the people to anticipate us."* He was about eight years too late. People began calling Thérèse a Saint as early as two years after her death.

The power of intercession given to Thérèse was undeniable. Truly, her prophecy made towards the end of her life, *"God will have to do my will in Heaven, because I have never done my own will on earth,"* was coming about. Within a short twenty eight years after her death, in 1925, the little cloistered Carmelite was proclaimed St. Thérèse.

†

Penny and I didn't know very much about St. Thérèse in 1976. We were sort of roped into devotion to this coquettish Saint. Penny was born a few years after the canonization of St. Thérèse; although she was christened Pauline and not Thérèse, her mother, who had been caught up in the growing devotion to the new Saint, gave *St. Thérèse* to Penny as a patron Saint. We still have a statue of the Saint in our home, which was given to Penny as a child.

In 1976, I finally convinced Penny to go to Europe. I had been trying to get her to go for years, but she never wanted to leave the United States. Finally, she agreed to go on a Pilgrimage. We had just come back to the Church the year before, and were hungry for anything that had to do with Church. So, we went off to Europe and the Holy Land; visiting Rome, Lourdes, Fatima, Assisi and all the Shrines in the Holy Land. I had planned three days in Paris at the end of the pilgrimage. I had been stationed in France with the Army in the mid-fifties, and wanted to share the romance of Paris with my darling. I never visited any Shrines while I was in France during my younger years, even though I had been stationed less than a hundred miles from Lourdes. Lisieux, which was way out to the northwest in Normandy, never entered my mind, though I had to pass there by train on one excursion I made to London by boat train.

I had our time in Paris pretty well set. I knew exactly what I wanted to do, and where I wanted to bring Penny. We would go to the Eiffel Tower, the Arch of Triumph, the

Champs Elysees and on and on. However, since we had fallen deeply in love with Church and all the Saints, I fully intended to include the Cathedral of Notre Dame and the Basilica of Sacre Coeur. But Penny had a different agenda. We had learned in Lourdes that the incorrupt body of St. Bernadette, the Visionary of Lourdes, was in Nevers, about three hours out of Paris by train. Penny insisted we visit the Shrine of St. Bernadette, and see her beautiful body. That was *one* of our days in Paris shot. I had loved little Bernadette for many years and I really wanted to go, but I didn't want to give up our days in Paris. In the end, Bernadette and Penny won out. We decided to go to Nevers.

Then, Penny remembered about St. Thérèse. We found out that Lisieux is also about three hours out of Paris by train; only it was in a *different* direction. St. Thérèse was her patron Saint. *We had to go to Lisieux!* That would leave only one day for Paris. You can imagine how upset I was. Bernadette was one thing, but I knew nothing about this Little Flower of Lisieux. However, this was Church and Penny was insistent; so we had to include St. Thérèse in the itinerary. Looking back now, I really believe that those two French Saints *Bernadette and Thérèse* had made a decision in Heaven to keep us away from Paris, as much as possible. And naturally, being who they are, *they got their way!*

The train trip to Nevers was boring, three hours there and three hours back. The time we spent at the Shrine of St. Bernadette, in the little Convent of St. Gildard, made it well worth the trip. But I wasn't looking forward to doing the same thing the next day to go to Lisieux. Finally, Penny could see my long face; as we arrived back at the train station in Paris, she weakened. She said we didn't have to go to Lisieux the next day. I rushed to cash in our tickets. In that way, it was firm. *We were not going.*

The next day in Paris turned out to be the *very worst* day we had ever spent at any time of our life. Everything went wrong! We had given the hotel the wrong dates as to how long we were staying there; they wanted to throw us out. We even tried to go home, but were not able to change our plane reservations. We knew that either we had made a mistake, or St. Thérèse was getting even with us for not going to Lisieux. Before we even left Paris, we made a vow to visit St. Thérèse the very next time we went on pilgrimage, even though we had no idea *when* that might be.

The day after we returned to Los Angeles from our pilgrimage, we had *business* appointments in San Diego. We stayed there two days, and went to the Church of the Immaculate Conception in Old Town. Something that we had never seen before, but must have been there, was a *life-sized* statue of St.Thérèse in the back of the Church. We decided, after Mass we would go to her and apologize for not having visited Lisieux.

What should we find at the foot of the statue, but a plastic bag with a small rosary called a *chaplet*, instructions on how to say a *novena* to St. Thérèse and a testimony from the lady who made up this kit, as to how devotion to St. Thérèse had saved her life.

We were praying for a teenager in our parish who had cancer of the bone marrow in the kneecaps. He couldn't do anything other teenagers could do. He was an altar boy, but couldn't kneel. He couldn't run along the sand at the beach, or take part in sports. His bones would chip whenever he tried to do this. So we decided to pray to St. Thérèse for a *healing* for this young man, David Hawkins. We were not too happy about being dependent on receiving a flower as an answer to our prayer. Actually, I don't think we *trusted*. We were afraid we wouldn't get a flower. But we were going to pray to St. Thérèse, anyway. So, we began the novena.

Keep in mind, that at this time, we knew virtually *nothing* about the power Our Lord Jesus had given this Saint.

The next day, we returned to Los Angeles. We had an appointment with one of the manufacturers we represented, a Jewish man who imported little gift items from Japan. Penny and I became deeply engrossed in our *business* meeting with the man. I noticed, however, that he had something wrapped in a cone-shaped piece of green waxed paper. Towards the end of the meeting, he reached for this object. He said to Penny, "I have something brand new here. It's never been sold in this country. Don't get excited. I'm not even sure how many of them I can get. I just want your opinion on it."

He opened the waxed paper, and handed her the most beautiful rose we had ever seen. The sweet fragrance filled the room. The man explained that the rose was made out of very thin wood shavings, and was perfumed. Penny excitedly began to talk about how many we could sell. *I immediately thought of our novena to St. Thérèse!* I stopped Penny in the middle of her conversation with our manufacturer. *"Penny, don't you see what that is?"*

She looked at me strangely. "Of course, it's a rose, well not a real rose, but it looks and feels and smells like a real rose."

"It's a rose, Penny, a rose! Remember our novena to St. Thérèse?"

Her mouth dropped open. We hugged one another, crying. The manufacturer thought we had lost our minds. Our prayer had been answered in *one day!* Penny was determined to tell the boy's mother the next day at daily Mass. I warned her not to. Suppose this was not an answer from St. Thérèse? After all, it was an *artificial* rose. We decided it was best not say anything to the mother, just yet.

The next morning after Mass, as if I had said, *"Find Ann Hawkins; run up to her, and tell her David is healed,"* that's exactly what Penny did. The mother looked kindly at us, and told us that there was no hope for David. As a matter of fact, she and her son had an appointment with his doctor that afternoon to talk about amputating his one leg. The pain had become excruciating the last few days. She asked us to pray for them at 2:45 in the afternoon, when they had the appointment.

We promised to pray for them, but at 2:45 that afternoon, we were deep into the building of fixtures for our semi-annual trade show to be held at the Los Angeles Convention Center. We had completely forgotten about David and his mother when, at about 5 pm, their car pulled up to our driveway. They both got out, and ran up the driveway in tears, crying out *"It's a miracle! It's a miracle!"* David was holding something behind his back.

The doctor had told them that David's cancer not only had *not* spread, but was actually in *remission*. He couldn't give them an explanation; but they didn't need one. David took a cone-shaped piece of waxed paper from behind his back, and handed it to Penny. *It was a rose, a live rose!* St. Thérèse had gotten us hooked.

A Post Script to that story is that we kept that rose on the prayer table in our living room, where it lived for four years without one petal dropping, with about two inches of water in the bottom of the vase, which never evaporated. It never smelled bad; the water never became stagnant. In 1980, our daughter Clare and our grandson Rob came to live with us. They brought their cat, Suki, who loved to eat plants. We were afraid the cat would eat the rose of St. Thérèse, so we put it away in a breakfront. It was not closed-in. There were open cane doors on the breakfront. Air could get through. Nevertheless, within three days, the rose died; the water dried up. Jesus and Thérèse had kept the rose alive, the water in the vase for four years. We did not have enough faith that they would protect the rose from a cat!

But we had gained a new friend in Thérèse. Since that time, we have prayed for her help in thousands of situations; she's never let us down. We vowed that her Shrine would be the first one we would visit if we ever went on pilgrimage again. As it turned out, the following year, 1977, we went back to Europe in search of the Shrines of the Saints, and *Lisieux* was on top of the list. We had fallen hopelessly in love with St. Thérèse. She and her peaceful little town have become a part of our pilgrimage itinerary until this day.

There is another interesting thing we'd like to share about Thérèse and the power Our Lord Jesus has given her. Lisieux is located in Normandy, right smack in the middle of the path of the fierce fighting that took place in France during the *Normandy invasion in 1944*. While the town took a beating from the ground warfare and the bombing overhead, the Basilica of St. Thérèse, Les Buissonnets, where she grew up; and the Carmel, where she lived her life as a Nun were not touched. *Praise the Lord!*

†

The Little Flower of Jesus

Saints beget Saints. We believe that statement to be true. The parents of Thérèse, Louis and Zélie Martin, both felt drawn to the Religious life. Louis wanted to enter a Religious order, but was turned down because he didn't know Latin. He moved to Paris, where he stayed for three years. It was too sinful a city for him. He couldn't stay there any longer, so he went to Alençon, where his parents had a jewelry business. He lived there for eight years in virtual seclusion. He opened up a watch and clock shop, which took up much of his time. He was very spiritual, and kept to himself pretty much. He enjoyed being alone on fishing trips, or spending time at Church. He did involve himself in a young Catholic organization in his parish. He had no qualms about closing his shop each Sunday, which was one of the busiest days in Alençon.

Zélie had suffered an *unhappy* childhood. She felt that no matter what she did, her mother never considered her as good as her sister. Perhaps because of this, she became an over-achiever, excelling in anything into which she put her energy. She was very hard on herself, suffering from Scrupulosity, which her daughter Thérèse inherited from her. At age 22, when Louis met Zélie, she had mastered the art of making Alençon lace, for which the region was world famous. She had her own little shop, and was doing quite well. She, too, had wanted to enter the Religious life, but was turned down, which only added to her poor self-image, seeing as how her *sister* had become a Visitation Nun.

It was Louis' mother who brought the two together. She was concerned about her son, who was now 34 years old. After a very short courtship of three months, Louis and Zélie were *married*. However, Louis wanted to live a *celibate* life with Zélie, as brother and sister. She wasn't happy about the idea, but begrudgingly agreed, for almost a year. Finally, the couple asked guidance from their Confessor, who convinced them that they were to live the *full* married life. They were so obedient that they had nine children in ten years. Only five of them survived, all girls, of which Thérèse was the youngest and the last. Our little Saint was born on the 2nd of January, 1873.

The family had lost four children, three in infancy, and one at age five. When Thérèse became very ill as an infant, they feared she might join her brothers and sisters in Heaven. They tried everything they could. Finally, the doctor insisted the child be breast-fed, so little Thérèse was sent to a wet-nurse in the country for over a year. She came back healthy, beautiful, and with a great love for the country. Her health was always delicate, however. Even as a child, she became sick from the slightest thing, and the illness always lingered.

Thérèse was everybody's *favorite*. The older girls, Marie and Pauline, wanted to *mother* the child. Céline, only four when Thérèse was born, became her closest friend. Pauline was Thérèse's ideal. She felt a great attraction to this sister. Thérèse had her own inbred love for God, and had talked about being a Nun at the earliest age. Her sister Pauline wrote to a friend when Thérèse was only four years old, that she could see a vocation in her. But it was when Pauline entered the Carmel, that Thérèse's vocation was sealed.

Thérèse's life at Alençon was a happy one. The family was *well-to-do*. The Franco-Prussian war had ended, and it seemed for a time that peace had come to France. Zélie's lace business had grown and grown so, that Louis sold his watch shop to take over the management of her business. But Louis and Zélie never allowed their good fortune to get in the way of their spirituality. Jesus and the Church were *primary* in their home.

Thérèse was a spiritual girl from the very beginning. She had a great love for everything that had to do with her Faith. And being who she was, it was not a quiet, subdued love. It was an alive, exciting, vibrant spirituality. She embraced with fervor Jesus, Mother Mary, all the Angels and the Saints.

Thérèse was spoiled by everyone. She was the youngest, the prettiest, the most coquettish. Not only her family, but her relatives, family friends, virtually everyone who met her as a child adored her. And she knew it! It became one of her strongest weapons to get her way when she wanted it. She was spoiled, but she was never a brat. Everyone wanted to do for her, and she just took it all in. She was also vain. She would have been hard-pressed not to have everybody fawning all over her. But in later years, as a teenager, and then in the Carmel, these became her two greatest obstacles to overcome.

She had a very *strong personality*, which she herself admits. When she couldn't get her way, she would roll on the floor in tantrums, to the point where she sometimes choked.

Her mother once noted: "*Thérèse is not as gentle as Céline and has an almost unconquerable stubborn streak in her; when she says no, nothing can make her give in, and you can put her in the cellar for the day and she would rather sleep there than say yes.*"

It became cute to talk about the naughty pranks that Thérèse did. Zélie wrote letters mentioning her pranks. Her sister Pauline wrote letters mentioning "naughty tricks" and misdeeds. The little Saint herself wrote letters, accusing herself of being impish, answering back, and playing tricks on her sisters. These were all *exaggerations*, which the family understood. However, there came a time during the Process for Beatification, that these innocent charges were used *against* her. It was only Divine Intervention, that most of the people who knew her were still alive to testify to her character.

In 1877, at four and a half years old, Thérèse's world came tumbling down on her. Her dear mother, after a lengthy illness, died. Thérèse took this very hard. In her own words,

"*The moving ritual of Extreme Unction[1] impressed itself on my soul. I still see the spot where I was*

---

[1]Extreme Unction - Renamed the Sacrament of the Anointing of the Sick - Completes the sacrament of Reconciliation, removes the remnants of sin, brings grace to the soul, gives strength to continue suffering the illness, as Christ suffered. Very often, reception of the sacrament restores health to the sick. The sick person is anointed with holy oil by the Priest, while praying for forgiveness of sins, and restoration to health.

*told to kneel; I still hear the sobs of our poor
father. . . I do not remember that I wept much. I
spoke to no one of the profound feelings which
filled my heart; I looked and listened in silence."*

Louis Martin felt it best to move his five girls to Lisieux,
to be close to Zélie's brother and sister-in-law, who could be
helpful in raising them. They rented a beautiful little home,
called *Les Buissonnets*, which still stands today. The
atmosphere was different from Alençon. There, their home
faced the main street. Zélie was outgoing, and there were
many friends visiting all the time. In Lisieux, they knew
nobody, except of course, Zélie's family, the Guérins. The
home was a distance from the main street, and very *secluded*.
For Thérèse it was good in a way, in that she had a big
garden, which was reminiscent of her infancy in the country.
For all of them however, it was a time of being alone, just
family. Louis went back to his old ways of solitude, a luxury
he was not able to enjoy while Zélie was alive.

The two older girls took charge of the household, under
the supervision of Madame Guérin. Thérèse had two more
playmates however, her cousin Jeanne, who was much older,
ten, and Marie, seven and a half. But soon, her sister Céline,
closest in age to Thérèse, went off to school, and our little
Saint found herself alone much of the time. She wrote about
this time in her life.

*"After Mamma's death my happy disposition changed
completely. I, who had been so full of life, so outgoing,
became shy, quiet and oversensitive. A look was enough
to reduce me to tears. I was only happy when no one
paid attention to me. I could not bear the company of
strangers, and only regained my cheerfulness within the
intimacy of my family."*

It was a time, however, that brought Thérèse closer to
her sister, Pauline. Marie, the oldest, and Pauline took
charge of teaching Thérèse during the mornings. It was

during this time that Pauline became her second *mother*. Thérèse always referred to her in those terms, even in the Convent. In the afternoon, she got to go out with her father for long walks. It was good for Louis, too, because he would have stayed alone up in the belvedere at the top of the house, if he were allowed to. But he enjoyed this time with his little princess, the last of his children. People stopped to stare at Thérèse no matter where they went. They always had a compliment to pay to her father, about how pretty she was. There had been a time when she loved to hear these flattering words, but now she wanted to hide behind her father. The compliments, however, remained in her subconscious.

It was during this time at Les Buissonnets that Thérèse had a Vision, which she did not understand for years to come. One day, she was up in her room. Her father had gone back to Alençon to visit friends. All of a sudden, she saw a man who looked exactly like her father, walking in their garden. But he was all stooped over, and wore something over his head like an apron. She called out to him, *"Papa! Papa!"* but he disappeared without turning back.

Her two older sisters, alarmed by the sound of her voice, ran into her room. She cried aloud what she had seen. She was on the verge of hysteria. Marie and Pauline ran downstairs and looked all over the grounds. They found no one. They spoke to the maid, who had a habit of finding ways of teasing Thérèse. She knew nothing of what the child had seen. Thérèse was confused and frightened by this Vision. She had never seen her father this way. She couldn't get it out of her mind. A time would come after she had entered the Carmel when this would prove to have been a *prophetic* Vision.

Thérèse felt a security at home, among family, which extended to the Guérins, but not much beyond that. She didn't want to be with other people. She was not *happy* with other people. This was all contrary to the *outgoing* personality she'd had before her mother died. At one time, she actually expressed a desire to be a hermit, to her sister Pauline.

Therefore, her entry into school was a *traumatic* experience for her. She was very good with her subjects, with the possible exception of Mathematics. But in everything else, she excelled. She actually threw herself into her studies to avoid relationship with any of her classmates. She couldn't stand playtime. She didn't get along well with the other children. And this from a girl who loved and was loved by all she encountered. There was something wrong. She did not feel safe in this atmosphere. She once wrote that this period, the time spent in school at the Benedictine Convent in Lisieux, was the saddest time of her life.

She read a lot. Actually, she *buried* herself in books, got *lost* in books. It was a way of escaping from the world she lived in. Her heroine was Joan of Arc, who was not yet canonized. *Did Thérèse know somewhere in her subconscious that one day she would be proclaimed Secondary Patron of France with St. Joan of Arc? (1944)* Joan of Arc was to play an important part in the life of our Saint. Thérèse felt a kinship with her always. On two different occasions during her life in the Carmel, she wrote, directed and starred in productions about Joan of Arc.

There were many ups and downs in her life during this period. She lost her sister Pauline to the Carmel in Lisieux in 1882. This was a very difficult time for her. Pauline had been her second mother. Now she was gone. Thérèse was only *nine years old* at the time. She had felt such a closeness to this sister. She thought Pauline would wait for her, until she could go with her. Once, some years before, Pauline had made that statement, not thinking anything of it. She had evidently forgotten this commitment she made to her sister. Thérèse had not.

When she was ten years old, Thérèse was stricken with an illness that was difficult to diagnose. It seemed for a time like it would kill her. She was in a constant state of hallucinations and violent trembling, her shivering body, ice-cold. It began on the Feast of the Annunciation, March 25, and stayed with her almost seven weeks. She was completely debilitated. She rallied once on April 6, because she wanted desperately to attend the ceremony of her sister Pauline's receiving the Carmelite habit. She was able to go to the ceremony, but when she returned, her relapse was so severe, all thought it was the end for her.

It got so bad that her family took turns praying around her bed. Then, in the month of Mary, on May 13, a miracle took place. She kept calling out "Mama! Mama!" Her three sisters knelt at her bedside, and prayed to the statue of Our Lady which was on the bureau. Thérèse tells what happened:

"Finding no help on earth, poor little Thérèse also turned to her Heavenly Mother and prayed with all her heart for her (Mary) to have pity on her at last. All of a sudden the Blessed Virgin appeared to me beautiful, more beautiful than anything I had ever seen. Her face expressed an ineffable goodness and tenderness, but what went right to the depths of my soul was The Blessed Virgin's ravishing smile! Then all my pain vanished, two large tears welled up on my eyelashes and silently rolled down my cheeks, but they were tears of pure joy. Ah! I thought, the blessed Virgin has smiled at me, how happy I am - but I will never tell anyone, for then my happiness would disappear."

Thérèse was completely healed on **May 13,** 1883, through an apparition by Mary. Another miracle would take place through *another* apparition by Mary, on another **May 13,** 1917, in a little town in Portugal, called *Fatima*.

Ironically, during this period, which she referred to as the saddest of her life, Thérèse had one of her most spiritually uplifting experiences. She received her *First Holy Communion*. This was an event she had waited for as far back as she could remember. The whole family took this very seriously. Her sister Marie prepared her for the upcoming event. From the Carmel, her sister Pauline sent home a book of daily sacrifices for Thérèse to do in preparation for the long awaited day. This went on from February until May, when she finally received the Lord.

It was an extra special day for the Martin family. While the youngest, Thérèse, was to receive First Holy Communion, the first daughter who had entered the Carmel, Pauline, was making her final profession. The day chosen was May 8, 1884. Thérèse refers to her First Holy Communion as the *"First sweet kiss of Jesus"*. As she got closer and closer to the Communion rail, thoughts of when her sister Céline had received her first Holy Communion went through her mind. How sad she had been that time when she could not receive the Lord with Céline. But today was her day, hers and Jesus'. She described her feelings,

"Ah, how sweet was that first kiss of Jesus! It was a kiss of Love; I felt that I was loved, and I said, 'I love you and I give myself to you forever!' There were no requests, no struggles, no sacrifices; for a long time Jesus and poor little Thérèse had looked at each other (from a distance) *and understood each other. That day it was no longer simply a look, it was a fusion; there were no longer two, Thérèse had vanished like a drop of water lost in the depths of the ocean. Jesus alone remained. He was the Master, the King."*

This time with Jesus became the most important time in her life. She anticipated when she would be able to receive Him again inside of her. This was at a time when daily Communion was not allowed. So there was never a chance of Thérèse taking this gift for granted, as if she ever would. She even made a diary of how many times she had received Communion in the first year and a half, *twenty two*.

A Special Relationship with Jesus

We want to take a minute here to share about Thérèse's special relationship with Jesus. While it's true that the quotations we're using here are from her autobiography, which was written when she was 22 years old, we have to believe that the feelings that are expressed throughout the story of her life were those that she actually experienced at those times.

From the time she was an infant, she loved Jesus above all others. But at this time that we're sharing about, 1885 to 1888, she was also blossoming into a beautiful young woman. She *had* to have this kind of relationship with Jesus, in order to be able to maintain her focus, in the light of all the compliments she was receiving, and the natural emotions that were being stirred up inside her. She herself was to say about her emotional state at age fourteen, in 1887, "*I was at the most dangerous age for young girls*", and "*My heart could easily have let itself be caught by affection*".

If she had not given herself completely to Jesus with a passion, and maintained that passion through all the temptations that were thrown her way during her teenage years, she feared she might have given in to the world, and its false glamor.

We must keep in mind that this girl had it all. She was breathtakingly beautiful, well-groomed, educated, used to the finer things in life. Nowhere do we read that she even went through that gawky stage that most children experience. It was more difficult for her to walk away from all the world had to offer.

Thérèse was very hard on herself. She had inherited Scrupulosity from her mother, which is defined in the Catholic Encyclopedia as follows:

Because of confusion over the morality of actions, scruples arise when a troubled conscience, prompted by imaginary reasons, causes one to constantly dread sin where no sin exists, or to hold a venially sinful action mortally sinful. A conscience with scruples is a conscience ruled by fear.

Many of the great Saints were victims of *scruples.* Thérèse was no different. This plagued her all her life. As a young girl, she had her sister Pauline to set her mind at rest. After Pauline went into the Carmel, Thérèse felt shy about speaking to her about her scruples any more, especially since some of her problems may have been with chastity. She then went to her oldest sister, Marie, who helped her with these battles Thérèse constantly had with her conscience. She never shared her feelings with her Confessors at that time. She didn't know how to talk to them about inner feelings. She depended on her sisters.

In later years, in the Convent, her Spiritual Director admonished her,

"I forbid you in the name of God to question your state of soul. The Devil is laughing heartily. I protest against this willful distrust. Believe, come what may, that God loves you!"

And then again, after listening to Thérèse during confession, he told her,

"In the presence of God, the Blessed Virgin and all the Saints, I declare that you have never committed a mortal sin. Thank God for what He has done for you, for if He abandoned you, instead of being a little Angel, you would become a little demon."

We talk about these points, not to minimize the saintliness of Thérèse, the Little Flower of Jesus, but to *maximize* her love for Jesus in the light of all the obstacles placed in the path of her life. If we lose track of the battles of this young, normal girl, if we make her into a Saint without struggle, we lose some of the *touchability* of this powerful intercessor. While it's true that she loved Jesus above everyone and everything else all her life, she fought with every grace from Heaven to *maintain* that love. It was not an easy battle.

Little Thérèse and Bernadette Soubirous are two of my favorite women Saints. I think the reason I love them so much is because of the inner strength they showed in suppressing their human shortcomings. And while we don't want to dwell on their *humanity*, we don't want to belittle it either.

Thérèse's Determination to Enter Carmel

Thérèse had determination, and a strong will. When she decided she wanted something, nothing could stand in her way. A case in point was her decision to enter the Carmel, after her sisters Pauline and Marie. She was up against insurmountable odds. First off, she was fourteen years old. Secondly, *Teresa La Grande*, Foundress of the Discalced Carmelites, had made a rule that no more than two from a family could be in the same Community. This *Thérèse La Petite* wanted to buck the wisdom of one of the greatest Saints in history, and the Mother of their Order, Teresa of Avila. But as we mentioned, when Thérèse put her mind to something, *look out!*

Her *first obstacle* was her father. She had to get his permission. Emotionally, this may have been her most difficult task. She loved this man so much, and he adored her. She knew he would be heartbroken to lose his little *"Princess"*. But the Lord was calling her.

Louis Martin had suffered a stroke shortly before the day that Thérèse had chosen to drop her bomb on him. He was tired and weak. In addition, the middle daughter, Léonie, the only one who did not enter the Carmelite order, was vacillating back and forth with a vocation. She had only recently returned from an unsuccessful attempt to enter the Poor Clares, and was now asking for permission to enter the Visitation Order.

Considering all that was happening, someone with less courage than Thérèse would have chosen some other, more opportune time to approach her father. But that would not have been Thérèse. She waited until after dinner on a Sunday evening, and took her father out to the garden in back of the house at Les Buissonnets. They sat on a bench. She held his hands, and looked deeply into his eyes. He didn't stand a chance. His only objection was that she was so young. But she convinced him that her calling was truly of the Lord. He didn't actually tell her what he was feeling. He did not want to lose this precious diamond, his little "Princess". But he thanked our Dear Lord for the honor bestowed on him that all his girls would be serving Him in Community.

Thérèse was not looking forward to her confrontation with her *second obstacle,* her uncle Isidore, Zélie's brother. He and his wife had been very active in the upbringing of the Martin girls after his sister's death. Thérèse, who had an urgency to enter the Carmel, waited for six months after getting permission from her father, before broaching the subject with her uncle. She was somewhat intimidated by him. She had good reason. *He turned her down immediately.* It was ridiculous, he said, for a girl of her young years to think she had a Religious vocation. He insisted she wait until she was at least *seventeen.*

Thérèse was crushed. She went into deep depression. She says of that time,

"... *it was night everywhere, the dark night of the soul; I felt, like Our Lord in His agony, that I was quite alone,*

without anyone in Heaven or on earth to console me;
God Himself seemed to have abandoned me."

Her sister Pauline noticed her depression during one of Thérèse's visits to the parlor of the Carmel. She had never been so low. Even Thérèse could not understand why. Pauline decided to write a letter to her uncle, who valued her opinion greatly. As soon as he received her letter, his heart opened, and he gave his consent for Thérèse to enter the Carmel.

Obstacle three was one which she probably never quite overcame. It was Fr. Delatroëtte, who had been the Superior of the Carmel since before she was born. Word came to Thérèse that he would not even consider a child of her age entering the Convent. He gave *twenty one* as the minimum age for entering.

The next day, Thérèse charged down to the Priest's office, with her father and Céline as support. Remember, now, she was only fourteen at this point. Fr. Delatroëtte would not budge. His decision was final. But he made a mistake. He left the door open. He should have known his adversary better. His parting words were, "*Of course, the final decision rests with the Bishop. If he agrees. . .*"

Thérèse jumped on this. Her father, knowing in advance what her next step would be, and to stop the floodgate of tears which had begun as they left the Priest's office, volunteered to take her to see the Bishop. In a dramatic gesture, the future Saint made a prophecy,

"I said I'd go to the Holy Father himself if the Bishop of Bayeux wouldn't let me enter the Carmel at fifteen."

Thérèse's interview with the Bishop of Bayeux, Bishop Hugonin, was her *fourth obstacle*. It is the first time we hear of her putting her hair up in a bun to give the impression of being older. It didn't help. The Bishop thought it was cute, but reserved making a decision until he had an opportunity

to speak to Father Delatroëtte. The Bishop promised
Thérèse's father an answer during their Pilgrimage to Italy.

Here we see the Hand of the Lord. He is working with
his people, putting everyone into position. Thérèse had
made the statement that she would petition the Holy Father.
We would say *coincidentally*, except we don't believe that
anything is coincidental with the Lord. So, instead, we say
we believe the Divine Plan called for Thérèse and Céline to
accompany their father on a Pilgrimage through France and
Italy, which would culminate in a visit with His Holiness,
Pope Leo XIII, for the occasion of his Golden Jubilee, fifty
years a Priest.

Again, *not coincidentally*, there was a great deal of press
coverage, because of the stand the Church of France was
taking by honoring their Pope. It was a time of political
uncertainty; the French Catholics were making a show of
support *for* their Pope, and *against* the Freemasons both in
France and in Italy. Thérèse could not have cared less about
any of this. She had a focus, and was working her plan. But
because of the press coverage, her audience with the Pope
was reported in the French press.

She was preparing to meet her *fifth obstacle*, Pope Leo
XIII. The audience line was very long that Sunday,
November 20, 1887. Thérèse felt her whole life hinged on
what she said to the Pope. She and Céline were on the back
of the line of the group from their Diocese. Men were on
one line, ladies on the other; so, the girls were separated
from their father. Thérèse's little heart pounded as she got
closer and closer to the Pope. She could see that His
Holiness said something to each of the pilgrims before her.
She *knew* she would have her chance to speak to him.
Suddenly, word came down the line that he was getting tired,
and there would be no more conversation. They were to
kneel, kiss his ring, and move on. *Thérèse's heart dropped.* It

was all over. But her older sister, Céline urged her on. *"Speak!"* she ordered.

The Bishop of Bayeux, who had not gone on Pilgrimage to Rome, appointed Fr. Révérony as his emissary. Father was standing next to His Holiness, introducing the people to him, and generally keeping the line moving. Thérèse had to pass by him. He gave her a stern look. He had a feeling she wanted to petition the Pope. Thérèse knelt, kissed the Pontiff's slipper, and then pleaded with him. *"Most Holy Father,"* she said, *"I have a great favor to ask of you."*

The Pope looked at her inquisitively, and then bent down to hear her request. By this time tears were running down her face.

"Most Holy Father, in honor of your jubilee, (nice touch Thérèse) *I want you to let me enter the Carmelite order at fifteen."*

Either the Pope didn't hear her, or didn't understand the meaning of what she said. He turned to the Priest, Fr. Révérony for an explanation. The Priest glared at Thérèse. "This child here is anxious to enter Carmel at fifteen, and her Superiors are looking into the matter at this moment."

Pope Leo XIII looked kindly at the angelic face, so full of hope that he would grant her request. "Very well, my child, do what your Superiors tell you."

She grabbed both his legs, and would not let go. *"But if you'd say the word, Most Holy Father, everybody would agree."*

The guards gave her a ceremonial tap on the shoulders, which meant to move on. She didn't budge. The Pope said, "All's well; all's well. If God wants you to enter, you will."

We get the impression from Thérèse's writing that she didn't feel the tap from the guards. At any rate, she kept her grip on the Pope's knees. Finally, the guards lifted her bodily, aided by the Priest, Fr. Révérony, who was furious. They *literally* had to drag her out of the audience room.

The incident was reported in a local newspaper, and as a result, every attempt to plead Thérèse's cause back home was met with *hostility*. Everyone went to bat for her, including Mother Marie de Gonzague, and Mother Geneviève, both of the Carmel in Lisieux, and her uncle Isidore. Everyone failed. Even Thérèse wrote a letter to the Bishop, pleading her own case. She heard nothing. She had wanted to be accepted before Christmas of 1887, but nothing came in the mail. She finally gave up that idea.

Christmas Day was a tearful day for Thérèse. She had wanted so badly to celebrate it from behind the Grille at the Carmel. But that was not to be. After she returned home from a visit to her sister Pauline at the Carmel, she found a little bowl in her room with a ship in it. On the ship, the baby Jesus lay, with a ball next to Him; a single word appeared, "*Self-Abandonment*". Six days later, on January 1, 1888, she was to receive word from the Carmel that she had been accepted. *The Bishop had given his permission.*

Nowhere do we read that Thérèse quite understood what had really happened. We have to believe that she did, because of her great wisdom and sensitivity. We know that she was so in tune with the Lord that it must have become clear what Jesus was doing with all the struggles Thérèse experienced in her quest for admission into the Carmel, *all seemingly to no avail*. Possibly because her gift of *acceptance* had been mixed with yet another obstacle, a delay proposed by her own *sister* Pauline, she never thought to expound on how the Lord had worked in her life.

Thérèse had used everything she knew to try to get what she wanted, *when* she wanted it. She used all her ingenuity, all the tears that had worked on previous occasions, the pouting, the manipulating and maneuvering, and none of it worked. Her final grandstand play, the disaster of the audience with the Pope, seemed to clinch it for her. *She had failed!* Even after that, her Uncle Isidore,

Mother Genevieve and Mother Marie De Gonzague sent a barrage of pleas for her admittance, but all in vain.

Then, when all her human efforts had failed, when she was at the end of her rope for ideas on how *she* could make it happen, she had received a word of knowledge, *Self-Abandonment*. It was as if, after all the amateurs had struck out, the *Lord*, the Power of all, had just touched the heart of the Bishop, and everything fell into place. Permission had been granted.

We believe He wanted Thérèse to know, and subsequently, us, His Children, that He is the Power. We are nothing, and capable of nothing. All our wheeling and dealing is worthless. He wants us to get out of the way, and turn the power over to Him. *And then watch the results!*

Life in the Carmel

When Pauline and Marie entered the Carmel, after having lived in their upper middle class homes in Alençon and Lisieux, they experienced a great *culture shock*. They had never known or anticipated, the austerity, the poverty of the Convent.

The Little Flower, however, the spoiled child of the Martin family, felt no shock at all, either in her own testimony, nor in that of either of her sisters who were there when she entered. Her *cell*, or room was miniscule, compared to that of Les Buissonnets. It measured 6.8 feet by 12 feet. It contained a bed, a stool, an oil lamp and an hour glass. *And that's it!* You really have to see her room at Les Buissonnets, to appreciate what she gave up to live this life. It was large, with a polished hard wood floor, dainty wallcoverings, a plush mattress on a big bed, a curtained canopy, and delicate area carpets. Everything that her room at Les Buissonnets was, the Carmel was not. And yet, there's almost no indication that she found it anything but exciting. She makes a statement about her entrance which explains her attitude about the Carmel.

"*. . . I'd no illusions at all, thank God, when I entered Carmel; I found the Religious Life exactly what I'd expected it to be. The sacrifices I had to make never for a moment took me by surprise - and yet, as far as you know, Mother (Pauline), those first footsteps of mine brought me up against more thorns than roses!*"

She loved her new life so much she wrote her sister Céline after a month in the Carmel,

"*My dearest Céline, there are moments when I ask myself can it be true that I am at Carmel; sometimes, I can't believe it! Alas, what have I done for God that He should so fill me to overflowing with His graces?*"

But her struggles were just beginning. The sweet little girl whom the Community had known for six years as Sister Agnès of Jesus' (Pauline) and Sister Marie of the Sacred Heart's (Marie) little sister, was now one of them. She was too young, too smart, too pretty, too vain, and virtually *worthless* at physical labor. In the minds of the Community, there was a clan, *the Martin clan*, three sisters from the same family, of a much higher social status and greater intellect than most of the rest.

The Prioress, Mother Marie De Gonzague, who had adored little Thérèse for years and had fought arduously for her admittance into the Carmel, became her greatest *critic*. The Prioress was fifty four and Thérèse fifteen when the child entered. They were from different worlds.

Thérèse writes of her Prioress, Mother Marie De Gonzague, very lovingly, but you can sense an undercurrent of hurt there.

"*But Reverend Mother was often ill, and couldn't spend much time with me. I know she was very fond of me, and said the nicest things about me; but God saw to it that she should treat me very severely without meaning*

*to. I hardly ever met her without having to kiss the
ground in penance for something I'd done wrong; and it
was the same on the rare occasions when she gave me
Spiritual Direction."*

There was never a question of the child's spirituality.
From the beginning, it was known by everyone at the Carmel
that this was a special gift from God. This same Mother
Marie De Gonzague, wrote of Thérèse just one month after
her entrance into the Carmel,

". . .(Thérèse) is perfect. Never would I have expected to
find such sound judgment in a fifteen-year old! Not a word
has to be said to her. Everything is perfect."

Why, then, did this woman become the source of her
greatest suffering?   Why was there such a *love-hate*
relationship between the two for the nine years Thérèse
lived in Community? Was she too spiritual? Was she too
perfect? That too, can create problems of jealousy, which
Thérèse never mentions.

But Thérèse was a sensitive girl, extremely so. She *had*
to know when she was being attacked.   There are *some*
references in her writings about the personalities of the
women with whom she lived; statements like "*Of course, one
does not have enemies in Carmel . . .*" and "*The lack of
judgment, education, the touchiness of some characters, all
these things do not make life very pleasant.*"

She does write very often about *suffering*. We're not
sure if she knew what she would have to endure *before* she
entered the Carmel, or *became aware* of it very quickly after
she entered. It's possible that during her parlor visits to the
Carmel, with her two sisters over a period of six years, she
was able to pick up on some of the undercurrents of tension
and the hardships of living with other women in Community.
It would have been hard for her sisters to hide their feelings
from their families, on these rare occasions when they felt
free enough to share their hurts.

Possibly, because of her great insights and acute sensitivity, Thérèse was able to discern very soon after joining the Community that *struggle and suffering* were to be a part of her everyday life. She shared some of her feelings about suffering.

"Suffering opened her arms to me, and I threw myself into them lovingly enough."

"And Our Lord let me see clearly that if I wanted to win souls I'd have to do it by bearing a cross; so the more suffering came my way, the more strongly did suffering attract me."

"For the next five years, it was this way of suffering I had to follow, and yet there was no outward sign of it."

". . . I think this way of suffering, by which God led me, will be a revelation to the people who knew me."

A natural and normal source of consolation and defense would have been her sisters, Pauline and Marie. Remember, Thérèse was only fifteen years old. Notwithstanding the other problems she faced in the Carmel, she was so much younger than everyone else. At first, her sisters treated her as they had at home. She was the youngest, the prettiest, etc. But our little future Saint would have none of that. She fought her own instincts to be spoiled. It was not going to happen here. She had not come to Carmel for Pauline and Marie. She had come for Jesus.

In an effort *not* to give in to her sisters' protective instincts, she avoided them. This was extremely difficult for Thérèse because she loved them so, especially Pauline.

The Little Way of St. Thérèse

The Lord gave Thérèse special gifts. *He* truly took over as Novice-Master. The easiest and most normal path for anyone to follow, in a situation such as she found herself, would have been to either hold in the hurts and anger she felt or lash out at her attackers. In either case, it would have made for a very bitter Sister, and the evil one would have had his way.

Jesus gave Thérèse a special secret, *an insight*, which became known as the Little Way of St. Thérèse. *It was to turn all negatives into positives, to offer all her hurts to Jesus for the conversion of sinners, Priestly vocations, and the success of the missions.* For example:

There was a sister who disliked her thoroughly and made every effort to cut her, whenever they would meet. Thérèse's initial reaction was to give this sister a wide berth, avoid her wherever possible. She walked long distances out of her way not to confront this sister. But then, she decided that a good way to offer her sufferings to Jesus was *to go out of her way to meet this sister.* When the sister insulted her, as Thérèse knew she would, our little Saint would only smile.

During meditation in the Chapel, an old Nun prayed the rosary, noisily. She made *sshshing* noises as she prayed. This drove our little Saint up the wall. She *dreaded* when this sister would come in, because it always broke her concentration. As a special gift to Jesus, she offered this trial to Him. She got to the point where she looked forward to this Nun's coming into the Chapel, so that she could have this little gift to give to her Lord. She came to *love* this Sister. When the little old Nun died, Thérèse was sad at having lost her.

Thérèse had a very sensitive stomach. She was used to eating the best food, prepared in a very appetizing way. Under the best conditions, Convent food never approached the quality she had been used to at Les Buissonnets. But there were times when food was prepared that *none of the Sisters could bear.* At these times, the cook would say, "*We can give it to Thérèse. She'll eat anything!*"

It goes on and on. For the rest of her life, she practiced *this little way.* And nobody ever knew about it. She kept it a secret even from her sisters. She once wrote,

"Perhaps it would have relieved my feelings a bit if other people had been conscious of it, but they weren't. There'll be a lot of surprises at the Last Judgment, when we shall be able to see what really happened inside people's souls; and I think this way of suffering by which God led me will be a revelation to the people who knew me."

Abandonment became the key word of her Religious Life. The Catholic Encyclopedia describes Abandonment as follows:

"It refers specifically to the first stage of the progression of the soul toward union with God whereby futility is found in all other than God.

. . . it involves a passive purification of the soul through willingly undergoing trials and sufferings and leads to a surrender of natural consolations . . ."

In an effort to practice her little way of *abandonment*, she constantly had to fight off the desires of her sisters to baby her and give her special treatment as they had done at home in Les Buissonnets. She had to go out of her way to avoid them, so as not to allow them to spoil her as they had done since she was an infant. The most difficult sister to avoid was her second mother, Pauline, Sister Agnes.

She had always loved Pauline. Early in her postulancy, she and Pauline were to work together in the refectory, or dining room. Pauline talked incessantly about matters of interest to both of them, family matters. Little Thérèse prayed silently, so as not to hear her. Pauline was hurt by this, but finally came to understand. At one point, Thérèse had to shock her sisters, whom she loved so much, by telling them *"I have come here for Jesus, not for you."*

She buried herself in this new way of life. She tried to become so small, so unnoticed, almost a part of the woodwork. She submerged her personality as much as she could. Her unspoken motto was "*No one must know, except Jesus.*"

"*Yes, I want to be forgotten, not only by creatures, but also by myself. I'd like to be so reduced to nothingness, that I have no desire. The Glory of my Jesus, that is all; as for my own, I abandon it to Him; and if He seems to forget me, well, He is free since I am no longer mine, but His. He will grow weary of making me wait, quicker than I of waiting for Him!*"

She aspired to Sainthood. Actually, she *knew* she would be a Saint. But she felt she had to do something. Her *little way* became her something, that which would bring her into the Communion of Saints, the inner circle of Jesus, the place where she wanted to be.

She was given Scripture passages which affirmed this.

"*If anyone is a very little one let him come to me.*" (Prov 9:4)

"*As a mother comforts her child, so will I comfort you; you shall be carried at my breast and fondled in my lap!*" (Isaiah 66:12-13)

And, of course, her *most* favorite scripture passage was the one which the Church gave to her for her feast day, that of (Matthew 19:13).

"*Let the little children to come unto me. Do not hinder them. The kingdom of God belongs to such as these.*"

Thérèse must have known things that she did not share with her sisters except in a roundabout way. Thérèse truly believed that she would die young. After the death of her father in the summer of 1894, she talked about death often. While it's true that she had always suffered bad health, and her respiratory problems began to surface about this time, there's more to it than that. In a letter to Céline towards the end of 1894, she stated, "*...If I die before you, do not think that I will be far from your soul...*" and then almost as an afterthought, she wrote: "*But above all, do not be alarmed, I am not ill.*"

We know that she had a special kinship with Joan of Arc. Joan died young. Thérèse wrote, directed and starred in two plays about Joan of Arc. It appears that she used these plays to expound her own spirituality. She used passages from Scripture in these plays referring to early death,

"But the just man, though he die early, shall be at rest...
Having become perfect in a short while, he reached the
fullness of a long career; for his soul was pleasing to the
Lord." (Wisdom)

Towards the end of the play, Thérèse put these words into the mouth of Joan of Arc,

"Lord, I accept martyrdom for love of you, I no longer
cringe from death or fire.
O Jesus how my soul craves for you; to see you, my
God, is my one desire.
All I want is to die for your love,
I want to die to begin to live, to die to be with Jesus
above."

A time would come and not be long in the coming, when these words could very easily be attributed to Thérèse talking about herself.

Autobiography of a Soul

The Lord used Pauline in a very special way. All that He had taught Thérèse had to come out. It had to be known. But none of the Martin girls, not Marie, not Pauline, not even Thérèse knew what the *Lord's plan* was. Thérèse had adopted her little way. She became smaller and smaller in the eyes of the world. Most people didn't even know she existed. This was good. This was what she believed the Lord was asking of her. But there was a problem! How would the world ever learn what Jesus had taught His Little Flower? How would anyone know about this Little Way of St. Thérèse? The Lord set the stage.

One winter evening, not long after Céline had entered the Carmel, the four of them, Pauline, Marie, Thérèse and Céline were sitting around the fireplace telling stories of their childhood. Thérèse had been designated master story-teller. She was so good at it. The following had to be the Lord's design, it appears so contrived. Marie spoke to Pauline, who by now was Prioress of the Community.

"Is it possible that you let her (Thérèse) write little poems for one or other of the Sisters, and she writes nothing about her childhood for us? *You will see, she is an Angel; she will not stay long on earth,* and we will have lost all these details which are so interesting to us."

What *really* prompted Marie to make a statement like that? It appeared to come from out of the blue. What possessed her to say, "*She will not stay long on earth.*" Pauline looked at Marie strangely. Her older sister was suggesting Thérèse write her life story. Why would she do that at twenty-two years old? How could Pauline as Prioress, permit that? Thérèse didn't take any of it seriously. All of a sudden, as if she were commanded by the Lord, Pauline, no longer the older sister, but the Mother Superior, said to Thérèse very solemnly, "**I order you to write for me all your childhood memories.**"

Thérèse made the only logical statement possible. "*What do you want me to write that you do not know already?*"

But out of obedience to her Superior, and though not knowingly, out of obedience to Divine Providence, Thérèse began to write about her childhood. She opened her autobiography, which she herself called, "*Autobiography of a Soul*", with the following,

"*Dearest Mother, it is to you, who are my mother twice over, (Pauline) that I am going to tell the history of my soul. When you first asked me to do it, I was frightened; it looked as if it meant wasting my spiritual energies on introspection. But, since then, our Lord has made it clear to me that all He wanted of me was plain obedience. And in any case, what I shall be doing is only what will be my task in eternity - telling over and over again the story of God's Mercies to me."*

And with that, St. Thérèse, the little flower of Jesus, began what was to become the story of her soul, an inspiration to millions of other souls in the not too distant future. Rather than just recount memories of her childhood, she did what she said she would at the outset. She told the story of God's Mercies on her, and on the whole world.

The reading of her life story can be considered somewhat romantic. The actual writing of it was anything but that. We're reminded of St. Paul's Letter to the Philippians, which is so full of love and joy and hope. We went to the place where St. Paul wrote it, the Mamertine prison in Rome. It seems impossible that such a cheerful, loving letter could have been written in a dingy, depressing place like that prison.

The same would have to be said of St. Thérèse, as she wrote the story of her love of Jesus, from her childhood memories. Her writing conditions were the worst possible, maybe not as bad as St. Paul's, but then again, close. She had to find a writing desk; she didn't have one. They dragged out an old one from the attic of the Carmel. She had a little school notebook, and a scratchy quill pen. She wrote in her little room at night, under the light of an oil lamp. *There were no rough drafts!* She prayed before she began. What we read today in her book, which has been retitled, "Autobiography of a Saint", is exactly what was given to St. Thérèse under the inspiration of the Holy Spirit.

It was good for her to do this; it was *necessary* for her to do this. It gave her cause to reflect on her life, on how the Lord had worked in her life from her earliest childhood. Could it be that what she wrote was dictated to her from above, and that in the writing, the realization of her role in history became known to her? Very often in our own lives, when we look back on seemingly disjointed occurrences over a period of years, we see our whole lives coming together, orchestrated as it were, into a beautiful symphony.

In the book, Thérèse writes,

"This was indeed the mystery of my vocation, of my whole life, and above all the mystery of the privileges Jesus has lavished on my soul."

She finished the first part of the book at the end of 1895. It took six of those little schoolbooks. As she finished each one, Céline read what she had written, and cried, "It will be printed; it will be used."

Thérèse ended the book with the following:

"There, Mother, that's all I can tell you about the life of your youngest sister. You yourself know far better than I do what I am, and what our Lord has done for me, you won't mind my having compressed my life as a Religious within such narrow limits. How is it going to end, this story which I've called the story of a little white flower? Perhaps it will be picked still fresh; perhaps it will be replanted in some distant soil, I can't tell. But I know that the Mercy of God will always go with me, and that I shall never cease to bless you for giving me to our Lord. For all eternity, I shall rejoice that I am one flower in the wreath you have earned; to all eternity I shall echo your song, which can never lose the freshness of its inspiration, the song of love."

The Beginning of the End

We sometimes believe there's not enough room in the body and soul to contain all the Lord will give us if we but ask. While Thérèse's soul was filled to overflowing with the love of Jesus, her *body* was falling apart. The constant coughing, which had always concerned her sisters and Aunt Marie, turned into Tuberculosis.

The first signs of it took place on Holy Thursday evening of 1896. During that night, she felt a strange sensation. She coughed up a warm liquid. She didn't look to see what it was until the following morning, because the lights were out in the Carmel, and she didn't want to break a rule. When it was light enough to see, she found blood on her handkerchief. She was elated to have been given the gift of sharing in the Passion of Jesus.

But her little way, which she had practiced so long, forbade her to tell anyone about her problem. She went around as beautiful and as happy as ever, though she was suffering physically. No one had any idea of what was going on inside her. She wrote poems and plays during this period. As her cough became worse, she tried to cover it up. A time came, however, when she could no longer hide her illness. She was taken out of her cell, and put into the infirmary.

Thérèse became the brunt of sarcastic remarks from some of the Nuns in the Carmel. Mother Marie de Gonzague, whose sieges of moodiness plummeted from bad to worse, from indifference to anger, took every opportunity to cut little Thérèse. Other sisters made statements like "I don't know why they are speaking so much about Sister Thérèse of the Child Jesus; she is not doing anything exceptional. One does not see her practicing virtue. You cannot even say that she is a good Nun."

In the face of all this, fevers, difficulty in breathing, sleeplessness, constipation, gangrene of the intestines, she maintained her attitude of well-being and cheerfulness, so that no one believed she was sick. Even her doctors were confounded by her appearance.

Thérèse had always suffered bouts with her spirituality. She became spiritually dry almost every time she went on retreat. But in this last year of her life, satan's attacks became *violent*. She found herself doubting everything she had ever done or believed in. Her mind filled with fears of having lived for nothing and dying for nothing. *She had thrown away her life on delusions.* Her sleepless nights were filled with suspicion of all that she had ever embraced.

Was her *little way* the right way for her? Should she have instead, been a Priest, an Apostle, a Doctor of the Church? She had always envisioned herself in the missions of Indo-China (Vietnam). The Carmel of Lisieux had a Mission in Saigon and Hanoi; was that what the Lord had been calling her to? Had she ignored what He *really* wanted of her, in favor of this *self-abandonment*?

She wanted to be a Priest; women were not Priests; but she felt such a desire to be closer to Jesus in this way. It was a question that haunted her! She searched for the Lord to answer her through Scripture. She finally found her answer in Paul's first letter to the Corinthians, Chapter 12.

"You, then, are the body of Christ. Every one of you is a member of it . . . Are all apostles? Are all prophets? Are all teachers? Do all work miracles or have the gift of healing? Do all speak in tongues, all have the gift of interpretation of tongues? Set your hearts on the greater gifts."
and then again in Chapter 13,
"If I speak with human tongues and angelic as well, but do not have love, I am a noisy gong, a clanging cymbal.
If I have the gift of prophecy, and with full knowledge, comprehend all mysteries, if I have faith great enough to move mountains, but have not love, I am nothing.
If I give everything I have to feed the poor and hand over my body to be burned, but have not love, I gain nothing."

Thérèse had been right. The *little way* was *her* way. She had peace, at last.

Jesus Touches Pauline, Book Two
When Thérèse finished her six manuscripts of God's Mercies in her life, she sewed them together into one book, put a picture of Jesus, and her coat of arms on the last page,

and presented it to her sister, Pauline. *The older sister threw it into a drawer without looking at it.* Thérèse was visibly hurt, but being who she was, stubborn, she never asked Pauline if she had read it.

Pauline had read it, and was taken back by the depth of spirituality contained in her baby sister. But she never mentioned it to Thérèse. However, in June of 1897, Thérèse finally admitted to her sister that she had been coughing up blood, and how sick she really was. Whereas Pauline was devastated because her youngest sister was dying, the Lord put it on her heart that this wealth of spirituality, bottled up in Thérèse, could not die with her.

She asked Thérèse to continue her writings about her life in the Carmel. Thérèse's natural answer was, "*What will I write about?*" By this time, there was no fear in Pauline as to what our little Saint would write about. The fear was *time.* She went to Mother Marie de Gonzague, who had just been re-elected Prioress of the Community. Using her very best diplomacy, she was able to convince her Superior that Thérèse should write about her life as a Carmelite; this biography to be sent to all the Carmels in the world upon her death. Pauline even suggested that it be addressed to *her,* Mother Marie de Gonzague. That probably clinched it. Pauline was granted permission for Thérèse to proceed.

Actually what happened was that the *entire* manuscript, the *first* which had originally been written to Pauline, and the *second* to Mother Marie, were *both* addressed to the Superior, Mother Marie de Gonzague. Pauline had to swallow her pride to do it, but it was Divine Inspiration. It was the only way it would have been printed after Thérèse had died.

And so, the little flower of Jesus began again, picking up where she had left off almost two years before. Only now it was different. She had a great deal more maturity in her soul, but her *body* betrayed her badly. She just didn't have the strength to put into it all she wanted. She was able to write for about a month. Finally, she realized that she had poured out all that would come out of her. She ended her brief manuscript with the following,

"I'm certain of this - that if my conscience were burdened with all the sins it's possible to commit, I would still go and throw myself into our Lord's arms, my heart all broken up with contrition; I know what tenderness He has for any prodigal child of His that comes back to Him. No, it's not just because God, in His prevenient (anticipating) *mercy, has kept my soul clear of mortal sin, that I fly to Him on the wings of confidence and of love ..."*

Thérèse finally won her battle over her doubts.

Oh! . . . I Love Him! . . . My God I love . . . Thee!

Thérèse suffered a horrendous death, and through it all, she comforted those who loved her. She tried to be as little trouble as possible. She finally had to give up denying her torment, because it was just too obvious. Her body was riddled with gangrene. Her bones protruded through her emaciated skin. She had open bed-sores. She fought to maintain her cheerful attitude. She was victorious to the end. During the last few days of September, 1897, her sisters, her relatives, all the members of the Carmel were praying the Lord would end her torture. The only one who seemed to have any *patience* with the ordeal was Thérèse. She waited for her Lover to come for her in His time.

Late in the afternoon, on a rainy September day in 1897, Jesus the Lover, came for His Little Flower. Her face became very calm. She was young again; she was beautiful. Thérèse looked up at the Crucifix. She spoke her last words,

"Oh! . . . I love Him! . . . My God I love . . . Thee!"

A Shower of Roses

Thérèse died on September 30, 1897. Pauline was allowed to have Thérèse's autobiography printed, to send to all the Carmels in the world. This was not unusual in a sense; the custom was to publish a short biography of a member of the Community. In this instance, because Thérèse had written this beautiful account of her life, *and* because it was dedicated to Mother Marie de Gonzague, Pauline was able to push it through. It took a year for the book to be printed. When the two thousand copies arrived at the Carmel, the comment that ran throughout the Convent was *"Whatever will we do with all these? We will surely have them left on our hands."* That was a gross overstatement.

Almost immediately the supply of books was gone. Requests came from Carmels all over the world for more. Thérèse's Autobiography began to be *lent out* to people outside the Carmelite Community. As a result, requests for the book on the little Carmelite began pouring in from Priests, laity, Religious of other Communities; it seemed like the whole world was catching the fever of Sister Thérèse. Just prior to Thérèse's canonization, over four hundred thousand books were in circulation. Within ten years of her canonization, over *two million* were in print.

Her prediction *"I will send down a shower of roses!"* came about, almost immediately. Wherever her name was mentioned, wherever people had her little book, wherever petitions were sent up to the Saint, *miracles* occurred, usually accompanied by the reception of a flower. Physical healings, spiritual healings and conversions were credited to the intercession of Sister Thérèse. Burned-out Priests came back to life. Missions in far-off places were given renewed energy. All of this was attributed to the Little Flower of Jesus. And it has never stopped!

Thérèse insisted the Lord had work for her to do. She had always felt that she would do more good in Heaven than she had done on earth. She told her sisters,

"God would not give me this desire to do good on earth after my death if He did not want to realize it . . .

If you knew what projects I have in mind, what I will do with things when I am in Heaven. I will begin my mission.

If God grants my desires, my Heaven will be spent on earth until the end of time. Yes, I will spend my Heaven doing good upon earth . . .

I will return! I will come down!"

Above left:
Les Buissonets
Thérèse's Home

Above right:
Thérèse - age 14
When she went
to see
the Bishop

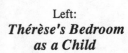

Above:
Thérèse's Toys

Left:
Thérèse's Bedroom
as a Child

Left:
***Mother Thecla
Co-Foundress
Daughters of St. Paul***

Right:
***Daughters
of St. Paul
Book Ministry***

Left:
***Bob & Penny
at
Daughters
of St. Paul
Metairie, LA***

Mother Thecla Merlo

Co-Foundress of the Daughters of St. Paul

"I want to become a Saint at any cost, only for the greater glory of God."

God uses all the tools in today's world to spread the Kingdom. *He* created the means we use to communicate; why shouldn't He take advantage of them? Through Mother Angelica, He has tackled telecommunications, and the Word is spread all over the world by means of *television* and sophisticated satellites out in space. Sister Briege McKenna uses *Ma Bell*, the *telephone*, to pray with people thousands of miles away, and the Lord heals them. And *then* there is Mother Thecla Merlo, co-foundress of the Daughters of St. Paul. She was a pioneer in bringing the Word of God to His people through the *written word*. From unbelievably humble beginnings, setting type and printing Diocesan newspapers in a remote section of Northern Italy, the Daughters of St. Paul have developed a major network of communications throughout the *world*, by way of books, films, television videos and audio cassettes. Wherever the Word of God needs to be spoken, in whatever language, by whatever means, the followers of Mother Thecla Merlo can be found.

The Lord takes us to Alba, a small town in Northern Italy, south of Turin, on the road to Genoa. By the world's standards, Alba is not one of the highlights of Italy, but to the local people, who are extremely proud of their town, it's very important. It is the birthplace of a Roman Emperor, Pertinax, who ruled towards the end of the Second Century. The town is known for its *tartufi bianchi*, white truffles, which are searched out and found by dogs specially trained in a white truffle training school near the town. The main attraction of Alba is its wine market. It also boasts one of *only* five schools of the study of wine in Italy. But for our purposes, Alba is a town blessed by the Lord. The Lord has sent us there to seek out a *powerful woman* in our Church.

The Theologian and the Seamstress

There was a young seminarian studying in Alba towards the turn of the century. His name was Giacomo (James) Alberione, and he had a Vision. He felt inspired to do something for his brothers and sisters in the new century, the Twentieth Century. As the world moved forward to a new era, Fr. James said a special prayer. He asked the Lord to use him in a powerful way. By the year 1915, he was moving according to the Lord's plan. He had said "Yes" to the Lord, and he was being used mightily. God fed more ideas into Fr. James' heart each day than most people experience in a lifetime. Fr. James needed *time* and *people*, and the strength that comes only through intimate communication with God.

The people of the town insisted he would never live long enough to see any of his grand dreams accomplished. He was tubercular, much too sickly, they thought. He *probably* agreed with them, which was another reason for his urgency. He had the ability to see great potential in people. He saw this in a young woman from a nearby village, Teresa Merlo. The Lord put Teresa in his path, and let it be known to Fr. James that this could be the one to help him build his Community. But the Priest didn't present it to her in that manner. He did not want to cause confusion. He told her he wanted her to help him teach girls how to *sew*. She was an excellent seamstress. This did not seem very threatening to her. *She said yes.* Then he said something vague about, " . . . *later, there will be printing, and furthermore a Congregation of Sisters working with the good press."* This latter part was said to the girl almost as an *"Oh, by the way,.."* not really important. But we can see that he had his Vision mapped out. *Teresa* was to be the one to build with him.

And while Teresa didn't understand completely what he meant, she knew the *Lord* was calling her to this.

Teresa was born in 1894, which made her about twenty one at the time of the meeting with Fr. James. She was a pretty girl, but also frail and sickly. She was a very spiritual girl from a very religious family, due to another *strong woman* in our church, her mother, Mama Vincenza. Both Teresa and her brother Constanzo were raised in a very strict religious manner. Constanzo had a vocation to the Priesthood, which he fulfilled.

Teresa wanted to be a Sister, but her poor health proved to be a stumbling block not once, but twice. After her first attempt to enter Religious Life was unsuccessful, because of Anemia, she was told to go home, take tonics and the right food, and then come back. Mama Vincenza filled her with all the best food to build her blood. But when she went back the second time, her health was diagnosed as worse than the first. It was recommended that she give up any ideas of entering Religious Life. The Lord had another road for Teresa to travel. She would have probably made a very good Sister with the Community she chose, the Sisters of St. Benedict Cottolengo. But that was not the plan the Lord had for Teresa from before she was born. She was unhappy about the rejection, but she accepted it. The Lord sent her back to her home town of Castagnito, to open a sewing school and teach Catechism, both of which she excelled in. This was to prepare her for Fr. James Alberione, and the new Community the Lord had chosen for her.

During the time that Teresa was going through the process of trying to enter a Religious Order, Fr. James moved ahead boldly with the Apostolate the Lord had burned into his heart. He knew the way to reach the greatest amount of people was through the press. It was so influential at that time, it was called the *Fourth Estate*. To his way of thinking, however, the journalists in Italy were *morally* ignorant, or spiritually *bankrupt*. He felt a need for a Religious Congregation whose sole work was the press. When he said "Press", he meant printing presses, and typesetting equipment. He got some used machines, and old metal type, and began his Apostolate with two young boys in a beat-up building in the center of town, and called it a printing school. Everybody thought he was crazy, but he could see his Vision beginning to unfold. At the outset, he brought in experienced printers and typesetters to teach his young apprentices their craft. But within three years, he had his *young people* working the presses themselves *efficiently*!

He felt the need to bring *women* into the Apostolate. He knew there was a place for them in Ministry, other than in cloistered Convents. He thought of St. Catherine of Siena, who had worked out in the world. Why couldn't he have women working for the Apostolate of the Press? He believed they could bring a femininity and sensitivity that was greatly missing. *He did not see the role of woman as being less than man.* There is so much work to be done for the Lord. He saw women and men side by side as Apostles in the Lord's new movement. He was so convinced of the contributions women could make to his Apostolate, he wrote a book entitled *Woman: Her Influence and Zeal.* Some of the teachings he gave to women in this book are purely *prophetic*. It was as if he were writing for the women of the 1980's or 1990's, rather than those of the 1920's.

> *"The women of today must be better instructed in the Faith than the women of past centuries. She must have a greater degree of foresight into the objections and difficulties that the faith of her child will encounter in the world. She cannot throw him into the midst of ravening wolves like a defenseless lamb; she must arm him with an instruction that is more complete."*
>
> Woman: Her Influence and Zeal

Because of his attitude, as communicated in his writings, the Lord sent him a small group of young women who expressed an all-consuming desire to be part of a new and modern movement.

Our Priest knew the Lord wanted him to begin a strong *Catholic* Press, but even *he* had no idea of the magnitude of the Lord's plan. However, he was a "Yes" person, and so he moved right along with Jesus' plan. He enlisted the aid of a local woman, Miss Boffi, to house the group of women who would work at the little sewing shop he was going to set up. Initially, their job was to sew shirts and uniforms for the Italian soldiers, fighting in World War I. These women were to eventually work their way into the Good Press Ministry. Miss Boffi didn't quite know what Fr. James was doing, but she *trusted* him, even though many in the town thought him a bit *eccentric*. However, Miss Boffi worked long hours at her job, and couldn't properly supervise the girls. That's when the Lord placed *Teresa Merlo* in Fr. James's path.

It's exciting to see things in hindsight. It's almost as if we can see with God's eyes. Here, we see Teresa and Fr. James following the Lord's plan, moving in different directions, only to have them meet on June 15, 1915, when Fr. James would ask her to join his group, and Teresa would say "*Yes*". Our Lord Jesus doesn't force anything on us. We have free will. But if we are *yes* people, the Lord has such great plans for us. It's so rewarding to be in the Lord's Ministry. The amazing thing about it is that we never know just what we're saying *yes* to. We're sure that neither Fr. James nor Teresa had any idea of the enormous Ministry they were walking into. They just said *yes!*

The little Ministry began to build quickly. As the war waned, the women spent less time sewing *shirts*, and began sewing *books* together. That was the method used for bookbinding in those days. Without being aware of it, they were beginning to work in the *Apostolate of the Good Press*.

Although the printing was done in one building, and the sewing in another, they were fulfilling Fr. James's Vision, men and women working side by side for the Lord.

But this also caught the attention of others in the little village, who had nothing better to do than look for things to complain about. They chose Fr. James's Ministry as their target. What were *men and women* doing working together? Did this Priest intend to have women working with ink and presses? Influential people complained to Fr. James's Bishop, Bishop Re, which fell on deaf ears because the Bishop knew Fr. James well, and was much more aware of the Apostolate of the Good Press than people thought. When that didn't work, their complaints went directly to *Rome*. However, Bishop Re was well thought of in Rome, so the complaints had no impact there. Not to be defeated so easily, the critics of the Ministry took the matter to the *state* authorities, but the Lord still triumphed in the end.

However, there were some touch-and-go moments that were cliff-hangers, when the little band of Apostles were not sure if they would be in existence the next day. Fr. James never hesitated for a moment; he barreled ahead. He knew he was doing the Lord's work, and the Lord would be triumphant. Bishop Re trusted the judgment of Fr. James. On the *Feast of the Immaculate Conception,* December 8, 1917, as part of his homily to his group, Father James said,

"I know that before coming to this house each of you heard criticism against it. Many of you had to fight real and serious opposition. Such trials are necessary to keep us humble and to remind us that God is the only One in charge.

"We frequently speak of promoting the good press. Now, some people are already working for this, devoting a part of their time and energies to this end; some for honor, some for gain, some for enjoyment. We want to work neither for enjoyment, nor for honor, nor for gain.

But by means of the good press, we seek the glory of
God and the reign of Jesus Christ in society."

It was during this time that the first book center
opened. The sewing school moved to a different location.
The ladies made some religious articles as well as the
soldiers' shirts. Books from the press found their way into
the center. The Diocesan newspaper from Turin and the
Daily Missal were available for sale. Teresa Merlo was in
charge of the book center. This little space in the sewing
shop was to be the prototype of the first of the book centers
of the Daughters of St. Paul, which would grow to be called
today, *St. Paul Book and Media Centers.*

The beginnings of the Daughters of St. Paul were
unusual, in that some of the girls who joined the women's
sewing shop, and later the typography shop, which printed
Diocesan newspapers, parish bulletins, etc., were not aware
they were in the process of formation for a *Religious Life.*
They thought that by entering the Institute, they were
enrolling in a *private school*, from which they would emerge
seven years later, carrying a teacher's diploma. Therefore,
they either loved it, if they were answering the call, or they
hated it, if they were *not* answering the call. *Teresa* knew
why she was there; a few others of the early joiners knew.
But many only realized it when they observed the *example* of
Teresa and the few committed girls.

Fr. James felt the most important job for the women
was to form a strong Community before doing anything else.
While it's true that he had an urgency for them to work in
the Apostolate of the Press, that had to be secondary to
forming Community. He once said to them,

"The most fortunate young women to whom God has
given the singular grace of forming the first nucleus of
the Congregation, must above all seek to be hidden, to
root out any ambition, to cultivate a deep spirit of
humility, of sacrifice, to seal their hearts with the most

pure love of Jesus, - in a word, to be His immaculate and generous spouses."

A moment of truth came for Teresa and her little band of compatriots. After the war, the Bishop of Susa, a little town on the Italian-French border, asked for the sisters of Fr. Alberione's group to come to his Diocese to do the typesetting and printing of his local Diocesan newspaper. *Panic set in!* Were they ready? *Were they capable?* Father James thought so. Teresa thought so. But they had to *convince* the rest. They made the decision to go. Without being aware of what the Lord was doing, this was the first time the men's group and women's group were separated. It was during this time that Fr. James began the formation of the male members, calling them the *Pious Society of St. Paul.*

The original group of women went to Susa, with Teresa in charge. Some important milestones were made during that time in Susa, away from their families and friends. The first book center, named after St. Paul, was opened there. It was called "St. Paul's Book Center." There was a portrait of St. Paul in the center. The local people began referring to the little band of Sisters as "The Daughters of St. Paul," which seemed natural enough, as they worked under the protection and inspiration of St. Paul. The name stuck.

Getting out the first issue of the newspaper , called *La Valsusa*, was nothing short of a miracle. The equipment the Sisters had to work with was more dilapidated than what they were used to in Alba. The people contributing articles to the newspaper were not used to *deadlines*. The Sisters had to work around this. But through much prayer, and Teresa's determination not to fail the Lord and Fr. James, what with working late into the night and near calamities, *two weeks after they arrived,* the newspaper was printed. A Priest, Canon Chiesa, who had worked with them on their spirituality at Alba, wrote them a congratulatory letter.

"You did a fine job. See how fortunate you are. In such a short time, you have mounted a pulpit to teach an entire Diocese! What preacher in the Diocese of Susa can boast of an audience as large as yours? You preach the Good Word to everyone. . . But remember that the Word must be enlivened by the Spirit, and put this Spirit into every word you compose, every page of the paper that you fold or address."

What a prophecy this Priest made! They were truly mounting a pulpit for the Lord. When have women been able to take on the role of preacher before? And who had ever had as large an audience as theirs? There was such power in what they were doing, spreading the Word of God through the Newspaper, contradicting the bad news of the secular press with the *Good News* of Jesus.

We must insert something personal here. For many years, our Ministry has attempted to put out a newsletter to the more than 25,000 people on our mailing list, who have read our books, seen us on television, been at one of our lecture series, or been on pilgrimage with us. We began it in 1984, but it proved too expensive, and took too much time away from our other duties. We stopped printing it, but we never forgot it. Then this year, some months before we began research on Mother Thecla Merlo and the Daughters of St. Paul, we felt the need to resume printing of our newsletter, which we call The Good Newsletter. Through a gift the Lord gave Brother Joseph, we were able to get a computer and laser printer capable of doing typesetting, which was one of the greatest expenses we had incurred in putting out our periodical. But we still had a major obstacle to overcome. How could we print 25,000 Good Newsletters even four times a year? The best estimates we could get were into the tens of thousands of dollars per issue. We just didn't have the finances.

Then the Lord spoke to Penny. Why not make it an actual newspaper, using newspaper format, and printed on newsprint? We contacted our local secular newspaper. They agreed to print it at a fraction of the cost we had anticipated. Brother Joseph only had the computer three days when we began typesetting the first Newsletter. The Holy Spirit instructed him how to use it. We spent many nights folding and labeling the Newsletter, our hands black from the ink. We sorted, bundled and banded frantically. We had such an urgency to get it out to the people.

In the Spring of 1989, our first Good Newsletter was sent out. The response from those who received it was overwhelming. We receive hundreds of love letters every week. The Lord has touched the hearts of thousands of people through this newsletter. We had no idea the power it would have. Especially in our time, when nobody reads anymore; they all watch television. We share about Church, the Saints, Mother Mary, and Miracles of the Eucharist. We have begun a column for pilgrims to share their experiences, and testimonies from people whose lives have been changed as a result of reading our books. Luz Elena writes a column in Spanish. We get requests for extra copies to leave in the vestibules of Parish churches. The Lord is working so powerfully.

Then we began this chapter on Mother Thecla Merlo, and the beginnings of the Daughters of St. Paul. The parallels are so strong between how the Lord directed them and how He's directing us. It tells us so many things, but the most important thing we've learned is that Jesus has a plan, and He's working His plan, and if we say "yes", we're a major part of that plan. Praise You, Jesus!

Back to Teresa Merlo and her band of printers. After a successful two years in Susa, they were summoned back to Alba by Fr. James to undergo formation for the Community. He had visited them often in Susa, but knew that it was just a

matter of time before he would have to give them intense
training. The formation had to be on a daily basis, rather
than spasmodic. It had to be peaceful, but rigorous. He had
to instill in them the knowledge that theirs was to be a
radical sign among Religious Communities. It was to be
different from any other group of women doing the Lord's
work. They had to go out *into* the world, rather than *retreat*
from the world. *They had to be in the world, but not of it.* Fr.
Alberione's Vision of what they were to be was so much like
what has evolved since Vatican II.

After Fr. Alberione had gathered the group who had
returned from Susa, he gave them a retreat, at the end of
which nine young women made their religious vows, one of
whom was Teresa. They were given the title, *Maestra*,
meaning Teacher, but so much more. Teresa was given a
new name, Thecla, in honor of the first disciple of St. Paul,
whose name was Thecla.[1]

At that time, Fr. Alberione installed Maestra Thecla as
the first *Superior* of the Daughters of St. Paul, with the
following words; *"From today on, Maestra Thecla will be your*

---

[1]St. Thecla - Butler's Lives of the Saints describes St. Thecla as a
flamboyant heroine of the early Church, a maiden who, inspired by the
preaching of St. Paul, and his discourse on Virginity, broke off her
engagement to be married, which caused St. Paul to be scourged for
trying to discourage virgins to marry, and wives to leave their husbands.
Her life is full of close calls with death by fire, by wild animals, by packs
of soldiers, always being saved through Divine Intervention. She is best
known for having died to her senses, so that nothing remained living
except reason and the Spirit. After a separation from St. Paul of many
years, tradition has it that she went to Rome, and upon discovering that
St. Paul was dead, went into a glorious sleep, from which she never
awakened. She is said to be buried a short distance from her master,
Paul. While there is no concrete proof that she actually existed, she is
referred to by such distinguished early Fathers of the Church as *Sts.
Augustine, Epiphanius, Ambrose and Gregory of Nyssa.* Her feast day is
September 23, *Penny's birthday, who was originally baptized Pauline.*

Superior General. I have appointed her for twelve years, and after that you yourselves will see to the matter."

The Infancy of the Apostolate

Mother Thecla's was truly a unique mission. She was to be the faithful interpreter of Fr. Alberione's Vision for the Daughters of St. Paul. She had to form the girls into responsible members of the Community. This was particularly challenging considering that most of the young girls were *country girls*, who had no experience or knowledge of printing. *Patience* was the key here, and much *love*. She had to ease the girls the Lord sent to serve Him, into the book-bindery operation, while at the same time keeping their spiritual development up front in her mind. As is the case with all the Lord's Ministries, they were just a *remnant*, a small band of disciples, and there was so much to be done. The valiant group worked into the night to accomplish what their lack of numbers could not.

Mother Thecla took upon *herself* responsibility for everything that went wrong, including the lack of vocations. She was too hard on herself, but when she saw that it was affecting her band of disciples, she stopped browbeating herself. However, her main goal from that time on was to *build* the numbers of her Community.

In that first year, 1922, Fr. Alberione made a prediction. *"The production and diffusion (dissemination) of the Gospel is your specific mission. There will come a time when you will distribute thousands and millions of copies of the Gospel to people of every nation and tongue. God has prepared great things for those who are faithful."*

Had the Lord given this Priest a Vision of things to come? Did he have any idea in 1922, of the vastness and scope his Apostolate would take in the next three-quarters of a century? Whether he knew or not, the Lord used him and these sisters in a powerful way, under the direction of Mother Thecla Merlo.

The Daughters of St. Paul Go Door-To-Door

It seemed, especially in those early years, that everybody in the Pauline Society, both the men from the Pious Society of St. Paul, and the women, Daughters of St. Paul, were wearing roller skates. They moved so quickly, taking advantage of every opportunity, depriving themselves of rest and sleep, all to get the Apostolate off the ground. It's difficult to believe, but their ongoing stream of motion *attracted* people to them, especially those who also *burned* to do good in this unique mission. Add to that the fact that Mother Thecla was never satisfied with the number of Sisters she had. She knew how much work there was to be done, and there would never be enough people to do it. In addition, every time Fr. Alberione got a new inspiration, Mother Thecla had to provide the bodies to make it happen. The following is a perfect example of how that came about.

In 1925, Fr. Alberione decided it was time to leave the nest. The first group of men went to Rome, to set up printing facilities and distribution centers there. They were followed almost immediately by a group of Sisters. They worked together, taking shifts to get the various periodicals, Gospels, and lives of the Saints printed and distributed. The Community in Rome began to grow rapidly. It was not without sacrifices, however. The facilities were not that good to begin with. The sisters rented a farmhouse that was too small. Some of the members had to sleep in a barn that had gaping holes in the roof. When it rained, they had to find dry spots in the barn to sleep on. But the spirit of adventure and love of their mission kept them going.

Meanwhile, back in Alba, the Community supported their fledglings in the field with prayer and new ideas. One of these was to come in 1928. After a frenzied three years of production, refining techniques, adding new equipment, the production *finally* exceeded the demand. They were printing more than they were distributing. A Marketing Plan was needed. Who else should give it to them but the Holy Spirit!

At that time, the most effective and least expensive way of selling merchandise in the secular market was door-to-door. Fr. Alberione saw the wisdom in this method of distribution. When housewives were so used to salesmen peddling pots and pans, beauty aids, brushes and etc., what a relief to see two smiling Sisters approach their door, to share the Word of God with them. It was an immediate success. We must give at least part of the credit, however, to St. John Bosco. It was about the time of his Canonization. What would be more of a natural to distribute among the people than a book on the life of this *powerful Saint*? Using Don Bosco as *a leader*, they were able to distribute many lives of the Saints all throughout the Diocese of Alba.

This approach worked so well that a group of Sisters were dispatched to Verona to do the same. At about the same time, the Daughters of St. Paul in Rome began going door-to-door. As their father in Faith before them, St. Paul, they were out to conquer the *Big Apple of Italy* (Rome) for Jesus. And their work was blessed mightily by the Lord.

Fr. Alberione and Mother Thecla saw the Lord's plan unfold in what would seem to be a natural evolution. When two young Sisters were sent out to far-off places like Messina or Catania (both in Sicily), Foggia, Bologna, or Genoa, and on and on, they carried a supply of books with them to disseminate door-to-door. They would ask for lodging with a local Religious Community until such time as they could afford a flat of their own, nothing pretentious, just a roof over their head where they could stay warm and dry, and where the books would be protected. Then they asked for more books to be sent from Alba. They went door-to-door evangelizing with books and periodicals, to support themselves, and also to get enough money to open a book center. While doing all this, they had to go to the city authorities to get proper permits to open a center.

Now, we must keep in mind that these were not women of the world. For the most part, they were innocent girls from the mountainous region of Alba. All they really knew in advance is what they were supposed to accomplish. They had no idea of the obstacles they would encounter on the way. Another thing is that it was not the norm to see habited women walking the streets, much less engaging in enterprise, even if it was for the Lord. They were the targets of much criticism from local busybodies, but they kept trudging along until they had accomplished their goal. One of their first goals was a Bible, or at least a Gospel in every home.

What made it work? How were these disciples able to leave the nest, go into foreign surroundings, and live and work, with only each other to turn to for companionship until such time as more women would be sent from Alba? These were not business women. They were servants of the Lord. We have to believe that the ingredients that made it work were *attitude* and *relationship*. From the beginning, these sisters were taught that they were under the tutelage and protection of their namesake, St. Paul. His journey was one of traveling to distant places to build Church, making relationships, and leaving *loved ones* behind. He spent his life looking back sadly on those he was leaving, and at the same time, looking forward enthusiastically to those he would encounter. Without the tireless efforts of St. Paul, the Church as we know it today, would not exist. His was an attitude of selflessness, complete *Self-Abandonment* to the Lord. We believe the Daughters of St. Paul were following his example, when he said, *"Imitate me, as I imitate Christ!"*

The other great strength these sisters possessed was *relationship*. Long before Vatican II, and the sweeping reforms that took place in *Religious Life*, the Daughters of St.

Paul acted as a Sisterhood, rather than a Hierarchical structure. While it's true that there was *headship*, and Fr. Alberione and Mother Thecla were the *heads*, the relationship was never one of masters and servants, but more of parents and children. The trait that Fr. Alberione saw in Teresa Merlo in 1915, that she probably was not even aware of, was her ability to *parent*. She was *in charge*, and there was no doubt of it in anyone's mind, not by anything she said, but by how she *loved* her daughters. They were her daughters, and they were dear to her. The Community embraced that relationship, and down through the years, even today, almost 75 years later, there is such a *love relationship* between the Daughters of St. Paul, you can't help but be drawn to them. Mother Thecla has certainly done her job well.

Father Alberione Spins the Globe

That Fr. Alberione was a visionary, goes without saying. He envisioned what would happen in Italy at the turn of the century. He put his plan into effect, knowing full well he was just following the Lord's directive. And it worked! In early 1931, he was asked by the Sacred Congregation for Religious to give an account of the Daughters of St. Paul and the Pious Society of St. Paul. He wrote the following report:

"In these years the Daughters of St. Paul have visited all the parishes in 246 Dioceses (he enclosed the list). A good number of Bishops have encouraged them, insisting that they visit the parishes of their Dioceses. The fruits of this Apostolate have been many. We recall some: the moral-religious periodicals of the Pious Society of St. Paul now have 1,300,000 subscribers all together; approximately 3,000 parish libraries have been set up; in addition, 600 parish bulletins are being printed and diffused; over 1,000,000 copies of the Gospel, the Letters of St. Paul and the Life of Christ have been printed and diffused; 50,000 copies of the Family Bible have been printed, and four new

editions are being printed right now. Every year, 600,000 copies of various lives of Saints are diffused among the families. A number of Bishops have requested the presence of the Daughters of St. Paul. This little good, which we would like to see multiplied in accordance with present-day needs, is for the most part the fruit and merit of the Daughters of St. Paul, who are invested with the same spirit as the Pious Society of St. Paul; spreading the doctrine of the Church by means of the press."

When Fr. Alberione put these figures together for his report, he had to come to terms with what he was saying. For the Daughters of St. Paul to have visited 246 Dioceses in Italy meant that 80% of Catholic Italy had been touched by this network of St. Paul. *Where do we go from here?* It was at that time he began *spinning the globe.* For any normal person, this would not seem that unusual. Many people are pictured sitting in their offices, spinning the globe, while they ponder on important things. But with Fr. Alberione, the spinning of the globe *was the important thing.* Unlike others who spin the globe, Fr. Alberione would stop at a given point, and search it with his finger. That can be scary!

One of the first hints we have that he was seriously considering the expansion of the two Congregations *worldwide,* came during informal talks with some of the men of the Society of St. Paul. He felt them out by sharing the potential they had in the rest of the world. They asked, with a lump in their throat, if he was planning his expansion for this generation or the next. He smiled, and told them, on the contrary, it would happen in a *short* time.

On August 20, 1931, the first two Priests of the Congregation arrived in Sao Paulo, Brazil, to begin the first international mission of the Pious Society of St. Paul, and the Daughters of St. Paul. Fr. Alberione's Vision was very pure. They were not to take part in any normal kind of missionary work. They were to *focus* on the Apostolate of printing for the various Dioceses, as they had done in Italy. In a letter he sent them just a few days after they left, he said,

> *"You will spread the divine word with the Press. Do not conduct a business but a spiritual business....Do not operate a commercial industry, but be very industrious for the salvation of souls....Do not look for money, but for everlasting treasures....I know you are good for nothing, but neither would I want you to believe yourselves capable of anything. I would fear this; I fear it now and will continue to fear it."*

He finished his letter with his favorite saying, *"Woe to the one who thinks himself capable."*

Within two months, the first two Sisters of the Daughters of St. Paul arrived in Sao Paolo, against the advice of the male members of the Pious Society. The men had written Fr. Alberione, asking him not to send *women*, because the Bishop was opposed to having them there. However, they forgot that Fr. Alberione was working on orders from a Higher Source; He knew what He was doing.

This sudden acceleration, on top of the breakneck speed at which the Pauline movement had been working from its inception, caused more manpower problems. It wasn't as if they had all these men and women waiting in the wings, chomping at the bit, anxious to get out into the field. Mother Thecla had to find suitable people, especially for such a delicate mission, as setting up overseas houses. She had always seen the problem of not having enough people to do the work. As the movement grew, she was in a constant quandry as to where to get people to man the new houses, or the type foundry, or the book centers, or wherever else they were needed. *The senior Sister who went on the first overseas mission to Brazil was only twenty-one years old, and had made her final profession three weeks before she left for Brazil.*

However, Mother Thecla knew her job, and trusted in the Lord to provide the people for it. She felt somewhat apprehensive about sending her Sisters so far away. They were an extremely close-knit family. She loved them so deeply. But again, the Lord and Fr. Alberione knew what they were doing. Thecla was a "*Yes*" person. She could not do other than to follow that "*Yes*", and so she sent her Sisters, two by two. In the ten months from the time the first group went to Sao Paolo, houses were opened in Puerto Alegre, Brazil, and Buenos Aires, Argentina.

During that same time, a Priest was sent to New York, to initiate the first *house* in the United States. He ran into a blockade from the first. Finally, the only way the Archdiocese of New York would sanction the Pauline movement in New York was for them to minister to the *Italians* in that city. They adapted an attitude that St. Francis of Assisi was famous for, "*If you can't get in the front door, go in through the back door.*" On June 17, 1932, the first two Daughters of St. Paul set sail for the United States. Mother Thecla's love for her Sisters is illustrated in a letter she sent these two before they left Naples for New York.

"I send you my best wishes, my wishes that the new land to which you will go and in which you will live may be your field of labor for holiness - your own, first of all...Don't be discouraged if you don't see the good you do. Most of the time people are helped through obscurity, through hidden sacrifices, instead of the fervor of a clamorous Apostolate.

Above all, let us try to lay aside our own ego, for this is what ruins everything. And then, certainly, the Lord will come, and with Him things will accomplish themselves, or rather, He will accomplish them.

If you want to keep peace and charity among you, let each one be willing to take blame. I beg you, for the love of our Lady, forget the examples of lack of fervor and self-sacrifice your Superior has given you. I ask your charity."

On June 28, these two Daughters of St. Paul, one of whom was Mother Paula Cordero, who is still living, arrived in New York harbor. The United States was locked in the great Depression, but the Sisters were able to find a little apartment in the Bronx. More Sisters arrived, and by October, 1932, there were *five*.

They began receiving invitations from Pastors in New York, New Jersey and New England to make visitations in homes of the parishes. The sisters brought inspirational literature, and sometimes took the parish census as well.

On October 1, 1936, Fr. Purificato of St. Anthony's Church, Herkimer, New York, wrote,

"I am most pleased to state that your good Sisters have been in this parish for some time. They have accomplished a twofold mission: namely, the distribution of Catholic literature, and through their zeal they have also brought back to the Church many families. Be assured that I appreciate their good work and I will always welcome them to this parish."

Within a few years, Daughters of St. Paul and members of the Pious Society of St. Paul were to leave for all parts of the world, including China and Japan. Mother Thecla gave *all* the same advice, to form a Community of love before all else, and strive for holiness with all their energies. She told them that it was nothing to go to the ends of the earth, even though this was extraordinary; it was nothing to set sail for the most distant continents, even though this was praiseworthy; *what counted was to live in charity towards one another so the Apostolate would be more fruitful.*

She told them that without their commitment to *religious* perfection, their Apostolate would have no effect; an Apostolate could only germinate from consecration, as a stream flows from the spring that is its source.

As the Pauline society grew, especially in Rome and overseas, it became obvious to all that the headquarters should really be in Rome. Fr. Alberione was the first to move his headquarters, and that of the Pious Society of St. Paul to Rome. Shortly thereafter, Mother Thecla followed suit, and moved the headquarters of the Daughters of St. Paul to Rome also. It didn't really matter where Mother Thecla was headquartered. She was to spend the next few years following in the footsteps of her father in Faith, St. Paul, *on the road.* But it was easier for her to make connections from Rome than from Alba, and although her *heart* was in her hometown, her *soul* was in her Apostolate, and that was now in Rome. All of this took place in 1936.

Mother began *visiting* her Communities. She had not seen most of the Sisters since they had left Alba for their distant voyages, to set up houses and book centers in various parts of the world. Although she had always answered all letters from her Sisters almost immediately, the personal contact was necessary. For the Sisters' parts, they were happy to see their Mother General, and share their accomplishments *first hand* with her, including new members from the countries they had adopted.

Mother Thecla always made it a point to determine if her Sisters were suffering too much. Their spiritual and physical health were her most important concern. And while the Sisters could not determine, out of loyalty to the Community, whether the house they lived in was too ramshackle, or if the equipment had to be replaced, Mother Thecla had no problem making decisions of that nature. She knew that they needed the most modern equipment to do the Lord's work. She was the first to make all her sisters learn to drive, get licenses, and use automobiles in the Apostolate as soon as they were practical. The Daughters of St. Paul were the talk of all the towns they inhabited, driving those big automobiles. But it didn't bother Mother Thecla, and so it didn't bother them. Besides, they could more easily transport their books from place to place.

We keep mentioning dates, because while the 1930's saw the greatest success in pioneering of the Pauline Society in such places as Italy, France, China, the United States, Brazil and the Philippines, those years also heralded in the most despicable period in the history of the world, the rise of Adolph Hitler, and the onslaught of World War II. Shortly after Mother Thecla returned home from the United States in May, 1937, international travel was banned until the end of the war in 1945. Two things flashed in Mother Thecla's mind; the safety of her Sisters in other countries, and the need to communicate with them. She made these her priorities during the war years.

While it would be impossible to think that a little thing like a war being fought in their own back yard could stop the motion of the Pauline Society, we must admit that the wheels slowed down considerably during that time. Priorities became basic; feeding, housing, surviving, and helping others to do the same. Mother Thecla could not recognize uniforms; she only saw children, *God's children.* As she approached them, she brought out the love on both sides. She saw Nazi soldiers who didn't want to kill anyone, and her own Italian brothers, who, though branded *Fascisti*, had no more idea of *why* they were risking their lives in the war than their German counterparts did.

Mother Thecla hid and protected Italians who were being hunted by the Germans; on the other hand, she soothed the Germans who came in search of the Italians, by feeding them, and ministering to them. When Cassino and the great Benedictine Monastery of Montecassino were in imminent danger of being destroyed, she took thirty Benedictine cloistered Nuns into her house, fed them, clothed them and sheltered them. When the Allied troops marched close to Rome, and the German soldiers retreated, she took one of the empty houses next door to hers, and outfitted it for the Benedictine Nuns to have as their own.

She had two favorite sayings during the War years; *"God will provide"*, which He did, and *"The Blessed Mother will slap away all the bombs,"* which she did. We have such *vivid* memories of the near-starvation the Italians went through during and right after the war, and yet Mother Thecla was able to give to all who came to her doors. While it's true that some of her sisters had to make midnight trips to Bolsena to get potatoes, chestnuts and other food, the Lord never let her down.

We're not sure if her thinking after the war was that they had lost so much time during the war they had to work triple time to make up for it, but her attitude and movement would make us believe so. She not only went into high gear right after the war, but looked for all modern means to get the job done faster and better. She contacted a motorcycle manufacturer to make a model that would accommodate two Sisters and bags of books. In her own words, *"Let us motorize the Sisters, so they may go about doing good."*

Now we know that Mother Thecla came from Alba, way up in the north of Italy, and we know that Mother Angelica's family came from Reggio di Calabria, in the deep south, but there is so much in common between the thinking of these two Sisters, they could be sisters. In the late forties, there was no television so to speak, but there were *films*. The Society of St. Paul and the Daughters of St. Paul, under Mother Thecla's tutelage, began a *film company*. They made films that were either catechetical in nature, or at least had moral values, to try to *counteract* the anti-Christian movies coming out of Hollywood or Cinecitta Studios in Rome.

This turned out to be one of the most ambitious undertakings of the Pauline society. For one thing, it was extremely expensive. Mother Thecla, always supportive of Fr. Alberione's new ideas, took it upon herself and her Sisters to finance the whole program. In addition, it was very *technical*, in an area where The Daughters of St. Paul were completely inexperienced. In an effort to give moral support to her Sisters, and also to be sure that everything was done according to Fr. Alberione's wishes, she spent much of her time on location with the filming crew. She even went in front of the cameras on occasions when a group of Sisters were needed in a scene.

Mother Thecla's philosophy on how to best operate the Apostolate has been carried out down to the present day.

". . . that we must always use the more modern means to do good; our constitutions, too, say this. Therefore, we must always be up-to-date in our activity, always progressing with the times."

In her ongoing pursuit to bring the Word of God to His children through books, and then films, Mother Thecla launched a new program in 1954, which was to bring Audio-Visual aids into the Apostolate. Records and filmstrips were instituted as a means of teaching, especially the young. Mother Thecla became very enthusiastic about this program. When one of the Sisters questioned her about the advisability of this, thinking it was going backwards from the progress they had made with the Catechetical films they were making, Mother Thecla corrected her.

"Oh no! This means of communication is widely used, especially in Catechetics, for the picture can be held in place and explained well until everyone has understood the lesson. They are both needed. We must also think of people who do not know how to read and those who cannot afford to buy a 16mm projector."

The late forties and a good deal of the fifties saw Mother Thecla traveling from country to country, house to house, visiting all her Sisters. During these times, she made the car she used, sort of a *traveling Convent*. In order to keep their focus and their spirits up, she led them in prayer, sang hymns, read from the Gospel, and told stories of the lives of the Saints. She had nothing but praise for the Sisters in the foreign houses and centers. This spurred them on to greater accomplishments for the next time she visited.

Mother felt the ongoing need for more vocations

She struck deals with the Blessed Mother to increase the number of vocations in any given month. On one occasion, she told her Sisters,

"We have to ask for them (vocations), ask them of the Blessed Mother with faith. Let us ask her to send us twelve vocations this months - twelve, like the Apostles. Tell the other Sisters too, and have faith. Nothing is impossible to the Blessed Mother."

Our Lady, not to be undone, gave them *fifteen* that month, for the fifteen decades of the Rosary. During a visit to the United States, Mother Thecla challenged Mary once more. She said to her sisters,

"Look for new candidates. The Blessed Mother is obliged to send them, since we have promised her the Queen of the Apostles Shrine. Let us have great trust in our most holy Mother."

On her way back to Italy that year, she made a side trip to the Cova da Iria in Fatima. She had a long conversation with Mary at the Shrine where she had visited the three children in 1917. We don't know what deals were struck between the Mother of the Daughters of St. Paul, and the Mother of God. The gist of the conversation was that Mother Thecla was looking for *hundreds* of vocations to fill all the needs of the Daughters of St. Paul throughout the world. She knew Mary could do it. P.S. *Mary did!*

Vocations abounded. New houses opened all over the world. The Bishops of the world had seen by this time, how important the Daughters of St. Paul were to their dioceses. Letters poured in from the farthest corners of the world, inviting the Daughters of St. Paul to this country or that. Bishops gave them their initial living quarters in many instances. They always worked within the framework of the Apostolate, though they were obedient to the local Bishop. But the Bishops wanted what they were offering. The family magazine which had been instituted before the Second World War in Italy, *Famiglia Cristiana*, became *Familia Cristiana* in Spanish, *The Family* in English, and on and on. Wherever they went, they continued to bring the people the same things that had proved so successful in Italy.

Mother Thecla was never one to decline an opportunity to do something for the Lord through His children. Although she spent most of her time on the road, when she was asked to do *just one more thing*, she threw herself into it with all her energy. At such times, when there was so much to do, she slept less; when worries attacked her, she spent more time on her knees in front of the *Blessed Sacrament*.

The growth of the Daughters of St. Paul all over the world was nothing short of *miraculous*. We read of Mother Thecla flying to the four corners of the globe, setting up houses and book centers, visiting those in existence, and planning new ones. Yet this little band of disciples grew rapidly at breakneck speed. How were they able to do it?

One incident that took place in India gives us a key to the ongoing success of the Daughters of St. Paul. Fr. Alberione and Mother Thecla went there on their way back to Italy from a trip to Australia. There they found that the first candidate from India had entered the Congregation there. Fr. Alberione looked around at their housing facility. It was much too small. He told them, *"You need larger quarters."* He suggested they look for a larger house to accommodate new candidates which were sure to come.

Mother Thecla answered softly, *"Yes, but the means are lacking,"* meaning they didn't have enough money to get larger quarters.

He looked at her incredulously. *"And what about faith? Is it possible that one can reason so humanly?"*

Mother Thecla immediately picked up on this, thanked Fr. Alberione, and said to the Sisters, "*Did you hear what the Founder said? Let us have faith!*" This became her pet phrase from that time on. Whenever things were low, and they were very often that way, her constant comment was "*Have faith!*" It was as if her Vision were somewhere else other than here on earth. She was given the gift of seeing the priorities and the end of the tunnel.

During her thirteenth trip to visit the various houses of the Daughters of St. Paul around the world, she was in the United States. The Superior in charge of these houses, Mother Paula, was sharing the difficulties of managing the huge province of the United States. Mother Thecla made a statement which just about wraps up her entire outlook on her life, and that of her daughters. She said,

"*There are difficulties, sufferings and worries; however, you have seen that there are many sufferings in Rome too....But one beautiful day it will all be over, and we will find ourselves all united in Heaven with the Blessed Trinity, with Mary most holy, with our dear ones and with the Sisters who have gone before us. This is our joy and our comfort. Courage!*"

We want to talk about the times we hear "*Whenever things were low*", or "*When worries attacked her*". These are just one-liners, but a book could be written about them. We're writing about the growth and success of a Ministry of God, so we don't burden ourselves with the negatives. This whole book could be written about the obstacles that were thrown in the path of our *Powerful Women in the Church*. There were so many negatives, they would have *destroyed* the dreams and ambitions of people with less vision and faith in the power of God.

Mother Thecla always *lived on the edge*, going from one crisis to the next, thanking the Lord for handling all of them, because she knew she could not on her own. However, her faithful servant, her body, which had worked double time for almost fifty years, began to break down. It is inevitable for all of us. But when a vibrant, alive person such as Mother Thecla starts to show her mortality, it's a sure sign from the Lord that all of us are just passing through this life. She had major surgery in 1957, which took two years out of her traveling schedule. She worked during this time, but not with the same intensity as before. Even when she did get back on the road, tiredness crept into her days. *But there was so much to do, and so little time.*

Our Lord gave them a warning

In June 1963, she was to suffer a cerebral spasm. It was so severe they thought they would lose her the day it happened. She was given the Blessing of the Sick. But her strong Italian stock, plus the fact that the Lord wasn't finished with her yet, enabled her to survive it. However, she was to suffer a painful death by degrees for the next seven months. God is so good! Had Mother Thecla died suddenly that June, the Community would have been in a state of shock, because so much was dependent on Mother Thecla. Our Lord knew how important the work of the Daughters of St. Paul was, He didn't allow that to happen. Almost immediately, the major work that Mother did was delegated to others. In addition, Fr. Alberione and the members adjusted themselves to the fact that she would not always be with them, something they had never considered before. They would not have wished her the suffering she had to endure, but Our Lord gave them a warning, so at least they were ready for it when it happened.

In the last days, her body had completely fallen apart. She was emaciated, but her eyes beamed with joy. She was viewed by all as having gone so deep into contemplation, she was in another place. It was almost as if her soul had left her body to experience the glories of Heaven, only to come back when she was in the presence of people. She smiled broadly, although she had to be in excruciating pain.

On February 5, 1964, Mother Thecla Merlo gave up her body and soul to her Savior, Our Lord Jesus. She was surrounded by her Community, with the beloved Founder, Fr. Alberione, the one whom nobody thought would live through the 1920's, standing by her bedside, weeping. She suffered terribly. Her Priest spoke to her softly.

"Mother Thecla, offer your life for the Congregation. Offer your life and all your sufferings, that all the members will be Saints." And with that, she died.

Mother Thecla left behind her a wealth of inspiration for her daughters. *She was a contemplative in action.* This is very important in that her action resulted from her contemplation. *Her daily hour before Jesus in the Blessed Sacrament was her food, her source of energy, from which the action came.* Without that *strength*, nothing could have been accomplished. The Daughters of St. Paul around the world all make an hour of Adoration daily. *It is their powerhouse also!* There are many today who would discount the value of prayer before action; indeed many who believe that prayer won't get you across the street. Thank you Jesus, we have in Mother Thecla, a perfect example of the awesome power of prayer. By all standards, secular and religious, *Mother Thecla was a winner!* She leaves behind her a powerful witness in her Community, spread to the four corners of the earth. And *she always gave the credit to Our Lord Jesus in the Eucharist.*

Mother Thecla has been given singular honors by the Church. But the greatest signs of her accomplishment on this earth are those she leaves behind to continue the work she began with Fr. Alberione in 1915. Her Community has grown in great proportions. But the numbers have never taken precedence over quality. *They are the most beautiful and dedicated women we have ever met.* The attitude and relationship she instilled in the women she has touched, has been the greatest witness to that.

Our first personal experience with the Daughters of St. Paul, the sisters who followed in the footsteps of Mother Thecla, was in Metairie, Louisiana. We were selling our books to their center, and we set up an autograph party there in the Fall of 1987. We had only scheduled a one-hour session, because we were on a tight schedule. One hour became two, and we were inching our way to two-and-a-half hours when our coordinator finally dragged us out of there. *We fell in love with them.* They are so warm, so loving. They reflect the image of their foundress so beautifully, and not just to us. For a lot of the time we were signing books, and we couldn't take time to talk too much. It was at this time that we could see them interacting with the customers, with their children. How many babies they lifted up, and hugged and kissed. We were also able to witness their attitudes and relationships with each other. That is the true sign of Community, *how they love one another.*

When things slowed down somewhat, we went into a little room they had in the back, prepared with cookies and coffee. Someone would call us out front if we were needed. We were able to share with them, and better yet, they shared with us. There was such love and joy among them, not just for us, but for each other. There is a Chapel in each of the St. Paul Book and Media Centers. The Blessed Sacrament is there in each of these Chapels. We felt a great peace, leaving the professional aspects of the center behind us, by just entering into the Chapel, and talking to Our Lord Jesus.

We returned to the St. Paul Book and Media Center in Metairie, Louisiana in January 1989. The faces had changed somewhat, as the Sisters move around a lot. But the feeling of love, the attitude and relationship were very much the same as during our previous visit. We promised that the next time we go back to Louisiana, we will spend the evening with the Sisters, giving a talk *just for them* on the power of Jesus in the Eucharist, as if they need it!

We visited the St. Paul Book and Media Center in San Antonio, Texas. The Sister in charge is named Sister Thecla, after their Foundress. Again, we found the joy and love that Mother Thecla inspired in her followers. People enjoy going into their centers, just to inhale some of that love. There are only two things we must warn you about in advance. Both things stem from trying to follow in their Foundress' footsteps. One is they are terrific salespeople for Jesus. We never go into one of the centers that we don't come out with our arms loaded with books. But then they have such beautiful books! The other thing to watch out for is if you have a young, unmarried girl with you. They believe that every single girl is a candidate for the Community. Every time we bring Luz Elena Sandoval with us, we can see the minds of the Sisters working. They want to recruit her for the Daughters of St. Paul.

We've seen this kind of love before in Communities of Sisters. The first was the cloistered Community of St. Clare of Montefalco, in Italy, which we touch on in another chapter of this book. The second was the Sisters of the Monastery of Our Lady of the Angels, Mother Angelica's Sisters, in Birmingham, Alabama. The third was in Little Rock, Arkansas, when we were privileged to spend an hour with the cloistered Community of Carmelites there. And the last was a group of cloistered Poor Clares in St. Cloud, Minnesota.

We love Our Lord's little contradictions. These women are such living proof that Communities dedicated to Our Lord Jesus, especially where the Blessed Sacrament is the Focus of their Community, can thrive. They have the secret which so many other women are searching for, *and it's not meant to be a secret*. It's there in the Blessed Sacrament. If you've given up on adoring the Lord in the Eucharist, try it again. *If you haven't tried it, don't knock it until you do!*

†

Prayer

Most Holy Trinity, Father, Son and Holy Spirit, we thank You for having created, redeemed and sanctified Your humble and faithful servant, Sister Thecla Merlo and for having constituted her Mother and Co-Foundress of the Daughters of St. Paul who are consecrated to the Apostolate of the mass media of communication.

Deign now to glorify her even here on earth, granting us, through her intercession the grace we ask of You....

O Mary, Mother, Teacher and Queen of the Apostles, support our plea with your maternal intercession. Amen.

Glory be....Hail Mary....

(With ecclesiastical approval)

Anyone who receives graces and favors through the intercession of Mother Thecla Merlo is asked to send this information either to:

REV. MOTHER GENERAL
FIGLIE DI S. PAOLO
Via San Giovanni Eudes, 25
00163 Rome, Italy
or to
REV MOTHER PROVINCIAL
DAUGHTERS OF ST. PAUL
50 St. Paul's Ave., Boston, MA 02130

Daughters of St. Paul
Above: *Working in Television Ministry*
Below: *Working in Printing Ministry*

Left:
***Mother Angelica Gives
Spiritual Direction***

Right:
***Mother Mary Angelica
of the
Annunciation***

Left:
***Mother Angelica
& Mother
Veronica show
Bishop Thomas
Toolen her
Plans for the
Monastery***

Mother Angelica, Alive!

"My only fear is that I may have passed up an opportunity the Lord has presented me."

"I just see God wants me to do something, or God permits something in my life, and it doesn't enter my mind to say, 'Why?'"

Mother Mary Angelica of the Annunciation

In the eyes of the world, the power behind Eternal Word Television Network in Birmingham, Alabama, is a huge white satellite dish in back of the studios. Large white pipes contain the cables which send the message from the studio to the satellite dish, beaming it up into the sky, to a satellite in space, spreading the Word of God all over the world. It has an awesome look of power about it.

But the energy force which feeds life into the studio, the cables, indeed, into everything that lives and breathes at EWTN is another White Sphere, much smaller in size, but much more powerful, located inside the Chapel. *It is Our Lord Jesus in the Eucharist.*

Mother Angelica maintains that the overpowering force that has made things happen in Birmingham since 1962, the Monastery, the Community of cloistered Sisters, their printing press operation, and on a much grander scale, the only Catholic Cable Television Network in the world, is the *Eucharist*, the Lifeblood of everything.

While the world knows this woman as a down-home, straight-shooting, tell it like it is, caring but outspoken television personality, who bucked all the odds to create a Catholic television Network in the suburbs of Baptist Belt

Birmingham, the Sisters in the cloister know her as their spiritual mother, their teacher, their friend, their *role model*. And although Convents are closing up all over America, the Sisters of Our Lady of the Angels Monastery are alive and well and growing under the tutelage of this powerful woman in our Church.

Everyone who has touched and been touched by this lady has their own story to tell. How I met Mother Angelica; what Mother Angelica said to me; how Mother Angelica has been a part of my life. Our story is no different. The Lord has worked in our lives through Mother Angelica, and we will never be the same.

The Mother Angelica we know and love

Our first encounter with Mother Angelica was a good friend making the suggestion, "Why don't you go on 'Mother Angelica Live!' with your book, *'This is My Body, This is My Blood, Miracles of the Eucharist'*?"

We had never seen Mother Angelica or EWTN as we were not privileged to receive her on our cable, but we had heard many good things about her. We also had no idea how we would go about getting on Mother Angelica's program.

One day we just *happened* to see a copy of a book order that had been sent to Mother Angelica's Nuns at Our Lady of the Angels Monastery in Birmingham. We called and who should we speak to but Sister Antoinette. The patron Saint of our book ministry is St. Anthony, her patron Saint. We asked her if Mother Angelica had read our book, to which she replied, *"Yes, Mother has read your book and made it available to the Nuns."*

"Do you think there might be a possibility we might be able to go on Mother Angelica's TV program?" we asked Sister, not daring to hope. Sister told us to pray!

Our answer came at a time when we thought our world was coming to an end. It was late 1986. Terrorism had struck! Nobody was going on pilgrimages, and we were broke. All we had left was our house, and *it* was in jeopardy. Through the grace of God and some of His earthly Angels, we had published our first book, *This is My Body, This is My Blood, Miracles of the Eucharist.* We were receiving just enough orders to keep us afloat day by day, but *just day by day.*

As part of our ongoing financial crisis, the phone was turned off because we had failed to get our payment in on time. We called the Telephone Company, told them the check was in the mail at which point they promised they would turn the phone back on at 1 P.M. The minutes ticked away *slowly* into hours. The sounds of silence were deafening. *Finally*, at noon, the phone rang . . . .

"Hi! This is Lori Andrews of EWTN. Would y'all like to appear on Mother Angelica Live! and talk about your book?"

Sometimes, we judge God waits until the eleventh hour (or is it the twelfth), but He is there for those who trust in Him! The whole idea of living on faith was fairly new to us. We weren't used to it yet.

EWTN sent us our plane tickets and we were on our way! A slight, freckle-faced, red-haired girl, filled with the Holy Spirit, met us at the Birmingham airport. When the beaming smile spoke with a familiar Southern accent, we knew this was Lori Andrews. After we unpacked at the guest house we were going to stay in, Madonna House (our Mother Mary telling us she was there with us), the three of us started out for the Network.

The grounds proclaimed Church! On a hillside in front of the Network there was a statue of Mother Mary surrounded by Angels.

I shared with Bob, "We're home! Mother Angelica feels the way we do about Jesus and His Mother."

"Don't get excited," he answered in his inimitable Irish way, "statues don't mean anything, just as buildings don't a Church make. Let's wait and see!"

"Would you like to stop in the Chapel before going to the Network?" It was that Southern voice again.

As we entered the Blessed Sacrament Chapel, Bob and I went down on our knees and as if a powerful hand pressed us downward; we were prostrate before our God, our King. There He was, our Lord Jesus in His Blessed Sacrament in a shining, gold-plated Monstrance. *He was here and we were home!* We were in love with God and His people and they were here at EWTN.

Later that day, when Lori Andrews was asking questions about our book, coming to a truth about our belief in the Eucharist, we asked her, "You are Catholic, aren't you?"

To which she answered, "No. I was hoping you wouldn't ask that. I didn't want to stifle you."

That evening on television, we said to Mother, "Suppose Lori hadn't *known* about the belief we hold as Catholics, that in that golden Monstrance was Jesus Christ, Body, Blood, Soul and Divinity? What would she have thought, that we were prostrating ourselves before a golden idol? We never told them, our brothers and sisters of other faiths!"

And here we were, Bob and I, on live television, not only telling our brothers and sisters who were *not* Catholic about the Heart of our Church, the *Living Jesus,* but our brothers and sisters of the Roman Catholic Faith, some of whom have had doubts in the Real Presence of Jesus in the Holy Eucharist. God bless Mother Angelica! Before we were two minutes into our interview, she was generously asking us back to do a television series based on our book, *"This is My Body, This is My Blood."*

On that first program we did with her, she shared this incident.

"Every morning, after Communion, I pray, 'Let everyone who passes this Chapel on the highway, feel Your Presence.' Well, one day, two women came down and asked my mother, Sister David, who was an extern Sister by this time, 'What kind of place is this?' She replied, 'It's a Monastery.'

They said, 'The funniest thing happened when our car got to the driveway; we felt, well, just a feeling and when we passed the driveway, it went away. And so, we've been going back and forth for about an hour. When we pass the driveway on this side, it leaves. When we return (to the driveway), it comes back. When we go, it leaves again.'"

Mother Angelica continued, *"Sister David brought them into the Chapel and said, 'This is our Chapel and that's Jesus.'*

The women asked, 'Where?'

Sister David went up and showed them the Monstrance where Jesus was. The women knelt down and said, 'We feel the same Presence!'"

Mother Angelica is a voice bringing Christ's Love to a world starving for love, proclaiming His Word to the hopeless giving them hope, calling God's children by a new name, lovable and loved. When Mother opens her programs, you are reminded of St. Paul. She speaks to her *family*, to the family she never had. She tells them she is so glad to be back with them and how much she missed them, her smile radiating her love for them. We have compared her to Mother Teresa. *Mother Teresa's work is to provide a happy death for the poor in body. Mother Angelica's is to provide a happy life to the poor in spirit.* Here is a woman in our time, faithful to the promise she made to her Spouse Jesus, to love His children as He loves her.

Who is Mother Angelica?

Mother Angelica is a Nun, a foundress, an adorer of the Blessed Sacrament. This is her mission and all stems from that love she has for our Lord Jesus in His Body and Blood, the Holy Eucharist.

We remember the first time we heard that Mother Angelica spent a minimum of five hours a day in prayer. Looking about this huge complex, this Network that brings the Good News to millions of the faithful of the Catholic Church, we foolishly inquired, "Then how does this all come about?" only to be countered with, "Mother and the Nuns pray, and Jesus in the Blessed Sacrament does the rest."

Why do people love you, Mother Angelica? Is it because you are a true imitator of Christ, speaking simply, directly, at times strongly, but always lovingly? Bob likes to call your teaching on the Word of God "Cracker-Barrel Bible Study", like a mother would tell her child on her knee, maybe the same way Mother Mary explained the Scriptures to her Son Jesus. Is this why, so often, when giving talks, sharing with the many people around our country, Mother Angelica, I slip and call you Blessed Mother? Now, I can hear you right now,
"I'm not Blessed Mother, hardly," your eyes shining with the love you have for the Mother of God.

"It's always painful to *really* love!"

Mother Angelica was born to John and Mae Rizzo on April 20, 1923, in Canton, Ohio. They named her Rita Antoinette. Did they name her, as was the tradition of Italians, after grandmothers, aunts or friends? Whatever the reasoning, she was destined to become the modern-day *Saint of the impossible*, like her namesake St. Rita, giving hope to the hopeless; and *finder of lost souls*, like her other namesake St. Anthony, helping those who are lost, find their way back to their mother, Mother Church through television.

Mother Angelica, or Rita, was born of two parents of Italian heritage. Her mother Mae, beautiful and talented, after years of childhood wounds and rejections, felt new hope with this healthy, happy baby. Her marriage which had promised to provide her with the happiness and acceptance she had longed for as a child, had soon turned nasty and explosive. Rita's father, John, handsome and seemingly strong, was to walk out on them when Rita was barely two years old. What with the strain of the poor self-worth Mae had brought to the marriage and the harping, destructive influence of her mother-in-law on their marriage, Mae, along with Rita, found herself alone, deserted, not knowing where to turn.

At the ripe old age of six years, Rita not only faced the trauma of her parent's divorce, but the fear the courts might take her away from her mother to live with the father she hardly knew. Rita the child, came out from hiding upon hearing the words, "We won! Come out. You can live with your mother!"

No home to call their own, she and her mother were to become *the poor cousins*, subjected to living with relatives.

Rita was humiliated by teachers, because of their poverty, she thought. Then she was to discover painfully, it was, instead, that horrible stigma of *divorce*. Rita's grades became worse and worse. She suffered not only in school, but at home, because of irresponsible words spoken by an Italian missionary to Rita's mother, "*divorce is the ultimate sin.*" You've got to remember this was 1929. Divorce was virtually unheard of at this time. If Rita's father had died, Mae would have been a widow, which had a certain respect attached to it. But this was like a black mark for all the world to see. There was no pardon from this sin. The tarnish of divorce was to be one of the worst battles Mae would lose to poor self-worth, something she never got over.

To the end of her life, Mae never wanted anyone to know she had been divorced.

But everybody needs to have a friend, *at least one friend.* Rita and her mother had that friend, Fr.Riccardi, the pastor of the local Catholic Church, St. Anthony's. He reached out to them, embraced them, tried to console Mae in her disgrace, and gave them back some of the self-worth which had been deprived them. They became very close. Mae tried to pay back his kindness and generosity by working at various Church functions. It was the Italian way. And Mae was so happy to be considered a person, a human being, and not an outcast.

The friendship was to be short-lived. Fr. Riccardi became involved in a dispute with the local Mafia, called the Black Hands in those days. They wanted to bury bootleg liquor on the grounds of the Church. He thwarted them at every turn. Their recourse was to have him murdered in a dramatic way, in his own Church during a Baptism.

Mae was completely destroyed by Fr. Riccardi's death. He was their only friend in the whole world. She retreated back into her shell. Again deserted, what did it matter if it was by death, Mae found it more and more difficult to cope. So Rita began the long hard road of becoming *the parent*, a role she has never given up.

Rita and her mother struggled. They worked long and hard hours, barely earning a living wage from their failing Dry Cleaning business. When they were lucky, they took in just enough money to afford (poor as it was) an apartment of their own, and some food to eat.

"I was very withdrawn, very non-caring. I didn't like people. I thought people were just a lot of trouble, and everywhere I went, they caused my mother trouble, or me trouble. I used to deliver the dry cleaning. I drove a car when I was eleven. When I went to the door with the clothes, they would say, 'Well, thank you, honey.

*Tell your mother I'll pay her next week.' I delivered a
car full of clothes and I would come home with
nothing. Then my mother was angry with me!"*

Children can be cruel! Rita saved up her pennies and
treated her *friends* to movies, trying to hold back the hours
and the movies from being over, her *friends* quickly leaving
her, not even calling back a *"Thank you"* or a *"See you later."*

*"I went to school alone. I walked to school; I did my
studies; I came home. I did very poorly, because when
you are in that situation, when you're hungry, cold,
worried about your mother, you can't concentrate on
anything. You don't care about the capital of Iowa.
Who cares! In other words, you are only interested in
surviving."*

As we were interviewing Mother Angelica, we looked
about her office at the Network. Pointing to the numerous
degrees and honors bestowed upon her, hanging on the wall,
we commented, "And look at all these degrees you have
now!"

To which she replied, *"That's God's sense of humor!"*

We asked her if she ever felt despair with her life. Had
the hopelessness, the helplessness ever gotten her down?

"Well," she said, "I think there are different kinds of
despair. There's the kind of despair that comes from the
idea that nothing's going to change, that you're going to be
miserable the rest of your life."

Thinking of all the people who have suffered similar
pain, we asked, "Did you ever think of yourself as junk?"

She recalled, pensively, "No, I never considered
anything. I didn't think, I just survived. Day by day, in the
miserable existence we had, I accepted this as my lot in life.
God and religion and piety were as far away as the world is
round."

We asked, "Did you ever judge people who went to
Church as hypocrites?"

"No, I was so hurt by them, I didn't care. And the Sisters at school, I'm sure I was the cause of much of their antipathy for me. I didn't like Nuns at all. To me, they were the meanest people on this earth. They never seemed happy, except for one Nun.

"When I was a young girl, maybe second grade, one of the Sisters sent me over to the Convent. I knocked on the door and this Nun opened the door and looked at me. I could smell food and I hadn't had any lunch to eat that day. She looked at me and asked, 'Are you hungry?'

"I answered, 'Yes, Sister.' And she brought me in. She gave me a bowl of something, like a porridge or something.   But to me, it was like chicken and dumplings.   It tasted so good!   I loved that Sister, because she cared. But that's the only one I can think of (that cared).

"Well, next to my grandmother, that is.   She cared. You see, my mother was trying so hard to make it on her own; it was hard.   I could always come home to grandmother. I had a saintly grandmother."

We asked Mother Angelica if her grandmother had been the affirmer in her life.

"She was always there when I was hungry. And when things got bad, my mother and I would always go home to grandmother. We'd stay there awhile; we'd move; we'd go to another rat-infested apartment."

We asked about her father, what were her feelings toward *him*?

"Well, I don't have a father image, you see. I saw my father maybe seven times in my life. I remember one time I went to where he worked as a tailor. He gave me fifty cents. I was supposed to pick up the $5.00 a week alimony (due my mother and me), which was a lot in those days. But what I got was 50 cents! And so when I

*went up to the courthouse (you had to go to the
courthouse), I said, 'There isn't any alimony,' The
clerk said, 'Your dad gave you $5.00 alimony.' I said,
'He gave me 50 cents.' "She said, 'I've got a receipt
here.'*

*"So, he had added a zero! That kind of made me
angry.*

*"The last time I saw him, he came to the Monastery. I
was a Nun. He cried. He came with his sister; I never
knew I had an aunt. I felt sorry for him. He came twice
and the second time he said to me, 'Tell your mother
I'm sorry.' He died a couple of months later."*

We wondered, when Mother Angelica saw him, did she
see any of herself in him. So often, children will look more
like one parent than the other.

*"My mother, when she would get angry, would say,
'You're just like your father! You look like him!' and I
knew I was in big trouble!"*

You're just like your father and I don't love your father.
Therefore, I don't love you. How many children of single
parents hear the words and *only know the meaning behind*
the words.

Even after Mae Rizzo entered Mother Angelica's
Community of Nuns, her anger against her husband did not
change. She carried the wounds of her husband's rejection
until just before she died.

With no earthly father to watch over her, Rita was to
have the love and watchful care of *The Father*, Our Lord and
Savior. One day, as a young girl, when crossing a heavily
trafficked street, tired and a little distracted, she did not see
an oncoming automobile until it was too late to avoid the
speeding, fatal impact. She closed her eyes, waiting for the
worst, when she felt hands lifting her up. Upon opening her
eyes, she discovered herself standing on the median, safe and
untouched. It was her first experience with the protective

love of her *Guardian Angel*. The bus driver who witnessed the event, later recounted the story to Mae. He said it was as if Rita leaped in the air, or had been hurled high above the car and onto the median.

Mother Angelica remembers her high school years as a time of poverty, living in hovels, struggling with too little of what they needed and too much of what they didn't want. Not being able to trust in people who had always lived up to her worst expectations, Rita grew up not knowing how to love, or what constituted love. Her life was rough! She thought God didn't care about her. She didn't care about Him! She didn't care about anyone else. She had no friends; she was a *loner*. Because her mother was always going to commit suicide, there was constant turmoil and heartbreak.

That's very hard for a young girl. We have to wonder how Rita ever got through her young years. We read about children who have been battered physically or mentally, and the effects their childhood has on their adult life. We hear of lifelong anger and bitterness that overpowers the victim, and taints everything that happens in their lives. And yet Rita was not affected. We have to believe that God had a plan for Rita, which could not possibly have worked if she had not gone through these years of suffering. He walked with her, step by step, took care of her and strengthened her with each adversity.

How love was ever able to become a part of her vocabulary is testimony to the Power of God. But it was always there. Even though her mother was in many ways depressed, depressing, contrary, and her love possessive, the child Rita who grew up into the foundress, always believed her mother loved her.

"Now, to me, my mother was a very loving individual.
She worked hard to make a living, which to me, was
proof she cared."

Her mother, not wanting to get hurt again, built up a wall, a defense mechanism, not even allowing Rita to get close to her. Although this had to be difficult for the child to deal with, Rita would talk soothingly to her mother, trying to talk her out of her deep depressions, reassuring her everything would be all right. Rita became the mother image to *her* mother, even before she was to become her Mother Superior.

"My mother was never secure in herself, in anything. She was proud of me in an Italian way, when she would talk to someone on the phone; but on a personal level, I never did anything right, or could do anything right."

We can just picture all the Saints that Mother Angelica has used as role models, hovering over the child Rita all her life, whispering in her ears, protecting her from harm, lifting her spirits when it seemed like nothing was worthwhile. When Rita reached nineteen years of age, St. Thérèse, the Little Flower, was to come very powerfully into her life.

Abdominal pains which Rita had had for years became so severe she could no longer keep them from her mother. Doctors had not been able to alleviate her suffering. Her mother Mae brought Rita to a convert who, through the intercession of St. Thérèse, had been healed of cancer. The Little Flower had only been canonized seventeen years before, and her strength as an intercessor was felt around the world. Rita could sense the overpowering Presence of our Beloved Lord in this room where the convert, Mrs. Rhoda Wise, had been miraculously healed. Mrs. Wise shared the story of her dramatic healing. As Mae and Rita began to leave, Mrs. Wise gave Rita the novena of St. Thérèse to recite for nine days.

Although praying enthusiastically at first, Rita began having difficulty believing the novena would work. Nevertheless, she went through the nine days. During the night on the eighth day, Saturday evening, she was awakened by the worst pain she had ever experienced in her whole life. She thought for sure she would die. Sunday, the ninth day of the novena, upon rising to go to Church, she stood upright, *without any pain.* It was gone! And to this day, Mother has never had that kind of pain in her stomach. The prayer that she says every day is,

> *"Dear Jesus,*
> *Increase my faith, my hope; heal me.*
> *Heal my mind; heal my spirit.*
> *Heal me!"*

This was a turning point in the young girl's life. The healing itself made her aware that there was a *Personal* God and that Personal God knew her, talked to her, and loved her enough to heal her.

"See, I had lived in a hopeless situation and never did anything about it, because it was hopeless. Some things you endure, and some things you live with. If you're born in that situation, you live in that situation. Then, you acclimate yourself that this is going to be your situation the rest of your life. There is never a thought that anything would or could change."

Jesus truly healed her. When He healed her body, He also healed her of all the hurts, all the painful memories; He healed her mind. In the hopeless world she had grown up in, He had given her hope. This was to begin the love affair Rita was to have with the Lord. *He loved her!* She, who would not trust anyone to get inside the hard shell she had hidden behind all these years, was now completely, vulnerably in love with the Lord.

She turned more and more to her Lord in His Word. Mother says now she believes that the Lord was preparing her for His miracles, the miracles He was going to perform in her life. He was asking her to have the faith that her newfound love, Jesus, could do it. And she has never lost that faith or the belief He wanted to do it.

"I fell in love with God and really began to thirst after Him."
Rita began to know success and acceptance in the job market. But somehow, it had no meaning for her. She was drawn more and more to Church. She would meditate on the passion of our Lord as she *daily* accompanied Him, praying the Stations of the Cross. *She had a thought!* A Nun!? Why, she couldn't stand Nuns, their coldness, their anger, their rigidity, their severity. No way, it must have been her imagination. But when the Supreme Lover calls, He plants that thorn into your heart and you want your heart to be united with His. And you are on your way. . . to becoming a Nun!

When Rita stole away to become a Nun, her mother's angry words, "How can you do this to me, leave me all alone!" were to become an ongoing guilt trip for Rita. Mother Angelica remembers, especially during holidays,

"I would call her up. My superior would allow me to call. 'How are you?' I would ask. She either had a cold or pneumonia. She would tell me she'd had a fried egg that day. Here it was Christmas Day. I had a big feast in front of me; my mother is home with a fried egg!"

Helpless, Rita went to her Lord in the Blessed Sacrament, asking comfort for her mother, never thinking to ask for herself.

"Lord, you know I can't comfort her. I've never been able to comfort her. And so I really have to depend on You to do it."

Rita had been accepted as a Postulant in the Adoration Monastery in Cleveland, Ohio. She followed the *little way* of St. Thérèse, scrubbing the floors, washing clothes in the laundry, baking hosts to be used for the Sacrifice of the Mass. She was so happy. She loved the life! Her knees started to swell badly. Her Superiors began to doubt her vocation because Sister Rita was not able to genuflect or kneel before the Blessed Sacrament. Sister Rita tried, but kneeling on those knees, the size of grapefruits, which felt like two sponges, was impossible. Not only was the pain excruciating, but they couldn't hold up her weight. Still, the rule was you had to be able to kneel and if she could not, well . . . .

"Isn't God good?"

"Back in those days, you were a Postulant 6 months." After three disappointments and 15 months, Sister Rita finally was allowed to become a Novice.

"Dear Sister," intoned the Bishop, "you shall no longer be known as Rita Antoinette Rizzo. Your new name in religion shall be *Sister Mary Angelica of the Annunciation*. You belong to the Lord now. God be with you."

The child Rita Antoinette, at birth named after two powerful "yes" Saints, had now been renamed after the greatest of all Saints, of all women who ever lived, the First Lady of our Church, Mother *Mary*. As if that were not enough, with the second part of her new name, "Angelica," she was named after the *Angel* who appeared to Mary, on the occasion of the *Annunciation*, asking in the Lord's Name for that "yes" which was to change the world! Angelica, the name she was given, that of the messenger called to bring the Word of God to His people - was that to be a prophecy of what He had planned for her, her mission of asking God's children for their "yes"?

Sister Angelica's problems with her knees continued. Her Superiors were seriously considering asking her to leave. But in March of 1946, rather than send her home, the Superior of a new Monastery to be built in Canton, Ohio suggested she be sent there. Under normal conditions, it would not have been allowed. First off, she was not fully professed. Secondly, Canton was her home town. Both of these were against the rules. But the attitude of her Superiors was, *What does it matter? If she doesn't make it there, she'll have to leave the order.* Sister Angelica left St.

Paul's Adoration Monastery on her beloved St. Francis' Feast Day, October 4th, for the new Monastery in her home town, Canton. She went to bed that night, and on the next day, October 5th, *awakened to find her knees healed, never to swell again.*

The infirmarian in this Monastery was the same one who had been in Cleveland. When Sister Angelica showed her the healing that had taken place in her knees, the other Sister proclaimed, "*It has to be a miracle. God must want you here.*" Of course! Why not? In her heart, Sister Angelica knew she had a vocation. She had just waited for her Lord to make it happen.

God had a plan for Sister Angelica, but He had to open her up more, free her once and for all from the insecurities of her youth, so that He could set her firmly in the path He had prepared for her from the beginning of time.

"*All the time, as a Postulant and a Novice, I had been withdrawn. But as a young Sister, not yet professed, my superior made me bursar in the Monastery. It meant that I had to take care of the money, be in charge of it, and work with people. I had to call people to get things done. It gave me more contact with people. From the time I knew there was a God, and that He loved me, I was confident that He would take care of everything.*"

That was the catalyst the Lord used to give Sister Angelica the confidence and the ability to get things done. It has been a gift she has continued to use, without which none of what we see today would have happened. In looking back on the events in the life of Mother Angelica, as with many of the women of the Church we're writing about, the Hand of the Lord is so *obvious.* We can see His Plan being executed so clearly. Sometimes it seems as if He's going the long way around to accomplish something, but then when all the pieces fall into place, and the Lord's plan has been realized, we say to ourselves, "*Wow! Yes, that's what He was doing!*"

Sister Mary Angelica of the Annunciation was to spend the next fifteen years in the newly established Sancta Clara Monastery. She would be called to help five of the Novices. Speaking to them of the interior of the soul where Jesus lives and how much He always wants to be with them, slowly all the bitterness and resentments they had felt, caused by the old ideas of Monasticism, started to fall away. Our Lord used everything she had ever suffered, all the hurts, all the wounds to help other Novices who came into the Monastery. With her kindness, persistence, and her innate ability to see beyond masks put up in defense, she was able to form the Novices into a family, a Community. She kept this little band of Nuns going, counseling, loving, guiding them with the books of such great Saints as St. John of the Cross, Teresa of Avila and Catherine of Siena.

But she was always to know physical pain. One day Sister Raphael noticed that Sister Angelica was limping very badly. Sister Angelica confided she had fallen on a soapy floor while using a commercial scrubbing machine. She recounted how the heavy cord had become entangled under the large brush, causing the machine to spin wildly, flinging her against the wall. Although the damage was not noticeable at first, it had aggravated a spinal birth defect and she confessed she was losing the use of her left leg altogether. No longer able to hide the pain, Sister Angelica was placed in a hospital for observation.

After four months, all the methods, painful and futile, having failed, the doctors decided that a spinal fusion was the answer. The night before the operation, the surgeon announced coldly, matter-of-factly,

"Sister Angelica, we're going to operate on your spine tomorrow. There's a fifty-fifty chance you'll never walk again, so in the morning, if you can't move your leg, don't be surprised. Good night." And with that, he turned on his heels and walked out.

After all the hell she had been through, what with braces that had not worked, with plaster casts on again, off again, standing up, then bending over to eat, her stomach upset, lying on her back, then lying on her stomach, no sleep, no eating, no help, was there now no hope? She prayed; she pleaded, "Jesus, if you let me walk again, I'll build You a Monastery in the South."

The next morning, after the operation, she wiggled first the toes on her right foot, then on the left. *She would walk!* The doctors had decided not to do a spinal fusion, but to remove an extra vertebra, hopefully allowing the curvature of the spine to straighten out. After more pain, more braces, crutches, tears and torment, Sister Angelica walked!

Now she had to focus her attention on the deal she had made with the Lord. She hadn't known why she had said, "in the South," but she had, and once having struck this agreement with the Lord, she started to dream of the new Monastery. She confided her promise to the Lord to her Mother Superior, who, having seen the leadership of Sister Angelica, granted her permission to begin *"when the time is right."*

"Someday we'll build our own Monastery, Sister"

The dream to build "a Monastery, where every Sister's one desire will be to love Jesus and to grow in union with Him, to be one family and share everything in the manner of the early friars around St. Francis," began to unfold. Some of the Sisters began to think of ways to help support the Community, like Sister Joseph sewing Altar linens, and Sister Raphael sketching faces of Jesus from different parts of the Gospel (which we have seen, and they are inspiring).

Sister Angelica became Mother Angelica, having been elected to the Council to advise the Mother Abbess on matters of finances, vocations, etc., along with five other Councilors.

The first step to founding a Monastery is to find a Bishop who will allow a cloistered Community of Nuns into his Diocese. According to Canon law, the Abbess of a newly founded Monastery must be at least forty years old and her vicar thirty-five, so since Mother Angelica and Sister Raphael, who was to be her vicar, were not of age, they needed special permission from Rome. They obeyed and waited. While waiting for the necessary permission from Rome, they started to look for ways to raise money to start their Monastery. *Fishing worms!* Mother Angelica found her first lead in Popular Mechanics. She had spotted an ad for making money by raising *fishing worms*.

"Reverend Mother," (Mother Veronica, who had become Abbess) Mother Angelica asked, *"may I order a hundred earthworms? We can raise them in the basement and sell them to fishermen to raise money for the new foundation."*

When Mother Veronica blanched at the prospect of having worms crawling all over the basement, Mother Angelica read further and came up with another idea.

"We could order artificial lure parts, put them together and sell them to fishermen."

Mother Veronica, breathing a sigh of relief, not only consented, but made the initial investment of five dollars for a sample kit. They were on their way!

A friend printed brochures for them and financed the purchasing of a mail list of 2000 fishermen, and the mailing went out. They waited patiently for responses. All they got was two replies. To the eternal optimist, Mother Angelica, who had expected at least 1,999 orders, her eagerness turned to disappointment. She and the Lord were not on speaking terms.

"How could He do this?" she would say incredulously. *"After all, it was for Him. I can't even look up at Him when I go in the Chapel."*

As if the Lord were saying, "There she goes again, that little Italian Nun born without patience. But what can I do, I love her,"

One day she received an envelope from Our Sunday Visitor. Dale Francis, the editor of the Catholic newspaper, sent a copy of the article he had written *about the Nun who would build a Monastery with fishing lures.* He *just happened to be* one of the fishermen who had received her brochure and the idea fascinated him. Orders began to pour in.

Mother Angelica has never been a stranger to pain.

"Pain makes me dependent on God for everything. It keeps me with Jesus. I can't do it without Him. It is a gift, a kind of security to keep me from becoming proud or arrogant or taking credit for what God is doing."

We believe that pain may also be one way the Lord uses to get Mother Angelica to sit still for five minutes, so He can get her attention. One evening, the pain in her leg and back was excruciating, forcing her to retire to her room early, where she had a vision. As she lay in her bed, she could see before her on the wall the entire layout of plans for the new Monastery. She jumped up, completely forgetting her pain. She got little pieces of graph paper, taped them onto a large sheet she had laid out across her bed and traced them. Then she made the electrical plan and the plumbing plan, putting down where each and every sink was to go, each electrical outlet. She cut out little pieces of cardboard and made a model. She put a roof on the Chapel. She placed partitions where she saw the rooms to be, even placed the chairs inside the rooms, everything to the last detail. This was to be the plan for the future *Our Lady of the Angels Monastery in Birmingham, Alabama.* You see, God wanted her to do it, so He put her flat on her back, giving her the necessary time to do it.

Word got out among the Sisters about the new Monastery. Another Councilor, with more seniority, decided *she* would build one. Reverend Mother Veronica, remembering Mother Angelica's promise to the Lord, *knew* the Lord wanted Mother Angelica to do it, but she really had a problem. She made this proposition; each of the two Mothers would write to a Bishop. The first reply would be considered God's Will.

"Y'all come!. . ." Archbishop Thomas Toolen of the Mobile-Birmingham Diocese responded first with these words and they were on their way to build God's Monastery in the South!

Money continued to flow in from the sale of fishing lures. The Nuns of the Canton Monastery (the Community Mother was a part of) agreed to allow Mother and her four Nuns to leave the Cloister, and gave them $50,000 to erect the buildings. Mother was on her way to Alabama, to the Bishop, her model in a box.

After much praying and searching, and more praying, the land was found, 15 acres in Irondale, a suburb of Birmingham, Alabama. The cost was $13,000, the exact amount they had earned making and selling fishing lures.

The Italian people of the city helped, cutting down trees, clearing, levelling the land, anything and everything, when they found out Mother Angelica was Italian. But when they got to know her, they fell in love with her for who she was, just the way Bob and I did, and you did, too. Right?

The Bishop, upon viewing the Monastery partially completed, told them to stop pouring the rest of the foundation. Although he had seen the model and agreed to the plans, he had no idea it would be that big, and he said, "Stop!" He wouldn't give them their own money to continue. But when Mother told the workers, they volunteered to finish the work and wait for their money.

So, from the beginning, God kept opening the right doors and the right hearts. The Monastery for cloistered Nuns was to become the heart of the people of Birmingham.

Was it the Sacred Heart of Jesus, the Holy Eucharist the Nuns and Mother Angelica adore twenty-four hours a day that made these people, barely 2% Catholics in this state, such strong disciples, like those few who stayed with Jesus when everyone else deserted Him?

What started with Joe Bruno's "Mother, I'm going to give you all the food you need for the Nuns for a year. Just come and get it," became, after a year, "Mother, we're not going to stop. As long as I have grocery stores, you can have whatever you need."

What began because another woman, Joe's wife Teresa, asked him *just to go with her to see what Mother Angelica and her Nuns were doing,* has continued to provide the Monastery with all their needs for going on *twenty-seven years.* I believe his stores have grown from thirteen supermarkets to more than five times that, with fifty drug stores to boot. When asked, "Are you still feeding the Sisters?" he answered, "I'd be afraid to stop."

The Monastery of Our Lady of the Angels closed its Cloister doors on May 20, 1962, the Nuns and their Chapel dedicated to perpetual Eucharistic Adoration.

"We trust You, Lord. We know You'll do it!"

Fishing lures were not what the South needed, so the Nuns started to *roast peanuts.* That little business flourished for 3 years until one day the buyer asked for a *kickback.* Mother told him, flat out, they were not going to lose their souls over *peanuts.* The Nuns sold all their peanut roasting and packaging equipment. Mother made a decision never to engage in any endeavor but to spread the Good News of our Lord Jesus Christ. They gave up their lives completely to Divine Providence and the Nuns will tell you He has provided for all their needs to this day.

We asked Mother Angelica if she didn't have the least bit of anxiety, if she didn't hesitate, or catch her breath, or think for just a minute, before she stopped her peanut operation, cutting the Community off from its only source of income? She shook her head. *"Not for a second! I wasn't about to lose my soul over peanuts!"*

There was so much joy in their Community. God was making family. Mother was always bringing out their natural gifts. Her primary action was that they become holy, as they were created by God for His purpose.

"You never read that Jesus *re-made* His apostles. Our Divine Lord used what He found in them and worked from there, grace building upon nature."

She read to them from the Scriptures, feeding them, nurturing them, teaching them how the Word was for them, to *form* them, that they might know Jesus and imitate Him in their everyday lives.

She taught them through the lives of the Saints, citing how their own unique call to holiness often caused the Saints pain and rejection, how Christ had called the Saints through who they were and who they could become. Sister Raphael shared with us how all the Sisters would listen in awe as Mother pulled out so many insights from the stories of the lives of the Saints. It was as if Our Lord Jesus were dictating the words to her.

She would often remind them that in order for someone to be canonized, there must be proof of *joy* in her life. Well, if joy is a prerequisite for Canonization, and we have no reason to doubt it, Mother Angelica will be in Paradise, recognized and canonized, a Saint alongside her two favorite Saints, St. Francis and St. Clare.

†

As we mentioned in the Introduction, we have never written about *living* Saints before. We talk of them often, because we truly believe that these special people are doing God's work on earth. There are times when speaking about people like Mother Angelica that we can't help putting them in the same category as the brothers and sisters before us who have been proclaimed members of the Communion of Saints.

There are so many parallels between the life of Mother Angelica and that of Catherine of Siena and Teresa of Avila. We mentioned previously about how, when we sat with Mother in her office, interviewing her, we saw all these honorary doctorate degrees that have been bestowed on her over the years, although she just about received a high school diploma during her years at school. Her reasoning for these degrees was "*God's Sense of Humor*," which may be so. Yet, in reading the lives of Catherine and Teresa, we note that neither of them had formal educations, but both are Doctors of the Church because of their writings. Both claimed to have been taught by the Holy Spirit. In light of this, we can't help but compare Mother giving credit to God's Sense of Humor, to Catherine and Teresa giving credit to the Holy Spirit. Actually, they're all saying the same thing.

We're all called to be Saints. It's a decision we make. Mother Angelica, Mother Thecla Merlo, and Sister Briege would probably be the last ones in the world to call themselves Saints. On the other hand, we who have so far to go to attain their level of relationship with the Lord, have no problem grouping them with those who have gone before them, their brothers and sisters, the Saints. Please understand that it's *Bob and Penny*, out of great love and admiration for these women, and not Mother Church, who call them Saint.

†

When Pope John XXIII opened Vatican Council II, change started to come about. He was calling Nuns to address the needs of the Church today. So Mother Angelica called a meeting of all the Superiors of different contemplative Orders to hear what their problems were and how they were solving them, looking for input. But ultimately recognizing they had a situation unique to where they had been called to serve, a 2% Catholic area, they knew they had to re-shape their constitution to their own lives.

The Nuns, realizing that in this predominantly Protestant area the veiled faces and grilled parlors had to appear foreboding, petitioned Rome for the necessary permission to modify the Rule. They were granted permission by Rome to adapt their habits to fit more into their environment, and to get rid of the grille, the turntables, and other kinds of separations. *For example, we were interviewing Sister Raphael in the parlor, instead of talking to her through a grille. We were choosing pictures with Sister Grace Marie, seated side by side, instead of passing them back and forth through a revolving turntable.*

Mother Angelica started to write books.

A Josephite Priest, who shall remain nameless, had been persistently *bugging* Mother Angelica to allow him to pray over her for the Baptism of the Holy Spirit.

When her reply, *"I received the Holy Spirit when I was Baptised, Father,"* did not deter him, and realizing *wishing him away* was not going to work, she resignedly agreed.

Sitting her down, he prayed over her. Having finished a few moments later, he started to leave.

She asked, *"Is that it?"*

"That's it," he answered.

"If I had known that's all there was to it, I would have agreed days ago," Mother admonished, a little playfully.

Father just flashed her a big grin, as if he knew something she didn't know, and walked away.

Shortly after this, God put her on her back again, only now she was in bed with a cold.

"I opened my Bible to John, 'In the beginning was the Word and the Word was with God and the Word was

God' . . . . Suddenly, a new experience of the Spirit came over me. When Sister Regina came in with some orange juice for me to drink, I couldn't talk. I got up from my bed, my cold completely cured. I walked back and forth in front of the fountains for some time, pondering on what had happened to me."

It was the week before Easter when she began praying over the Nuns and one by one they experienced a new relationship with the Holy Spirit.

Charismatic groups were springing up all over the country. Questions were being asked by Catholic members of families where loved ones, embracing this new movement, were leaving the Church and joining other denominations. Mother could see what we saw in the infancy of the Charismatic Renewal. The people of God were on fire. They were excited with the *feelings*, the emotionalism, the Gifts of the Spirit. But not being knowledgeable of their own Faith and its tenets, ignorant of the Sacraments and the in- depth spirituality of their own Catholic Church, they were leaving to join the brothers and sisters of other denominations. Mother Angelica began to give her time freely and diligently to groups who turned to her for guidance back to the solid teachings of the Church. She explained how the Sacraments were an essential part of growing in the holiness they were truly seeking.

Mother began to write teachings on Scripture as a guide for lay people to use in their everyday lives. She compiled them into a booklet called *Journey into Prayer*. When she presented the booklet to the committee formed to address the needs of the Diocese, she was shot down, the Bishop laying the idea aside for *some time in the future.*

Mother was crushed, but only momentarily. The Sisters believed in the booklet. So with the Bishop's approval *they* had the little booklet printed locally. One book led to another. *Mini-Books* began to develop when a friend came up with the idea of taking twelve pages of excerpts from the larger books.

When asked how she goes about writing the books, Mother Angelica replied, *"The sentences just seem to form in my mind. When they do, I simply write them down. When the light turns off in my head, I know I'm finished."*

No book has ever been edited. Sister Veronica would type and Sister Raphael would give the manuscript the once over for any possible spelling or punctuation corrections. Three of the Nuns would go over the proofs from the printer. Sister Raphael would design the cover. Now completed, the book was then presented to the Community for their approval, and then it was printed.

People found the books **all over the country,** in airports, in bus stations, train stations, park benches, everywhere and anywhere where people could pick them up. Everyone who came to the Monastery was given books to distribute.

The letters started to pour in, "I was at the end of my rope; I was about to commit suicide when I picked up this little book. I'm going to start over. God bless you," and on and on. We could probably write a book on all the graces received by people as a result of Mother Angelica's Mini-Books.

The Lord spoke to Mother Angelica through the words of the local printer who had been doing all their printing, "We can't do your printing anymore."

A meeting was held at the Community. Mother laid out the problem. *"Unless we print the books ourselves, we won't be able to have them anymore."*

A printing press was bought along with cutters, staplers, and typesetting equipment, at a cost of $13,000.00 with $200.00 in their bank. The barometer Mother used as to what machine to buy was one that had the least amount of switches and gadgets.

Mother and the Community believed in the books and they placed their faith in that belief. But the banks didn't. Her reasoning was simple. *"They've got money, and we need it!"* Mother went from bank to bank, trying to get financing for the equipment, to no avail. But as the machinery was trucking its way towards Birmingham and the Monastery, the eleventh hour God arrived with a $10,000.00 check, via a loan by a friend who just happened to come by *to chat.*

Cameras to make half-tones that nobody knew how to operate, followed with sinks too big to go through the door, but somehow did. Slitting machines were cutting books into sizes the machines could not possibly do. This was truly God's work and He was having fun! The need for books and more books grew, what with the distribution of 150,000 booklets at one Eucharistic Congress alone. They added binding machines, and heavy duty folders. With just enough contributions coming in to cover the cost of printing, there was barely enough to erect a building necessary to house all the equipment and books. But build they did and each week as the workers' wages came due, they had received just enough money to cover them. And so, they lived one day at a time, just as the One they were called to imitate did before them. And it worked!

Mother Angelica never compromised her beliefs. Back in 1979, an Episcopalian asked her to give talks to her group. They would meet with Mother on Monday each week; she talked to them for an hour, and they asked questions for another hour. She was teaching them how to pray, how to cope with life's problems, teaching them about *grace*, the Scriptures, the Lord and our relationship with Him in prayer.

Things were going so well, that although they had planned to come only during Lent, they wanted to continue as an ongoing study. They loved it, were so excited, never wanted to leave, until Mother began teaching on her first Love, the Blessed Sacrament. They couldn't accept it. They couldn't handle the heights of prayer we, as Catholics, are called to. Although they professed a personal Savior, when confronted with Our Truly Present and Personal Savior, they, like the rich young man in Scripture, walked away. And I am sure Jesus was sad for them, just as He was for the young man in the Bible. We like to think that maybe some of these women have been watching Mother Angelica and EWTN; and they are now part of the Roman Catholic Church, fully united with us in receiving Our Lord Jesus, Body, Blood, Soul and Divinity in the Holy Eucharist.

"Unless we are willing to do the ridiculous, God will not do the miraculous."

One morning at lesson she instructed the Nuns, *"So often we toss our ideas to a committee we have in our head and begin to talk ourselves out of everything by reasoning."*

Her philosophy has always been to do God's Will. It's really simple. Is this for Jesus' Church and the furthering of His Kingdom? She gets an *idea* how this can be done. She goes ahead with her plans, allowing God to make them happen. *He* has to open the doors. If they do not open or if they close in her face, well, she goes on to the next inspiration.

God *just happened to get* Mother Angelica an invitation to appear on a television program for an interview. It was a tiny station, but from it came a grand idea.

"I've got to have a television studio."

The Nuns who have gone along with all of Mother Angelica's ideas, even with more than a little trepidation, had trouble with this one. *"A television studio!"* But they believed it was from the Lord and if He wanted it, it was all right with them. They started with a half-hour tape that cost $1000 to produce. It was shown by a religious television network who *just happened* to have been praying for a Catholic program for their network. That one program was to grow into the network's requesting *sixty* more half-hour programs. This was going to cost $60,000 which she didn't have. But that had never stopped Mother before, so . . . .

The Nuns built a set, made the sixty segments, and began taping seventeen more segments, when the local television station whose studio they were using to tape their programs decided to air the controversial, blasphemous movie, "The Word." No amount of reasoning would dissuade the manager from airing this movie which was about the fictional finding of a scroll which claimed that Jesus Christ did not die on the Cross and that the Resurrection was a hoax. Mother never has wanted *anything* enough to compromise her Lord and Savior. So, she advised the manager that if they did not agree *not* to air this movie, she would discontinue her taping with their station.

As Mother Angelica told us, he threatened her with, "You'll never be on television again. There's not a studio for a hundred miles who will touch you. You need us!"

Mother Angelica's answer, *"No, I don't need you. I only need God. I'll buy my own cameras and build my own studio,"* was to lead to the beginning of the Eternal Word Television Network. Ironically, (or God's Sense of Humor) the name that Mother was fighting against, *"The Word"*, became the cornerstone of the Name which she was to defend, *"The Eternal Word"*.

News got out about Mother Angelica leaving the studio and why. She had been the lone program to cancel and stand up for Jesus and His *Eternal Word*. A caller from Florida, upon finding out why Mother cancelled, promised to spread the word among the prayer groups in Florida and that's how the building of that first little studio was begun. *Just enough, just in time* (our Ministry's motto, too), became EWTN's journey. Just enough money would come in each week, just in time, to pay for the labor and materials.

As Mother Angelica and the Nuns got deeper and deeper into setting up a television network, four figures became five figures, became six figures, became seven figures. They were now talking over one million dollars. We asked Mother Angelica did she ever feel just plain scared!

"No, I don't think that anything ever scared me. I think I always thought, from the time I knew there was a God, that He loved me. I figured He always did and He would take care of everything now. Because, see, I've never known the end of the tunnel; I've never seen the end of the tunnel. I just see God wants me to do something, or God permits something in my life, and it doesn't enter my mind to say, 'Why did You do this?' Only one time I did that, and I never did it again. It was here at the Network and everything was going wrong. We were very low on money; banks were after us, creditors; I had a lot of pain. We were just having problems every which way. It seemed everyone was against us, the Church, bankers, lay people, everybody saying we can't do it; this is foolish!"

As Mother Angelica spoke, I could see a sadness unlike anything I have ever seen on her face. It was there; she was fighting back tears.

"So, I went before the Blessed Sacrament; I was very angry, and I said, 'Lord, I told You, I'm not the one for the job. Why me?' And suddenly, as I felt this so deeply, I heard the Lord say very distinctly, 'Yes, and why Me?' I never asked again."

I wonder if this could have happened on that Saturday, when this man called for his monthly payment of $48,000.00 for the transponder (which beams the signal to the satellite in the sky). The Sisters explained that Mother Angelica's mother, Sister David, had died, and they were burying her that day. Not even that would stop the ranting, demanding, threatening, *"On Monday, no money no transponder."*

Day by day, crisis by crisis, met through her faith in the the Lord and His Loving Power, Mother Angelica's Eternal Word Television Network has grown from a few hours each evening to *twenty-four* hours a day. Mr. Joe Bruno and his brother Lee Bruno, have donated a mobile television studio, named appropriately, *Gabriel I,* and a state-of-the-art mobile satellite uplink vehicle named *Gabriel II,* which are enabling Mother and EWTN to go *after* the Catholic news, taping it on the spot, and beaming it up to the satellite. The Lord has called her now to bring His Eternal Word to the *whole world.*

When we questioned Mother with, "Some say you're too orthodox, others too charismatic, and yet others, too fundamental," she replied firmly,

"I am Roman Catholic, and I feel to be Roman Catholic today, you're going to be labelled something. I think a Roman Catholic is fundamental in some areas."

(Author's note: especially in some areas of Scripture, like those pertaining to the Holy Eucharist, which we take literally, as opposed to our brothers and sisters who call themselves Fundamental.)

"A Roman Catholic is liberal (as to different expressions in the Church, i.e., Charismatic Renewal, Cursillo, Legion of Mary, Marriage Encounter, etc.) in as much as they are not tied down to one thing."

(Author's note: A deacon's wife, a convert, said 'One of the things that attracted me to the Catholic Church was that although you could find one or the other of the gifts in each of the Protestant Churches, in the Catholic Church, you have them all, encompassed in the one, true Church.)

"We as Catholics are called to be observant and obedient. I'm a stickler for obedience. I believe in obedience. I believe it's the only thing that works.

"I believe that God has given us a Church and a leader and I think that we follow that leader, and we follow that Church. If it is guided by the Holy Spirit, and I

think it is, in spite of the human weaknesses; which are not a fault of the Church, but those who minister to the Church. If you follow the Church, then you are pleasing to the Lord. I'm not going to spend the rest of my life in disobedience. Now, if there are people who do not believe in the Truth of the Faith, that's something between them and God. But it is my duty to give them the Truth."

At what cost, Mother, or does it matter? Here is a woman in our time who, we believe, does not count the cost.

"I have to answer to God alone. There won't be anyone with me."

We can see Jesus smiling, *You have spoken well of Me, my daughter. Come, enter, I have a special place for you.*

One day, Bob was complaining to Mother Angelica.

"To serve the Lord is not to know any sleep on earth. He keeps you busy twenty-four hours a day, seven days a week."

Mother Angelica first consoled, *"Well, you can rest in Heaven, Bob."*

Bob asked her, "Are you sure, Mother?"

Then she took it back with, *"No, I think God will have work for you there, too."*

Mother Angelica, like St. Thérèse, the Little Flower of Jesus, you will continue doing good on earth. The love you have for your *dear family* will be pouring out even after you are *working* in the Kingdom. We can see you right now, like that other prophet, standing before the Throne of God, "They'll get it yet, Lord. Just one more chance."

We shared how hungry we found our brothers and sisters of the Church, hungry for the Good News and to learn more about their Faith, filling the Churches and halls where we have travelled, bringing them the Love of Jesus in the Eucharist and Mother Mary. People are scared. They don't know anymore if what they hear is the Magisterium, the true teaching of the Church, or someone's opinion. She shared her concern with the wave of modernism and secularism.

"Not only that, but there's New Age. It's New Age here in the United States, and Islamism in Europe. The Moslems are taking over."

When we talked of our concern about how many people were being fed this New Age philosophy without knowing it, she interjected,

"Because I think at least the Network is there and growing, and people can get the Truth if they want it, I only look to what God wants us to do. And I think what God wants of us is to get the word of the Church to everyone."

We told Mother Angelica what we hope to accomplish with this book. It is a reaffirmation of the role women have had down through the centuries in forming and maintaining our Church. We shared some of the insights we've received about how important women have been from as far back as the Old Testament days. Since this is a book about powerful women in the Church, we asked Mother if she had anything to say to the women of the Church.

"Well, we have the same, I call it, Luciferian sin, which is, 'I will not serve.' That's the basis for all the problems of women, men and children, teen-agers. I say Lucifer, because they have allowed the enemy (Lucifer) to take over, with pornography, drugs, alcohol, so-called false freedom, permissiveness, and all the rest. Once a society begins to be led by that kind of stuff, then it becomes decadent. That's how Rome fell, and that's how every nation fell. Abortion, euthanasia, when man plays God (Author's note: Wasn't that Lucifer's game in the garden with Adam and Eve?), that's the evil of New Age, the great apostasy."

(Author's note: Actually New Age is not new. It is an evil, an old heresy dating back to the early 1900's. It espouses pantheism, modernism and Hinduism. It would make us believe that we are in control of our lives, that we are the god who controls what happens. What a responsibility, what a weight to carry, what a mess! What happens when you realize you can't do it? Do helplessness, hopelessness, and despair follow? After all, if you are your own god, then it follows there is no All-Powerful God to turn to, Who saves, Who cares, Who hears all and responds to all.)

Mother Angelica continued,

"And so people become victims when they do not pray, when they do not receive the Sacraments, when they are not obedient to the Magisterium of the Church. And you open yourself to the enemy, the world, and the flesh; it's still the same. The enemy can't use anything original."

Mother Angelica affirmed the urgency we have had to evangelize, to spread the Word, to convert as many people as quickly as possible. When we wondered why there does not seem to be the evangelization here in the United States that there is in the Third World countries, she replied,

"Well, I think the only way to evangelize is to evangelize! We (the western world) talk and do things on committee, and we don't get anything done."

"Look at how they love one another."

Her Community is her *priority*, her vocation. Mother Angelica rises about an hour and a half before the Sisters. She and the Sisters spend about five hours a day in quality prayer time.

"We spend time before the Blessed Sacrament, adoring our Jesus; saying the Divine Office, attending Daily Mass, so it piles up. We are either thinking of God, or talking to God for that time (at least five hours)."

Mother goes to the television studio at 2 P.M. each day, having been with the Community until that time. She has not relinquished the formation and the instructions of her Nuns, spending an hour a day teaching them from Holy Scripture, and the lives of the Saints. She is each Nun's spiritual director, giving them an ear to speak to, arms to console and reassure them, wisdom to guide them closer to their God.

And so, we had the big secret, how God could work with a cloistered Community of Nuns. It was the power of prayer, God proving to His people He could do anything if only we turned it over to Him and prayed! It was for God's Glory that He chose this Community. It is obvious this is not where you would expect a television network to begin or to grow. Cloistered Nuns? What could cloistered Nuns possibly know about television?

So, it is apparent, or should be, God's doing it. To Him goes all Honor and Glory. Everything that has happened or will happen has been for Him, through Him, with Him and in Him. These Nuns have what - no, *the One Who* makes change. They have the ingredient missing in action or movements without prayer.

"Without that prayer foundation," Mother Angelica says, *"all is fruitless."*

As Lenin said on his death bed, when he mourned the failure of the Russian revolution,

"If only we would have had one hundred St. Francis' of Assisi, it would have been a success."

I have a dream!

Mother has had a dream since 1979. She felt called to begin two additional Orders in Birmingham; one of Priests and Brothers, the other of Extern Sisters. But, as in all things, she waited for the Lord to open the doors.

From the time Mother Angelica first came to Birmingham, Alabama, she has had a *good friend.* Her name is Sister Mary Gabriel. She and her School Sisters spent many happy hours at the Monastery.

The friendship has grown these twenty-seven years, into the fulfillment of part of Mother's dream, a Community of Sisters whose Apostolate is to serve the needs of Mother Angelica and EWTN. Sister Mary Gabriel, now *Mother Mary Gabriel,* is co-foundress, with *Mother Angelica* of the Sister Servants of the Eternal Word. One of the Sisters we interviewed shared what their commitment is.

"Our charism is that we are servants to God, and to the Eternal Word. The most direct way we are serving is being a servant to Mother Angelica's Ministry."

They are involved with reading scripts, reading and answering letters and generally filling the physical and sometimes spiritual needs of the Network. The work and the constitution of Mother Angelica's new Community is alive and evolving. But nothing is too great or too small. They may be involved in production one day and housekeeping the next. Most importantly, the priority, like that of Mother's other two Orders, is their prayer life. In addition to their work for the Network, they share in the daily, strong, five-hour commitment to prayer, with Mother Angelica and the Nuns of the cloistered Community of Our Lady of the Angels Monastery.

They live in separate living quarters from the cloistered Order of Nuns. The Blessed Sacrament is exposed in their own chapel. When they don't have commitments at the Network at night, they spend more time before Jesus in the Eucharist. They try to have all-night Adoration two nights a week.

Their philosophy is a complete contradiction to much of what is happening in religious communities today.

There is a strong bond, a unity, with the Magisterium of the Church, and the Holy Father as head of the Church and Vicar of Christ on earth.

There is a designated Superior, and that Superior is in headship. She is not just another member of the Community. They believe that God appoints a Superior, has appointed Mother Gabriel as Superior, and that God speaks and works through that Superior.

They wear full-length habits, as requested by our Holy Father, to make a statement to those who have modified habits to the point of being unrecognizable. The habits are an aid in focusing on the Vows they have taken.

They take very seriously the Vows of their Community. Poverty is fairly easy as Mother Angelica is always on the edge financially. Ironically, her financial condition hasn't changed that much from that of the young girl, Rita Rizzo of fifty some-odd years ago, but the attitude is so much different.

Obedience is something we were able to sense very strongly among the Sister Servants in general, and particularly in the one we interviewed. It's such an important part of the structure. In order to accomplish what they feel called by the Lord to, they *must* take obedience very seriously.

Chastity is an ongoing struggle against our lower nature, our gift from our ancestors, Adam and Eve. But we see here in this Community such strong tools to keep out the lure of the world and the flesh. Although they are smack in the middle of Television, their focus on prayer and spirituality is the stronghold.

Another beautiful and Spirit-filled friend who has become a source of love and knowledge to the faithful who watch Mother Angelica and EWTN, is Father Michael McDonagh. Mother and Father Michael have known each other since 1977. They met at a Charismatic Conference in

Florida. They both felt from the beginning that the Lord had put them together for a reason. They were kindred spirits.

Over the years, Fr. Michael has come to Our Lady of the Angels Monastery for annual visits, and in 1984, was asked to be on the Board of Directors of ETWN.

They shared the other part of her dream, to start an Order of Priests and Brothers of the Eternal Word, but they waited for the Lord to open the door. It seemed that if the door were ever opened for a Community of Priests and Brothers, Fr. Michael would be the one to lead them.

When the Lord showed her that the time was right, Mother Angelica telephoned Father Michael and the wheels of motion began to turn, the wind of the Holy Spirit began to blow, sending forth a gush of fresh air into our beloved Church.

Fr. Michael's path would have been seemingly more difficult, in that he was a Parish priest in the Diocese of St. Petersburg, Florida, which has been growing in leaps and bounds. There never have been enough Priests for all the parishioners, and the situation has been getting worse with the great influx of Catholics moving in from the colder states. He tried to brace Mother Angelica for possible disappointment at the hands of the local Bishop, who was not trying to get rid of Priests, especially one of Fr. Michael's caliber. But perhaps Fr. Michael was not aware of just how much power emanates from the Eucharist in the chapel at EWTN. He surely is now.

When Fr. Michael made his request of his Bishop, he didn't apply any pressure at all. He assured his Superior of his confidence in whatever decision the Bishop would make, and promised not to be upset if it was a "No."

Six weeks later, his Bishop called him in. He said to him, "*As much as I don't want to let you go, I think I **have** to let you go.*" Thus, the dream that the Lord put into Mother

Angelica's mind in 1979, began to see its fruition in 1987. The Lord is willing to wait, but when He has something He wants done, He moves Heaven and earth and everything in between to get it done.

The way the two new Orders are growing is a miracle in itself. At a time when we are told there is a crisis of vocations in our Church, that Seminaries are empty and Convents are closing, these three Orders are building larger facilities to try to accommodate all the new vocations. *And all those who have joined have been by word of mouth!* There is no recruiting done. Somehow, Our Lady sends the ones she feels will be good for the Orders. Fr. Michael has a waiting list, because there is just not enough room for all who want to join them.

The Order of Priests and Brothers was begun in 1987 and Father Michael and Mother Angelica have already sent three of the Brothers to a Seminary to study for the priesthood.

It is said that St. Francis attracted the fairest by his life-style, that of living the Gospel faithfully. Mother Angelica, with Mother Gabriel and Father Michael, in the true tradition of Jesus and Francis, have attracted as well, the most beautiful, happiest, and most loving bands of disciples to do the Will of God. Two of the young people at the Monastery, one man and one woman, are children of friends we have made in Louisiana. When Penny met the young woman, whose family we know, at Our Lady of the Angels Monastery, she blurted out, "You're so beautiful. . . ." The young Postulant blushed. Penny quickly countered with, *"But that's as it should be. Jesus' Brides should be the most beautiful."*

So now we know the secret of the success of EWTN, Our Lady of the Angels Monastery, the Sister Servants and the Order of the Eternal Word. *Only it was never meant to be a secret!* Mother Angelica has been giving away the secret for years, only not enough people listened. Or they thought it was just too simplistic.

Plug into the Power Source, which is the Eucharist, and all things will flow. The Healing Power that went out of Jesus as the woman with the hemorrhage touched His cloak, is the same power He gives us through the Eucharist. It surges through our souls to our veins and arteries, and continues out of our bodies into everything we touch. The power of the Eucharist is what makes it all happen.

"We are in the worst of times; we are in the best of times."

We are in the time of St. Francis. At times of great need, the Lord raises up prophets and great Saints and we often kill them. We believe Mother Angelica is one of those prophets. She has not had the easiest of lives. Plainly she is a contradiction in our times, God writing straight with crooked lines. She was born out of pain, into pain, to bring hope to a Church in pain. Many of the very people whom she thought she would be able to depend on for loving support, fellow religious of the Church, have either ignored her and ridiculed her at best, or set out to block her from doing "God's Work", that of bringing the Catholic voice to the world through EWTN.

The people she has found that she *has* been able to depend on, are you and me, the little people. From the time she landed in Birmingham, Alabama, her support has been the small monthly donations she receives from people all over the world who believe in what she is doing. To many who do not feel the call to give everything up and follow Jesus, *this is their only way to spread the Good News,* by keeping Mother Angelica afloat with their donations.

Every now and then, the Lord sends a Joe Bruno, or the Knights of Columbus, or many others to bail her out when finances become rough. But by and large, hers is a grass roots movement, depending on the people of God, the very people she is called to serve, *and they have come through!*

Bob and I feel so blessed to know, to love and to be loved by a Saint in our time. We have been touched by Mother Angelica, and we and the world will never be the same. We love you, Mother Angelica. Thank you for your ongoing *"Yes"* to the Father.

"Someday the whole world's going to know this woman, because she has such a deep knowledge and relationship with Our Lord." . . . Sister Mary Raphael

Right:
*Sisters of Our
Lady of the Angels
Monastery
at Prayer*

Left:
*Pizza Time
at the
Monastery!*

Right:
*Sister Servants
of the
Eternal Word*

Left:
*Praise Jesus
for the
Fourth of
July*

Above: ***Sisters of Our Lady of the Angels Monastery
and Sister Servants of the Eternal Word***
Below: ***Order of the Eternal Word***

Left:
***Sister Briege
(in the center)
Final Profession***

Right:
***Briege's First
Holy Communion
1952***

Below:
***Briege and Bishop
Obiefuna - Nigeria 1989***

Left:
Briege - Age 6

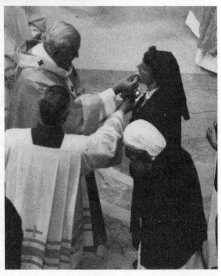

Right:
***Briege Receives Eucharist
From Pope John Paul II
1982***

Sister Briege McKenna

"Jesus, I'm going to find you, whatever it takes."

The power of the Lord is mighty! He takes His people from all over the world and places them in strategic positions, to spread His glory to all His children.

Why else would He take an Irish colleen from a little hamlet in Northern Ireland, move her to Tampa, Florida as a headquarters; *and then send her out of the country*, all over the world, to be the instrument of His Healing Hands? Why does He send her to parts of the world where she doesn't speak the language but is understood so well?

How can Jesus use a *woman* to minister to His Priests? How can this Religious bring back faith, belief and devotion to the Eucharist to *oftentimes* spiritually broken men? We go to St. Augustine's famous statement for part of the answer,
"God writes straight with crooked lines"
and to the words of Mary in her Magnificat,
"He has shown might with His arm;
He has confused the proud in their inmost thoughts.
He has deposed the mighty from their thrones
and raised the lowly to high places.
The hungry He has given every good thing,
while the rich He has sent empty away."
We have to believe that if the situation is contradictory in the eyes of the world, it is of God. And Sister Briege McKenna is one of God's delightful contradictions, *a powerful woman* in our Church.

We doubt if George and Brigid McKenna had any idea what the Lord had in store for their child when a baby girl was born to them on Pentecost Sunday, June 9, 1946. They most likely thanked Our Lord Jesus for a healthy baby, prayed that she would grow up untouched by the evils in the world, and marry well within her station.

Her life as a child was much like other children from her circumstances. She was a good girl, but a cut-up. She had a great love of Our Lord Jesus from her earliest days. She was taught her faith belief by her dear mother at first, and then by the good Sisters. A highlight of her life came when she was not yet seven years old. She received her First Holy Communion. The very Real Presence of Jesus inside her created a burning in her heart which has been with her all her life. The Eucharist was to become her greatest strength as she went through life. In reflecting, Briege gives credit to the *Power of Jesus in the Eucharist* for all the meaningful things which have ever happened to her.

Christmas is a very special time for most of us, but for children, even teenagers, it is a glorious time. It was the same for young Briege, until one Christmas, which she will never forget. It was 1959. Briege was thirteen. She shared with us that two days before Christmas of that year, Brigid McKenna told her daughter she would be in Heaven for Christmas. Young Briege could not figure out what her mother might be talking about. But on Christmas Day, her mother died. Briege was crushed. She wept bitter tears. But she was to be given a Christmas gift that evening, which would be with her for the rest of her life. She heard a voice speaking very softly, very gently.

"Don't worry. I'll take care of you."

She didn't know where the voice came from. She was too young to realize that it was the Lord speaking to her. She only knew she felt a *peace* that she had never felt before. The next morning, when she awakened, her vocation was sealed. She knew she wanted to be a Nun.

We asked Sister Briege if she had felt the desire to be a Nun prior to this time. She could not recall a time before her mother's death when she had ever thought about a vocation to the Religious life. But a parish Priest once told her that she had talked about being a Nun when she was eight years old. She has no memory of this. Was there a Nun she could remember who was a role model to her? She could not think of any Sister in her early days who would have influenced her to become a Nun. So it becomes apparent that the inspiration was given her directly by Our Lord Jesus on that Christmas night of 1959, when He spoke to her, and comforted her in her grief.

To most of us hearing this, we would catch our breath and say to ourselves, "What a special girl. The Lord spoke to her." and we would be right, but only partly right. *The Lord speaks to all of us.* That's His gift to us. Our gift to Him is listening, and acting on the word. The special part about Briege is that she said "Yes." She has continued to say *yes* throughout her life, from that day to this, even at times when the word choked in her throat.

Jesus carefully picks His very exceptional people. While Briege speaks often of St. Teresa of Avila, there are many parallels between her life and that of the other Thérèse, the Little Flower of Jesus. Both girls lost their mother at an early age, as had Teresa of Avila. Both girls attempted to enter the Religious Life at fourteen years old. Thérèse entered at fifteen, and Briege at fourteen and half years of age. Both had a great love for the missions, and although Thérèse never left the Carmel at Lisieux, she is co-patron of the missions. Briege, on the other hand, spends a good deal of her time ministering to the Third World countries.

But it didn't begin that way. After two short years in Community, in 1964, she developed excruciating pains in her feet. At first, it was diagnosed as *growing pains*. After all, she was only seventeen years old. But it got worse and worse. Finally, it was determined that she had *rheumatoid arthritis,* and it was crippling her. Her condition became so serious that at one time, she had to wear plaster boots to bed at night to avoid irreversible deformity.

She suffered this condition for six long years, during which time she made her final profession and volunteered to be part of a new house her Community had opened in Tampa, Florida. Everybody thought that the warmer climate of Florida would be better for her arthritis than the cold, wet weather of Ireland. And so Briege packed up her meager belongings; and amidst much weeping, she left her beloved Ireland, and came to America.

The climate in Tampa proved to be far worse for her condition than Ireland had been. She suffered through three years of it. She took cortisone, which did more harm than good, and finally, just lived with the pain. Her condition seemed *hopeless.* Coupled with the constant physical pain, or possibly because of it, her spirituality began to wane quickly. The evil one had a field day with Briege. She began by questioning her vocation, and then whether Jesus really existed. *If He was real, why wouldn't He heal her from this agony? Was there real power in the Gospel, or is it just a history of Jesus? Does healing really take place, or is it all a fake?* But deep down inside, her belief, or her hunger to believe, was strong. She went through her prayers, but *felt* nothing. She steered away from any conversation regarding the Power of God. *She was living proof of the non-power of God.* But that was hurt and anger speaking. Finally, her fighting Irish came to the surface. She spoke to Jesus in the Blessed Sacrament.

"Jesus, I'm going to find You, whatever it takes."

The strong will of the Irish, which helped them keep their Faith through hundreds of years of persecution during the Penal times, was ingrained in Briege. She turned it in the direction of God and Faith. She embraced the Charismatic

Renewal, which was very new at the time. She felt the great need for excitement, for emotion in our Church.

Through the Renewal, the Lord led her to a retreat in Orlando, Florida, on December 9, 1970. She listened to many talks on the Healing Power of the Holy Spirit. Speaker after speaker proclaimed the Power of Jesus *to heal.* Briege listened intently. But she had a thought, *Don't pay attention to them. Pay attention to Me.* She closed her eyes. She said only four words. **"Jesus, please help me!"**

She felt a hand touch her head. She opened her eyes. There was no one there. She began to feel a surge of power shoot through her body. She describes the feeling as *"a banana being peeled."* Her stiff fingers began to loosen up. Her feet, which had become badly deformed, relaxed and straightened out. Sores on her elbows disappeared. Her heart pounded wildly. She jumped up to her feet, tears streaming down her face. She was healed! She cried out,

"Jesus! You're right here!"

The Lord, in one fell-swoop, healed Briege physically and spiritually. She never again experienced the agony of arthritis, which had crippled her for six years, nor did she ever feel the spiritual dryness which had accompanied it. But the greatest part of the miracle for Briege was the knowledge that Jesus loved her and would always be with her. He would always keep the promise He made to her that Christmas night her mother died, *"Don't worry. I'll take care of you."*

That's not to say she was never down again. Ministry is like a roller coaster, full of valleys and high places. But Briege is a "Yes" person. She *claimed* that "Yes"; she stood on it; she could live through that "Yes". And Jesus could work through her.

It was a brand new world for Briege. She was like the blind man who had been healed by Jesus. Everything was light and bright. Colors were vibrant and brilliant. The whole Church took on *new life* for Briege. The Eucharist was awesome. Reconciliation was gentle, a gift of love from Our Lord Jesus. The Holy Spirit through the Charismatic Renewal was powerful.

There was only one charism that Briege could not throw herself into, *healing.* At first blush, it seems strange that she did not want to get involved in healing, when she was witness and living proof of the great power of healing the Lord was willing to give us. But when we consider her background which was conservative, and her Community which was "respectable" and "strict", it might not be that strange. In addition, she was afraid of being accused of *sensational*ism. There are those who dwell on the sensational and phenomena. Sister Briege wanted no part of that. She had been *healed*, but she was not a *healer!*

As a matter of fact, when Sister Briege was healed, she had no intention of telling anyone about it. But it was so obvious and dramatic a healing, it was impossible to hide. In addition, that would have been an insult to her Love, Jesus, Who gave her the gift. We must praise and glorify God for the gifts He gives us.

That same Irish stubbornness which had been used for Sister Briege's physical and spiritual healing, came back, only this time it was fighting the *Lord's program.* Briege would have nothing to do with healing. Jesus sent messages in bright neon lights, and still she would not accept them.

She found herself all alone in the Chapel one day, when she heard her name called. She looked around. There was no one there. The voice came again. It was coming from the direction of the Tabernacle. She heard the voice tell her, *"You have My gift of healing. Go and use it."*

Her response was, *"Jesus, I don't want any gift of healing. Keep it for Yourself."*

She came to California, clear across the country, to an area where she was not well known. She sat next to an

Episcopalian Priest during a prayer meeting. After it was over, he turned to her, "Sister, I've never spoken to a Roman Catholic Nun before, but I have a message for you. You have the gift of healing, and you know it because the Lord spoke to you in your Chapel in Florida."

When she denied it vehemently, giving all the reasons why she could not have the gift of Healing, the Priest said to her, "Jesus will never force you. He reveals His will, but you are free to choose to follow Him or not."

That may be so, and we have no reason to doubt the Episcopalian Priest, but that's not the Jesus we know. When He wants something, He *never* lets go until He gets it. True, He will not force you, but He also won't let you live until you say "Yes". We have found that to be the case in our own lives, and what subsequently happened to Sister Briege bears it out.

A few days later, after Mass, a woman came up to Briege, and spoke to her. "Sister, I don't know you, but when you went to Communion, the Lord gave me a picture of you with a line of people coming to you. The Lord told me that you are being called into a great healing ministry."

On the plane back to Florida, the Lord gave Sister Briege a mental image of how she was treating the gift of healing. In her own words,

"Then He (the Lord) gave me an image of a house. I have a great imagination, which I believe God uses to speak to me. In this image of the house, I was inside and a man came knocking at the door. I opened the door and he seemed to be a very nice man so I asked him in.

I told him, 'See, all these rooms. Make Yourself at home; go anywhere You like in my house.' I followed the man as he walked through all the rooms. There were many of them and they were very pretty. Suddenly he came upon a locked door. On the door in large dark type was PRIVATE PROPERTY - DO NOT ENTER. *He turned to me, and*

*as He turned, I recognized Him to be Jesus. He asked me,
'Briege, why can't I go in this room?'*

*I replied, 'Come now, Jesus, look at all I've given You.
I want to keep a little something for myself.'*

*I heard Him say in this image, 'You know, Briege, if you
do not open that door, you will never know what it means
to be truly free.'*

*I remember looking at the image and saying to myself,
'Now what is in that room?'*

The Lord said, 'I'll show you.'

*Inside that room was my reputation, what others
thought of me. I didn't want Jesus in that room because I
was preserving my good name and my reputation. I
wanted to follow Jesus, but I wanted control of my life. I
wasn't going to be a fool. Anything to do with the Cross,
with picking up my Cross, that was out of the question.*

*I heard Jesus saying to me, 'I thought you gave me your
life.'"*

A natural reaction to hearing something like the above
would be, "Wow! If the Lord had spoken to me that way, I
would have thrown all caution to the wind, and do what He
told me."

But when you think about it, hasn't the Lord sent us
messages in blood and ink? Don't we know when He's
asking us to go beyond ourselves in certain ways? Don't we
find reasons why we don't want to convert our lives, and just
follow Jesus? Aren't the excuses we give ourselves about the
same as Sister Briege gave? Reputation? What people
think of us? I know for myself, the Lord is asking me to go
far beyond where I am now, and give 100% more than I'm
giving. But I have a fear of being uncomfortable, being
unliked, making waves.

"But...," we may say, "Sister Briege experienced an
outstanding and dramatic miracle, an obvious physical
healing." That's true, but think back over your past life.

Hasn't there been a time when you felt the Lord's Hand in your life. I know Penny and I have. If the Lord hadn't hit us with a two-by-four, in a very dramatic way, we wouldn't be back in the Church today. Think! In *your* life, has your spouse ever been unfaithful, and then come back? Have any of your children been victims of drugs and alcohol, and come back? Has anyone in your family ever left the Church, and come back? The Lord has worked powerfully in all our lives. What is He asking of us, and are we saying "Yes"?

But back to Sister Briege, she persisted in *stonewalling* the Lord. When she returned to Florida, she continued to get messages. People came up to her, whom she had never seen in her life, and told her she had the gift of healing. Apparently, the Lord felt it was time to bring in the big guns. We asked Sister Briege *when* she finally accepted that the Lord had given her the gift of healing, and wanted her to use it. She said it happened when she went to a parish women's guild meeting to give a talk. She marveled at how she had spoken for an hour without once mentioning healing.

But a few days later, a woman, who had been at the talk, telephoned her. She told Briege she had walked out because she thought Briege too young to be giving talks on prayer. She also shared that she had been contemplating suicide. The night of the talk, however, the woman said, she saw Briege walk into her bedroom. Briege told her she had not been there; she said she had been at home in bed. The woman insisted it was Briege. She said that even when she closed her eyes, Briege was still there. She told Briege that she had asked her, "*Why do you not believe in Jesus?*" Having completed her sharing, this woman, who had been in despair, perked up suddenly and said, "Do you think it's possible that God could help me?"

At this point, Briege had a talk with the Lord in her inimitable Irish way. "*Oh Jesus, use me all You want during the day, but don't have me roaming through people's homes in the middle of the night!"*

To which Jesus replied, *in His inimitable Irish way, "But I thought you said that if I'd do the telling, you'd do the praying!"*

This was the turning point for Briege McKenna. She went to a Priest for affirmation. But it couldn't be a Charismatic Priest! She even made sure he was fairly conservative. He affirmed what the Lord had been saying through all the messengers He had sent her. The Priest even said to her, "You know, if I was God, I'd tell you to get lost."

The Priest told her that Jesus was not asking her to do anything but be an instrument. Do what Mary did, say yes.

Briege shared some of her doubts. *"But Father, how can I know when to pray? I can't just go up to people who are sick and tell them I can pray for physical healing."*

He smiled at her and said, "Sister, you don't have to tell people. If Jesus called you to this ministry of healing, then He will lead you to the people and He will lead them to you."

And lead them He did!

Briege said yes, and the floodgates opened. Jesus sent people from far and wide, and *although* they were healed, and *although* Briege was still doubtful whether it was through her, she continued to say yes. As she built her courage, He built her confidence. He gave her healings she thought were impossible. He was trying to get a point across to her. One woman stood up at a prayer meeting and asked for prayer for a woman who was blind and paralyzed. Blind and paralyzed? *No way!* But the woman was healed. The Lord was trying to tell Briege that healing is not a matter of mastering your craft. You don't get a Masters or a Ph.D. in healing. You don't get better as you go along. It really has nothing to do with you, other than your just standing there, and letting Him work through you so that He can do it. *He doesn't need training! He's perfect at it!*

There's one *thing* we can get better at, that our *powerful women* in the Church have gotten better at and continue to get better at. That *thing* is discerning when the Lord is telling you that *really important something* He has for you to do. Mother Angelica says we form committee meetings in our mind, to talk ourselves *out* of doing what we know Jesus wants us to do. The *powerful women* we have met and read about, spend their whole lives trying to perfect a *Self-Abandonment* to the Lord. They turn their lives over to Him completely. They know when the Lord is speaking to them, and they act on it at once.

A major breakthrough in this area came to Sister Briege during the next summer. She went home to Ireland for vacation, but her reputation followed her. People were coming by her home in Newry, and calling her to this hospital and that prayer meeting to pray for healings. Her father wasn't too happy with the idea. He thought she should be allowed to have a holiday while she was home. She liked to visit her Aunt Lizzie who had been like a mother to her since her own mother had died. But as soon as word got out that she was going to be there, as many as sixty cars would be parked outside her aunt's house, waiting for her to show up. Healings were taking place every day. Well-wishers worried about her, however. They weren't sure how the Bishop would take all this healing if he were to find out what was going on.

Sister Briege decided it was time for a conference. She went to the Cathedral to talk to Jesus. To her first question, *"I'm home on holiday. Is it Your will that I should be doing this (healing)? I don't want to do anything against Your will,"* He answered her by sending in a man who had hurt his wrist. Not knowing who Sister Briege was, the man asked her to pray for him, simply because she was a Nun. After she had prayed, he went over to another part of the Church to say the Rosary. In the middle of his prayers, he called over to her, "God, that was a powerful prayer. Could you write it out? The pain and the swelling are gone."

Briege heard the Lord say, "*That's why I brought you home, to touch My people.*"

But then she asked Jesus a second question, which has opened up a brand new area of healing for her. She asked Him to teach her how to pray for people. She looked up at the Tabernacle. In her mind's eye, she saw a huge, pink telephone. At first it bothered her. But she couldn't stop looking at it. Then she saw large words, printed as if they were headlines on a newspaper.

"The telephone is a means of communication.
People talk to each other on it.
I can also use it. You use the phone.
People will hear you, but experience Me."

Briege immediately thought of the words of the Centurion in Matthew 8:8. "*Lord, I am not worthy that you should come under my roof. Say but the word and my slave will be healed.*" We hear these words. We repeat a version of them at Mass every time we prepare to receive the Eucharist. But then we say so many words. Do we actually pray, understanding and believing what we pray? Or do we just mouth *words*?

Briege was at a point in her relationship with Jesus where, though she might question something He told her, she pretty much believed He would make it so. She immediately put this new concept into work. In many instances in Ireland, she prayed with people for others who were ill, but who were great distances away, and healings came about. When she returned to her motherhouse, she was told that a man from England wanted to come to see her, and have her pray over him. She said it was not necessary for him to come. Just let him call her, and they would pray together over the phone. When the man called, she prayed with him, and a healing took place.

†

Author's note: When we interviewed Sister Briege for this chapter, it was by telephone. She is in Florida; we are in California. Our schedules were such that it was not possible for us to meet personally, and so we decided to do the interview by telephone. I had done most of the research on Sister Briege, so I had a whole battery of questions to ask her. But the day she called, I had come down with a virus called Bell's Palsy, which paralyzed the entire left side of my face. It had actually only happened a few hours before Sister Briege called. I had just come back from the Emergency Room, and was lying down. I was in a state of panic. I couldn't talk right. I couldn't chew. I couldn't close my left eye. I had to use a patch to keep the eye closed and moist. Saliva dripped out of the left side of my mouth. The feeling was the same as if I had been given an injection of novocaine by a dentist. The whole left side was dead. Needless to say, I didn't want to speak to anyone. I gave Penny the questions, and asked her to talk to Sister Briege.

The strange thing is that I knew about Sister Briege's phone ministry, but never for a moment did I think it was for me. I don't know why; I just didn't. Penny got on the phone with Sister Briege, and explained what had happened. Naturally, the first thing Sister Briege wanted to do was pray over me. I got up out of bed, began praying with Sister Briege, and then continued on with the entire phone interview. I'm not going to say that I received feeling back in my face on the spot. But the next day, when I went to the doctor, he ruled out many serious problems I could have had, like stroke, tumors, or brain damage, which would have involved major delicate surgery, and determined that feeling was beginning to come back into parts of my face. I truly

*believe that the healing began with the prayers we said
with Sister Briege that day. Praise Jesus!*

We have to stop for a minute here to share on a most
important aspect of healing.   It's essential that we
understand what is happening.   When Sister Briege was
given this word of knowledge by the Lord, He made it clear
to her"...*that all I had to do was unite with them before Jesus.
He is not limited by time and space.*"   In this, He proved to
her, and to us that He is truly the Healer, and Sister Briege,
or Fr. Ralph DiOrio, or Fr. Bob De Grandis, or any of the
other people who have been given this gift, are only
instruments.   If healing can take place through Sister Briege
on the phone, it's got to be the Lord.   So she sits there, with
earphones on, so that her hands will be free to go to
Scripture, or write things down while she is praying with
people.   The day that we spoke to her, she said she had had
a thought (Holy Spirit?) that she should call us before she got
so busy with her other calls.   She said she had spoken to fifty
six people from all over the world the day before.   The Lord
was moving through *Ma Bell!*

The Healing Power of Jesus in the Eucharist

During our interview with Sister Briege, she told us that
when she gives a healing service, neither she nor the Priest
pray individually over anyone.   The Priest walks through the
assembly with Jesus in the Blessed Sacrament exposed in the
Monstrance.   He blesses each and every person.   While he
does this, Sister Briege stays up at the microphone and prays
over   everybody.   The   healings   that   take   place   are
unbelievable.

In January of 1989, Penny and I gave a Day of
Recollection with Fr. Harold Cohen in Metairie, Louisiana.
At the end of the day, we did basically the same thing.
Penny, Luz Elena Sandoval, and I stood up at the
microphone, and prayed for healings from many things, drug

and alcohol abuse, terminal cancer, heart disease, separation and divorce, while Fr. Cohen walked through the assembly with the Blessed Sacrament exposed. Penny and I have never claimed to have the gift of healing, but that day, Jesus worked powerful healings with that group.

Another instance we would like to mention concerning healing through the Eucharist. Father Ralph DiOrio gave a healing service in 1986 in Little Rock, Arkansas. They filled a huge auditorium for the service. There were thousands of people there. But before the healing service began, the Bishop of Little Rock processed through the auditorium with the Blessed Sacrament in the Monstrance, and blessed everyone there. Healings took place by the droves. One man, who had been away from the Church for 30 years, and had only come to disrupt the service, claimed that a bright bolt of light shot out from the Monstrance, and about knocked him down, very much like the conversion of St. Paul. He got up later, crying, and confessed what had happened.

After the Bishop had left the auditorium, what was there left for Fr. DiOrio to do? All the healing had been done by Jesus in the Eucharist. Fr. DiOrio spent the next two and a half hours praising the *Healing Power* of Jesus in the Eucharist.

In our talks, we tell people that we have the greatest respect for Sister Briege, Fr. DiOrio, Fr. De Grandis, and many of the other men and women in our Church whom the Lord has given the gift of healing. If there is any way that you can attend one of their healing services, do so by all means. But if you can't physically get to be where these people are, and if you can't possibly get Sister Briege on the phone, go to Jesus in the Blessed Sacrament. All of these people will tell you that *He* is where the power is.

In Sister Briege's book, *Miracles do Happen*, she talks about an instance that brings this point home so clearly. We have to preface this with a message the Lord gave her one night when He wouldn't let her sleep. She knew the Lord wanted to talk to her. At about four in the morning, she got up, and knelt at the side of the bed. *"Jesus,"* she asked, *"What is it that You want to say to me?"* She felt the Lord saying,

"You must make Me known in the Eucharist. People are coming to you. People will come from all over looking for healing. They will say, 'Oh, if only we could get Sister Briege to touch us', or 'If Sister Briege could only lay hands on us, then we'd be healed.'

"Many are making false gods out of people in healing ministries. They are seeking after people and not Me. I come every day in the Eucharist. I promised to give you life and to give it to you more abundantly, to fill you with strength for your pilgrimage.

"I want you to go out now into the world and point to Me in the Eucharist. I want you to tell people to take their eyes off Briege McKenna and fix their gaze on their Eucharistic Lord, to put their faith in Me. You can disappoint them, and you will disappoint them, as will any person who attracts people to themselves. But if you point them to Me, then they will never be disappointed."

Sister Briege knew from this that the Lord wanted her to direct people's attention on the Gift He had given us from the beginning, the Power of His Body and Blood in the Eucharist.

Now we want to share an instance where Briege focused a woman in on the Healing Power of Jesus in the Eucharist. She and Father Kevin Scallon were in Australia giving a series of talks. The woman came up to Sister Briege and asked her to pray over her. She had a malignant tumor of the stomach and was swollen badly. She was young and afraid to die. She said to Sister Briege, "Sister, I'm so scared of dying. If only God would take away this awful fear that I have!"

Sister Briege knew a Mass was beginning in the parish church right next to the hall where they were speaking. She told the woman to go to Mass.

"Go to meet Jesus in the Eucharist. While I can't tell anyone they will be healed the way they want because I'm not God, Jesus will supply you the strength to face whatever is on your road of life. If you are to go through the door of death, He will give you the grace to go through that door without this awful fear. And if you are to live, He will give you the grace to live."

This was on a Saturday morning. That night, Sister Briege and Fr. Kevin were giving a rally in the hall. The same woman ran up to Briege and threw her arms around her. "It's happened! Sister, it happened!"

Sister Briege asked her, *"What happened?"*

The woman said,

"I went to Mass as you said. When I was walking up to Communion, I said to myself, 'In a few minutes, I am going to meet Jesus. I'm going to take Him in my hand, and I will ask Him for His help!' When I looked at the Host, I said, 'I know You are really here. Today, when You come into me, take away this fear. Heal me if You want, but please do something for me.'"

The woman continued,

"I had no sooner put the Host on my tongue and swallowed It than I felt as though something was burning my throat and down into my stomach. I looked down at my stomach and the growth was gone." *The woman was healed!*

We believe the Lord uses Sister Briege as *chum.* Penny and I were in El Centro, California, giving a weekend retreat. It was sponsored by the local prayer group. The leader got up to introduce us to an unusually large crowd they had that night. He said, "We're using Bob and Penny

Lord as *chum*. For those of you who are not fishermen, chum is bait. You all came to see and hear Bob and Penny Lord, but what we really want is to expose you to our prayer group, and get you to come back again."

Penny and I have used that in our talks. We tell the people who come,

"We're using Miracles of the Eucharist as *chum*. You think you're here because of Miracles of the Eucharist, but what you're here for, what we're here to do is to re-focus you on the Eucharist, and the power that Jesus gives us in the Eucharist."

We believe the same to be true of Sister Briege. Not long after she began her healing ministry, a beautiful couple, Ingrid and Peter Orglmeister, asked her to go to Brazil to give a series of talks. They were to be her interpreters. They were surprised when she did not give talks on healing. Her talks were about prayer and the Eucharist. This is how the Lord works. He gives you credibility. He gives you a drawing card. Then when people come to hear what they *think* they wanted to hear, He has you tell them what *He* wants them to hear.

The Lord draws us to Him step by step. The more we say "Yes", the more He uses us. But He prepares us first. Sometimes we're so excited to work for the Lord, we're chomping at the bit. We have a saying in our ministry. If we received a message from the Lord to go to Africa, Penny and Brother Joseph would be on the first plane. Then they'd read the second part of the message, which was "*Learn to speak Swahili first.*" Luz Elena and I, on the other hand, would learn Swahili before booking our airline tickets. This is a roundabout way of saying that the Lord went through great pains to train Sister Briege in her ministry.

She was invited by Mother Angelica to spend some quality time with Jesus at Our Lady of the Angels Monastery in Birmingham, Alabama. Briege thought it would be a great time to read up on the gift she had been given, that of healing. She brought with her all these great books by very famous people who have a healing ministry. She told us that the more she read, the less she remembered. And then the Lord sent Mother Angelica to the rescue. She brought Sister Briege into the Chapel, where the Blessed Sacrament is exposed in Adoration all the time. Mother pointed to Jesus in the Blessed Sacrament.

"There's the Teacher" she told Briege. *"Don't be trying to copy other people's styles. Come to Jesus; let Him teach you."*

The Lord touched Briege in a very special way that day. She made a commitment to spend quality time with Jesus in prayer. She promised to spend two to three hours of personal prayer a day before the *Blessed Sacrament.* That's the key, *before the Blessed Sacrament.* It sounds impossible, two to three hours before the Blessed Sacrament. What can you say? What can you do? I fall asleep. But Jesus *teaches* us there. We don't have to say anything. We can, but we don't have to. Very often, Jesus has to wait until we shut our mouths, before He can get through to us. The logic behind it is if you want to work for Jesus, what better way to find out what He wants you to do than *listen* to Him tell you. And where can you hear Him more clearly than in front of the Blessed Sacrament?

There was a Priest who expressed doubt as to whether Archbishop Fulton J. Sheen spent an hour a day before the Blessed Sacrament. Mother Angelica and her Nuns spend anywhere up to five hours a day in prayer, at least one of which is before the Blessed Sacrament. Sister Briege makes it a part of her day to spend two to three hours before the Lord. We've spoken to cloistered Carmelite Nuns, and Poor Clares, who spend at least one to two hours a day before the Blessed Sacrament. *I wonder why that Priest had such a problem believing that Archbishop Sheen spent one hour before His Lord in the Blessed Sacrament?*

The Lord needs that time with Sister Briege. There are things He wants Briege to talk about. There are many people He wants to touch through Briege.

Sister Briege and the Royal Priesthood

It was during prayer that the Lord put on Sister Briege's heart the plight of the Priesthood. You don't have to be a visionary to know the attacks on our Priesthood today. The Priesthood is the last stand of the Church. Satan has tried in so many ways to destroy the Church. He's tried to destroy the Eucharist, and then the credibility of the Word, and at the same time the family. He's been after Mary since day one. But the easiest, and most secure way to destroy the Church is to destroy her Priests. Without them, we have no Eucharist, and without the Eucharist, we have no Church.

The Lord used Fr. Harold Cohen of New Orleans in a powerful way to place Sister Briege in the path of His Priests. Fr. Cohen had met Briege in the early '70's, and saw the Spirit working in her. He found a simplicity in her, a way of relating to people and sharing the Lord that just charms people. She has the gift of storytelling. Fr. Cohen and Sister Briege developed a good working relationship over the years. So when he suggested she work with him on a Priests' Retreat he was giving, she reluctantly agreed. Actually, she tried to get out of it. She didn't know what possible input she could give. *"I'm only a First Grade teacher!"* she protested. She admits to having been very nervous. Fr. Cohen could not shake the feeling that the Lord wanted Briege on this retreat. So, when she agreed, he felt confident, and they began.

The first night out, Fr. Cohen gave the opening talk, and then came down with a bad case of the flu, and was in bed the *entire weekend*. It was too late to get anyone else to take his place. He told Briege she would have to take over the retreat. She was in a state of panic! She did not feel prepared at all. Add to that the fact that many of the Priests did not want to be on the retreat in the first place. They were sort of *encouraged* by their Bishop to become more familiar with the Charismatic Renewal. They were not happy that a Sister would be on the retreat. But now it was a whole different ball game. She was not part of the retreat; *she was the retreat!*

Just picture Jesus up in Heaven, so amused at what is going on. Here is a Nun who didn't want to be on the retreat, giving the retreat to a bunch of Priests who didn't want to be there either. *Probably the only one who wanted to be there was Fr. Cohen, who was flat on his back in bed.* But it's times like these where the Lord can work powerfully. And no one can take credit for the results except Him, because no one else has anything to do with it.

Briege says He gave her a crash course in the Priesthood that weekend. All the problems that could have been encountered in a Priestly vocation confronted her. By Sunday evening, the forty Priests had all learned to love Sister Briege, and had renewed their love for their vocation. She instilled in them the pride of the Priesthood. She refocused them on the power they had been given through the Sacrament of Holy Orders. It was truly a renewal for them, and a beginning for Sister Briege.

Today, Sister Briege spends most of her time giving retreats to Priests and Bishops all over the world. The Lord has given her the gift of raising up men who are suffering in their vocation. She *revitalizes* them, brings them back to the beginning, to the reason they became Priests in the first place. Through her, the Lord is able to clear out all the diversions that have been thrown at them during their years as Priests and refocus them on the priorities of their calling. She points to all the means of help Our Lord Jesus has provided for them, most especially His Precious Body and Blood in the Eucharist. She loves them as a sister in Christ.

The Lord has made Sister Briege a rounded-out woman of the Church. She has opened herself to all the gifts, all the flowers the Church has to offer. She is a traditional Catholic, with a great love and devotion to Mary. She doesn't question orders given her by Jesus and Mary. Because of a message given her by Mary in a dream, she hands out thousands of Miraculous Medals on every mission she gives. The Rosary is one of her strongest weapons, and greatest friends. She is supportive of Ministries who bring brothers and sisters closer to Jesus.

"Briege, Who is first in your life?"

But she has paid her dues. The Lord has asked for complete self-abandonment to *Him*, and she has said yes. He insists that He be the first and foremost in her life. While it's not too difficult to say yes to Jesus, it's not always easy to *act* on that yes. She recalled a time when the Lord called her on her promise to make Him first. She was in South America, at the beginning of a series of missions. Word came to her that her Aunt Lizzie was dying. Briege felt she had to go back to Ireland to see Aunt Lizzie one more time before she died. She had contacted her Superiors in Tampa, been given permission to return to Tampa and then continue on to Ireland. She told her companions, Ingrid and Jill, that she would be returning home, and that they would have to cancel out a good part of her schedule.

She decided, or did the Lord decide for her, to go to Mass before returning to Tampa. As she approached the Altar to receive Communion, she could feel Jesus speaking to her. *"Briege, who is first in your life?"* In her mind, she had a good Irish conversation with Jesus. It went like this.

Briege: *"You are, Jesus."*

Jesus: *"Then I don't want you to go home. I brought you here. This is where you should be."*

Briege: *"Oh, but Jesus, I have to go home because my aunt is dying and I'll never see her again and I promised to go and I have permission from my Mother General."*
Jesus: *"Briege, who is first in your life?"*
Briege: *"You are, Jesus."*
Jesus: *"Well then, I do not want you to go home."*

There is no question what Briege did. She did as she has been doing from the time she first fell in love with Jesus. She said yes. There was a sadness about her. She loved this aunt very much. But a peace came over her at the same time. Jesus had taken the decision out of her hands. She knew what she had to do.

However, there is a P.S. to this story. At about the same time Briege said *yes* to Jesus, Aunt Lizzie came out of the coma. She stayed in the hospital, in critical condition, until Briege was able to get back to Ireland at the end of her speaking tour in Brazil. When she walked into the hospital, she said to her aunt, *"Well, Aunt Lizzie, I'm home to see you."*

Aunt Lizzie answered, "I know, and it's about time. I waited seven weeks for you to come."

Then she told Briege that she had been ready to die when Jesus told her she had to wait for Briege to see her before she could come to Heaven. Aunt Lizzie died two days after Briege had seen her. There is an expression, "God is an Englishman." Well, we don't see how that's possible, because we know that *God is an Irishman.* And there's no way He could be an Englishman *and* an Irishman. Or could He?

There are many stories of Briege's adventures through the years. There is so much proof of God's love for us, as projected through this one daughter, whose ongoing *"Yes"* resounds throughout Heaven and Earth. She is one more living example of the *Power* of God and the *Love* of God for His children.

Sister Briege has written a beautiful, inspired autobiography, called **Miracles Do Happen**[1], which goes into great detail about her life and her philosophy. She calls herself a *Signpost to Jesus*. We believe that to be true, except in Sister Briege's case, it's more like a neon-lit billboard. We just want to share one more story about Sister Briege, and then we'll quit. The reason we want to tell you about this is because it involves *two* powerful women in the Church, Sister Briege and Mother Angelica.

In 1984, Briege was in Bolivia to give a retreat. She got caught in the crossfire of a Civil War in La Paz. She and her two companions were not able to get out of the city. The airport was closed. So they barricaded themselves in an apartment, and prayed for seven days. Meanwhile word got back to the United States, of what had happened to them, and people began to pray in droves. One of these people was Mother Angelica. She prayed also, but the Lord moved her one step further. She called the State Department in Washington, and put pressure on them to get Briege and her companions out of Bolivia. Within two days a woman from the American Embassy in La Paz came to Briege, and told her that she would be evacuated with other Americans the next day. The Lord is powerful, and He gives this power to those who say "*yes*." Our powerful women in the Church are those who constantly say "*yes!*"

What Makes Briege Run?

There's an urgency about Sister Briege. We've seen the same thing in Mother Angelica. We've heard that Mother Teresa of Calcutta is also running frantically all over the world, as if she's racing against the clock. My Penny's favorite expression, which we intend to put on her tombstone is, "*There's so much to do, and so little time.*" We believe they know something that we don't know. The Lord

---

[1]Servant Books - P.O. Box 8617 Ann Arbor, MI 48107

has given them an insight and a passion to touch every brother and sister in the world, *now!*

Sister Briege is always on the go. When she's home, she has those telephone earphones wrapped around her head constantly. When she's not at home, she's giving retreats, or days of recollection, or missions, or Priests' retreats. In the meantime, speaking tours and retreats are being planned for her in Europe, South America, Australia, the Middle East, Africa, anywhere and everywhere the Lord is calling her. This has been going on for years, and shows no signs of letting up.

Sister Briege has a personality that is beyond belief. She is buoyant, joyful, alive, and full of the love of the Lord. She is not impressed with Briege McKenna at all, but is always amazed at the way the Lord works through her. Because most of her mission is one of healing, physical and spiritual, she comes in contact with people who are in great pain and agony. Deformity and cancer-ravaged bodies are the norm for Briege. Yet, she maintains this beautiful, joyful exterior.

In the course of writing this chapter, everything has been thrown at our Ministry. I told you about my Bell's Palsy, which has been with me for three months, and has almost completely incapacitated me. I'm almost out of it, praise Jesus. The other day, we were called to visit an old friend, Angel Juan Maldonado, who is dying of Cancer. We have been bringing him Communion every day and praying with him. He is in the last stages of the illness. He is a skeleton. He can't walk; he can hardly talk. He has to have water after receiving Our Lord Jesus in the Eucharist in order to swallow the Host. We have only been visiting him for a few days, and we have been devastated by the savage deterioration of his body. We know the Lord has sent us to this man for a reason. The only positive that Penny and I have gotten from this experience is *priorities*.

When the time arrives, as it has to in all our lives, when the body finally loses the battle to whatever illness, cancer, heart attack or stroke, we must come to terms with priorities. *What is really important now?* No matter how much money we've got, how many cars, how big our house is, how much power we've been able to amass, it's all passing. We can't take it with us. We can't even take our emaciated bodies with us. What is important?

We believe this is what gives Sister Briege such impetus. She talks about having met heads of state who are ill, in need of prayers and healing. She talks about the rich, who are so poor spiritually, and virtually ignored. There are no programs for the rich. We haven't spoken to Briege about this, but we believe the Lord is telling us to share this with you. We think, that through her exposure to so much physical and spiritual agony, Briege has been given the gift of cutting through all the nonsense of life, to get to the core, the important issue at the end of the tunnel, *our immortal soul.*

In our talks, we tell people that we know the end of the story. It's no great mystery. Jesus will triumph! It's in the Bible. But how many dead bodies will we leave behind? Penny says she used to have a great argument with Jesus about the Scripture passage, (Luke 18:34-37) "*I tell you, on that night, two will be in one bed; one will be taken, the other left; two women will be grinding corn together; one will be taken, the other left.*" Penny could not understand how Jesus could take one and leave the other one? That was not the Merciful Jesus she knew. And then the Lord spoke to Penny. "*You're right, I would not take one and leave one. The ones who will stay behind are the ones who do not know Me, and so they will not come.*"

We believe that to be true. Our job is to make Jesus known to people, to make Him personal. We believe that Sister Briege has been given that insight, that urgency not to let anyone stay behind. She's a very young woman, and we believe the Lord will use her in a powerful way for many years to come. She's out there in the brush, trying desperately to spread the word of Jesus to as many as she can. But she can't do it alone. She's only one person, and the world is so huge. There are other sisters whom the Lord has been calling. *You know who you are!* You have but to say "*yes*", as Sister Briege, and Mother Mary before her, and all the *powerful women* in the Church have done. The Lord could do it without us, but He chooses not to. Will you be a Sister Briege McKenna? You don't have to be Irish, but it helps. Will you say "Yes"?

Above:
Briege in Mexico - 1976

Above: ***Briege & Fr. Kevin Scallon
with Prime Minister of Trinidad***

Right: ***Briege & Fr. Scallon
with Native Babies***

Below: ***Briege at Priest's Retreat
Nigeria - 1989***

Epilog

During the writing of this book, we have known attack unlike any we have ever known before. It was as if all hell broke loose.

On Good Friday I fell on our tile floor at the foot of the steps and hit my head on the oak post of the bannister. I thought I was going to die. No sooner was that crisis over, Bob woke up one morning, two weeks later, with half his face paralyzed, not able to close one eye. After all the battery of tests brought us the hope this would all *pass*, as they made us aware of how the Lord had *spared* us from so much worse, *then* we had to live with the slow process of healing that was to take place.

Through all the months of hope and discouragement, I discovered a very brave, selfless human being who prayed only to be able to do "Your Will and Your Work, Lord." That person was Bob, my husband. As we struggled to write through all the fear and pain, I found strength and example from the lives of these powerful women before me, who had lived to serve Mother Church. When I questioned "why us," I read our chapter, on you, Mother Angelica and on our other sister Saints living on earth and in the Kingdom, who also had wondered "why us," but said "yes."

Most of all, I found You, Jesus, in a new and more intimate way. I heard You and Your words, "How long I have waited for you to take time to talk to Me, to be with Me." Oh, we go to Mass, spend time in the Blessed Sacrament Chapel, say the Rosary and the many novenas to the Angels and Saints, each day, but had we given up total control, surrendering ourselves totally to Your Will? Were we being called, like the water our Priest pours into the

Chalice on the altar to be consumed, to be submerged in Your Precious Blood, to disappear so that You could *appear*? Were we being asked to follow You through the Cross, as our sisters before us?

Each time Bob and I finished a chapter, we felt a sadness at having to leave that special woman. Then, when we'd begin writing of the next *powerful woman in the Church* our excitement would build again. We developed such a unique relationship with these women; we didn't want to let go of *any* of them. We pray they have touched you the way they have touched us.

Now it's over, at least Volume I is finished. We know we will bring you Volume II, because there are so many women in our Church we can be proud of, whom we can embrace and after whom we can model our lives.

We told you about the thread that connected these women together. It *was* and *is* the *Eucharist*, the strength Jesus gave them and gives us in times of struggle, adversity, and downright despair, His very Body and Blood. It's a *Power Source* we must plug into. We can spin our wheels and go round in circles, trying to do the impossible, only to find that Jesus allows us to do these things with such ease, by energizing ourselves with the *Eucharist*.

In researching these sisters, as well as the many *powerful men in the Church*, we found without exception, a deep and committed devotion to *Our Lady*, Mother Mary. We have not found anyone who truly loves Jesus, that does not revere His Mother as well. They took the most direct route, *to Jesus through Mary*, having found that they could not really know the Son without knowing the Mother.

Two strong feelings have come out of this book for us. One is *pride* in those who came before us; the other is *hope* in those who will follow. We feel *strength* from those women of the Church who have fought against the powers of hell, and triumphed. Because of them, we have *hope* for our

Church of tomorrow. We know the Lord will always raise up *women* like those in this book.

Who are the Powerful Women in the Church of tomorrow? *You are the Powerful Woman in the Church.* Right now, we know the Lord has placed you out there, in strategic positions, to glorify Him by your lives. There are Teresas, Thérèses, Bernadettes, Ritas, Catherines, Clares, Mother Angelicas, Briege McKennas, Mother Theclas, and so many more the Lord would use in His Service.

You know who you are, Powerful Woman of the future. You can feel it. When you read about one of your sisters, living or dead, a surge of energy went through you. There was a familiarity, a kinship you felt, that could not be denied. Your heart started beating a little faster as you related with their joys and struggles, their closeness to Jesus and Mary. We're waiting for you to step forward and make your mark on our Church. Our Church has always been under attack. We may possibly be in the last days. Every moment counts. Your sisters before you have known of the urgency of the moment. They lived their lives as if the second coming of Jesus was just around the corner. *And it may very well be!*

Those who are true lovers of Christ are not worried about their own individual salvation. That's been assured. *(Those whom God has chosen, He has justified; and those He has justified, He has glorified. Romans 8:28)* Their concern is for the brothers and sisters who may be left behind. We're losing people left and right to cults. We're told the Mormons have 39,000 evangelists in the field.[1] The Jehovah's Witnesses have made strong inroads with our Hispanic brother and sisters. The Moslems expect to be the second largest religion in the United States in eleven years.[2]

---

[1] US Catholic - June, 1989
[2] Time Magazine - May 13, 1988

Saints and Other Powerful Women in the Church

How will we turn the tide? *You must touch them, powerful woman in the Church!*

In our talks, we tell people to forget the numbers, but to put faces on those who have left.

"*If Jesus were to come tonight,*" we ask them, "who do you know who would not be coming with us to the Kingdom? Is there a brother or sister, a mother or father? Perhaps you have a son or daughter, a grandson or granddaughter, a niece or nephew, a husband or wife? When I mention these names, does a picture flash in your mind? Those are the *first* ones you have to approach. They have to know Jesus, so *they* don't stay behind when He comes. You have to bring them back!"

We're told that by the year 2000, there will be six billion people on earth. Two billion will be Christian of some kind. That means that 2/3 of the world will not know Jesus. How can we reverse those figures? *You must teach them, powerful woman in the Church!* Whether you make your mark by praying in the cloister of the Convent, as did Thérèse, the Clares, and Bernadette; or reform the Church as did Catherine and Teresa; or go door-to-door as did Mother Thecla; or minister to Priests and Bishops and Third World countries, as does Sister Briege; or proclaim the glory of God through space by means of television like Mother Angelica; or be faithful to your vocation as obedient daughter, wife, mother, and Religious, as did Rita; wherever the Lord calls. You know *who* you are! You know *where* you are!

This is not the time to sit in a circle and argue among ourselves about *who did what to who*, as the *enemy* of Christ *picks off* Christians from behind. We don't have that luxury! We don't know how much *time* we do have. We do know one thing. You can do it, *powerful woman in the Church*!

Jesus loves you; Jesus needs you; Jesus wants you!

Bibliography

Alvarez Tomas CD/Domingo Fernando CD - *Saint Teresa of Avila* - Editorial Monte Carmelo - Burgos Spain 1982

Angelini, Anastasio Fr.- *Life of Saint Rita*
  Poligrafico Alterocca, Terni, Italy 1953

Armstrong, Regis OFM/Brady, Ignatius OFM
  Francis and Clare - Paulist Press, Ramsey, NJ 1982

Baldwin, Anne B. - *Catherine of Siena*
  Our Sunday Visitor - Huntington, IN 1987

Bargellini, Piero - *The Little Flowers of Saint Clare*
  Messagero Editions, Padua, Italy 1972

Bodo, Murray - *Clare: a Light in the garden*
  St. Anthony Messenger Press, Cinn. OH 1979

Broderick, Robert - *The Catholic Encyclopedia*
  Thomas A. Nelson New York, 1976

Butler, Thurston & Atwater - *Lives of the Saints*
  (Complete Edition in four volumes)
  Christian Classics, Westminster, Maryland, 1980

Daughters of St. Paul - *St. Rita, Saint of the Impossible*
  St. Paul Editions, Boston, MA 1973

Gaucher, Guy - *The Spiritual Journey of St. Thérèse of Lisieux*
  Darton, Longman & Todd, London 1987

Kavanaugh, K. OCD/Rodriguez, O. OCD - *St. Teresa of Avila* - ICS Publications Washington, D.C. 1976

Knox, Ronald - *The Story of a Soul*
  Fount Paperbacks - Great Britain 1977

Laurentin, Rene Fr. - *A Hundred Years Ago Bernadette*
  Fetes e Saisons - Editions du Cerf, Paris 1979

Lord, Bob and Penny - *This Is My Body, This Is My Blood*
  Journeys of Faith, Westlake Village, CA 1986

Lord, Bob and Penny - *The Many Faces of Mary*
  Journeys of Faith, Westlake Village, CA 1987

Lord, Bob and Penny - *We Came Back to Jesus*
  Journeys of Faith, Westlake Village, CA 1988

Lucarini, Spartaco - *A Woman for our Time*
   St. Paul Editions, Boston, MA 1974
Mc Kenna Briege/Libersat Henry - *Miracles Do Happen*
   Servant Books, Ann Arbor, MI 1987
New American Bible - Thomas A. Nelson, New York 1970
Omnibus of St. Francis of Assisi Franciscan Herald Press 1972
O'Neill, Dan - *Mother Angelica, Her Life Story*
   Crossroads Publishing, New York 1986
Raphael, Sr. M - *My Life With Mother Angelica*
   Our Lady of the Angels, Birmingham AL 1982
St. Gildard Convent - *Some of Bernadette's Sayings*
   St. Gildard Convent, Nevers, France 1978
Sheed, F.J. - *Collected Letters of St. Thérèse of Lisieux*
   Sheed and Ward, London 1977
Trochu, Francois - *Saint Bernadette Soubirous*
   Longmans, Green and Co., London 1957
Walsh, William Thomas - *Saint Teresa of Avila*
   Bruce Publishing Co., Milwaukee, WI 1943
Werfel, Franz - *The Song of Bernadette*
   Pocket Books, New York 1940

Bob and Penny Lord

We Came Back to Jesus is the third book in Bob and Penny Lord's Trilogy, based on the Prophecy of St. John Bosco, which is about **the Body of Christ, the Mother of Christ, and the Church of Christ.**

Their first, *This Is My Body, This Is My Blood, Miracles of the Eucharist,* is about **the Real Presence of Jesus in the Eucharist.**

Their second, *The Many Faces of Mary, a Love Story,* is about **the Mother of Christ.**

The third, *We Came Back to Jesus,* brings it all together. The focus is on **Church,** how Bob and Penny left the Church after the death of their 19 year old son to an overdose of drugs, the long road back, and how Mother Church embraced them, showering them with all the gifts the Church has to offer.

Readers say this is the reason the first two were written.

"I got to page 30, and had to stop because the tears kept coming out like a deluge......it was a personal relationship"
Msgr. Vito Mistretta - Citrus Heights, CA

"The book is lovely.....I do hope it reaches many and touches their hearts." **Fr. Richard Rohr - Albuquerque, NM**

"I got goose bumps as I read through it. There were so many memories....and so much love....and so much hope."
Fr. Chuck Gallagher - Elizabeth, NJ

"All your books are Super, but this one adds a luster....because this is giving the other two Roots....You bared all of your own personal selves....you actually showed us How God works in our lives..."
Anna Buonicore - Saddlebrook, NJ

This may well be their most important work thus far. It is a book you will not only want to read over and over again, but will want to give to your loved ones and friends.

207 pages - Hard Cover - $12.95 ea   Paperback - $7.95 ea.
California Residents add 6% Tax - Make Checks Payable to Journeys of Faith
Please include $2.00 for postage & handling

Journeys of Faith

31220 La Baya Drive, Suite 110 - Westlake Village, CA 91362